THE COLLEGE OF COMMERCIAL ARBITRATORS GUIDE TO BEST PRACTICES IN COMMERCIAL ARBITRATION

Hon. Curtis E. von Kann

Editor-in-Chief

James M. Gaitis, Esq., FCIArb. &
June R. Lehrman, Esq.

Editors

JurisNet, LLC

Questions About This Publication

For assistance with shipments, billing or other customer service matters, please call our Customer Services Department at:

1-631-350-0200

To obtain a copy of this book, call our Sales Department:

1-631-351-5430
Fax: 1-631-351-5712

Toll Free Order Line:

1-800-887-4064 (United States & Canada)

See our web page about this book:
http://www.arbitrationlaw.com

JurisNet, LLC
71 New Street
Huntington, New York 11743
USA
www.arbitrationlaw.com

DEDICATION

The College of Commercial Arbitrators fondly dedicates this book to the memory of the Honorable Winslow Christian (April 12, 1926 – November 15, 2005), distinguished lawyer, judge, arbitrator, and former President of the College, who conceived the Guide, launched its creation, but died suddenly before it could be published. This work is part of the rich legacy he leaves to the profession he loved and served so well.

SUMMARY TABLE OF CONTENTS

Chapter 1

INTRODUCTION

by Winslow Christian and the Editors

....1

Chapter 2

APPOINTMENT, DISCLOSURES, AND
DISQUALIFICATION OF NEUTRAL ARBITRATORS

*by James H. Carter, Ruth V. Glick,
June R. Lehrman, and Bruce E. Meyerson*

....7

Chapter 3

NON-NEUTRAL ARBITRATORS

by Richard Chernick and James M. Gaitis

....27

Chapter 4

DETERMINING JURISDICTION
AND ARBITRABILITY

*by R. Doak Bishop, Robert B. Davidson,
Barry H. Garfinkel, and June R. Lehrman*

....43

TABLE OF CONTENTS

Chapter 1

INTRODUCTION
*by Winslow Christian and the Editor*s

Chapter 2

APPOINTMENT, DISCLOSURES, AND
DISQUALIFICATION OF NEUTRAL ARBITRATORS
by James H. Carter, Ruth V. Glick, June R. Lehrman, and Bruce E. Meyerson

Chapter 3

NON-NEUTRAL ARBITRATORS
by Richard Chernick and James M. Gaitis

Chapter 4

DETERMINING JURISDICTION AND ARBITRABILITY
*by R. Doak Bishop, Robert B. Davidson, Barry H. Garfinkel,
and June R. Lehrman*

Chapter 5

CLASS ARBITRATION
*by Robert B. Davidson, James M. Gaitis, Deborah Rothman,
and Francis O. Spalding*

Chapter 6

PRELIMINARY CONFERENCES
AND PRE-HEARING MANAGEMENT IN GENERAL
*by David N. Brainin, James P. Groton, Gerald F. Phillips,
Deborah Rothman, and Curtis E. von Kann*

Chapter 7

MOTIONS
by Louise E. Dembeck, Eugene I. Farber, and Carroll Neesemann

Chapter 8

DISCOVERY
by R. Doak Bishop, Scott Donahey, Louise A. LaMothe,
John M. Seitman, and Stanley P. Sklar

Chapter 9

THE HEARING ON THE MERITS
*by Henri C. Alvarez, William L.D. Barrett, Louis A. Craco,
James P. Groton, and Curtis E. von Kann*

Chapter 10

AWARDS
by Thomas J. Brewer, Richard A. Levie, and James M. Gaitis

Chapter 11

POST-AWARD MATTERS
by Paul J. Dubow, James M. Gaitis, James R. Madison, and David E. Wagoner

Chapter 12

INTERNATIONAL ARBITRATION
by Gerald Aksen, Axel H. Baum, and Lucy F. Reed

PREFACE

Formed in 2001, the College of Commercial Arbitrators is a non-profit organization composed of prominent, experienced commercial arbitrators who believe that a national association of commercial arbitrators can provide a meaningful contribution to the profession, to the public, and to the businesses and lawyers who depend on arbitration as a primary means of dispute resolution. Its mission includes promoting professionalism and high ethical practice in commercial arbitration, adopting and maintaining standards of conduct, providing peer training and professional development, and developing and publishing "best practices" materials. The present work is the College's principal vehicle for fulfilling several aspects of its mission.

Many seasoned and knowledgeable practitioners generously contributed their time and insights to the creation of this Guide. The College expresses its deep appreciation to all of them for making this publication possible.

Our initial thanks go to the American College of Construction Lawyers, which four years ago began preparing a guide to best practices in construction arbitration and then unselfishly delivered its work product to us when our College undertook compilation of a practice guide for all commercial arbitrators.

The College is also deeply grateful for the extraordinary leadership of my predecessor as President, Honorable Winslow Christian, who had the vision to recognize the great value of such a guide and the tenacity to enlist the necessary drafters and inspire them to diligent and insightful production.

The heart of the project, of course, was the willingness of numerous Fellows of the College to take time from their busy professional schedules to collaborate with one another in reducing to writing the successful practices they have developed, through years of managing commercial arbitrations, so that others may profit from their experience. Without the contribution of these Fellows, this Guide would not have been possible: Gerald Aksen, Henri C. Alvarez, Markham Ball, William L.D. Barrett, Axel H. Baum, Bruce W. Belding, R. Doak Bishop, John P. Bowman, David N. Brainin, Thomas J. Brewer, James H. Carter, Richard Chernick, Winslow Christian, Louis A. Craco, Robert B. Davidson, Louise E. Dembeck, Scott

Donahey, Paul J. Dubow, Eugene I. Farber, Walter S. Gans, Barry H. Garfinkel, Eugene S. Ginsberg, Ruth V. Glick, James P. Groton, L. Tyrone Holt, Robert A. Holtzman, John Kagel, Louise A. LaMothe, Richard A. Levie, James R. Madison, Bruce E. Meyerson, Carroll Neesemann, Gerald F. Phillips, Lucy F. Reed, Thomas D. Reese, Kathleen A. Roberts, Deborah Rothman, John M. Seitman, Stanley P. Sklar, Francis O. Spalding, and David E. Wagoner.

Finally, I wish to extend my personal gratitude to the three Fellows who took on the daunting task of putting it all together. Editor-in-Chief Curtis E. von Kann and Editors James M. Gaitis and June R. Lehrman not only contributed substantively to the drafting of every chapter in the Guide but also devoted enormous talent and energy to refining the many discrete drafts submitted by the College Fellows and integrating them into a cohesive, harmonious monograph that expresses with grace and clarity the wisdom of the College. Their tireless efforts turned the College's aspirations into a truly significant achievement.

J. Michael McWilliams

President
College of Commercial Arbitrators

ABOUT THE EDITORS

Editor-in-Chief Curtis E. von Kann, a graduate of Harvard College and Harvard Law School, practiced civil litigation for sixteen years, primarily as an associate, then partner of Hogan & Hartson in Washington, DC. In 1985 President Ronald Reagan appointed him a Judge of the District of Columbia Superior Court, where he presided for ten years over a wide variety of trials. Following retirement from the court, he served as Independent Counsel in the investigation of President Clinton's campaign chief of staff.

Since 1997 he has been a full-time arbitrator, mediator, and neutral case evaluator in the Washington, DC office of JAMS, where he has served as sole arbitrator, tribunal member, and tribunal chair in a broad range of commercial arbitrations. Judge von Kann is a Fellow of the College of Commercial Arbitrators and of the Chartered Institute of Arbitrators in London, is a member of the JAMS National Arbitration Committee, and has lectured and published on many ADR topics.

Editor James M. Gaitis is the recently appointed Director of the International Dispute Resolution and Management Programme, and Principal Teaching and Research Fellow, at the Centre for Energy, Petroleum and Mineral Law and Policy, University of Dundee, Scotland, UK. He is a Fellow and Chartered Arbitrator of the Chartered Institute of Arbitrators and a Fellow and member of the board of directors of the College of Commercial Arbitrators. In addition to being an oil & gas attorney with over 27 years of experience, Mr. Gaitis has 16 years of experience serving as an arbitrator in complex energy and oil & gas arbitrations involving upstream, midstream, and downstream issues. He is listed on a broad variety of international and domestic arbitration rosters and panels and is the author of numerous articles relating to arbitration law and international and domestic arbitration procedure.

Editor June R. Lehrman is an arbitrator and mediator in the Los Angeles, California office of JAMS, where she arbitrates and mediates complex commercial, business tort, healthcare, and employment cases. Ms. Lehrman joined JAMS after more than a decade of private practice experience as a full-time neutral in business disputes. Prior to her practice as a full-time neutral, Ms. Lehrman was a litigator at Rosenberg, Chittum & Hecht and at Irell & Manella, both in Los Angeles. Ms. Lehrman is a frequent lecturer on dispute resolution topics and has authored numerous articles on commercial arbitration and related subjects. She is a Fellow and member of the board of directors of the College of Commercial Arbitrators.

ABOUT THE CONTRIBUTORS

All contributors are Fellows of the College of Commercial Arbitrators and have substantial experience as arbitrators. Some do their ADR work exclusively through particular providers, such as AIMAC or JAMS. Some are independent arbitrators and mediators whose appointments come to them directly or through various providers. Others practice law with certain firms or organizations and also serve as arbitrators.

The names, locations, and affiliations of all contributors are shown below.

Gerald Aksen, Esq.
Independent Arbitrator and Mediator
New York, New York

Henri C. Alvarez, Esq.
Partner
Fasken Martineau
Vancouver, British Columbia
Canada

Markham Ball, Esq.
Senior Fellow
International Law Institute
Washington, DC

William L. D. Barrett, Esq.
Partner
Hollyer, Brady, Smith & Hines
New York, New York

Axel H. Baum, Esq.
Partner
Hughes Hubbard & Reed
Paris, France

Bruce W. Belding, Esq.
Independent Arbitrator
Sausalito, California

R. Doak Bishop, Esq.
Partner
King & Spalding
Houston, Texas

John P. Bowman, Esq.
Partner
Fulbright & Jaworski
Houston, Texas

David N. Brainin, Esq.
Of Counsel
Locker, Greenberg & Brainin
New York, New York

Thomas J. Brewer, Esq.
Independent Arbitrator and Mediator
Seattle, Washington

James H. Carter, Esq.
Partner
Sullivan & Cromwell
New York, New York

Richard Chernick, Esq.
Vice President and Managing Director
JAMS Arbitration Practice
Los Angeles, California

Hon. Winslow Christian
Formerly, Justice of the California Court of Appeals
(now deceased)

Louis A. Craco, Esq.
Independent Arbitrator and Mediator
Manhasset, New York

Robert B. Davidson, Esq.
Executive Director
JAMS Arbitration Practice
New York, New York

Louise E. Dembeck, Esq.
Founder and Chief Executive Officer
American International Mediation, Arbitration and
Conciliation Center for Dispute Resolution
New York, New York

M. Scott Donahey, Esq.
Independent Arbitrator and Mediator
Palo Alto, California

Paul J. Dubow, Esq.
Independent Arbitrator and Mediator
San Francisco, California

Eugene I. Farber, Esq.
Partner
Farber, Pappalardo & Carbonari
White Plains, New York

Walter G. Gans, Esq.
Independent Arbitrator and Mediator
New York, New York

Barry H. Garfinkel, Esq.
Partner
Skadden, Arps, Slate, Meagher & Flom
New York, New York

Eugene S. Ginsberg, Esq.
Independent Arbitrator and Mediator
Garden City, New York

Ruth V. Glick, Esq.
Independent Arbitrator and Mediator
Burlingame, California

James P. Groton, Esq.
Partner
Sutherland Asbill & Brennan
Atlanta, Georgia

L. Tyrone Holt, Esq.
Managing Principal
The Holt Group
Denver, Colorado

Robert A. Holtzman, Esq.
Of Counsel
Loeb & Loeb
Los Angeles, California

John Kagel, Esq.
Independent Arbitrator and Mediator
Palo Alto, California

Louise A. LaMothe, Esq.
Independent Arbitrator and Mediator
Santa Barbara, California

Hon. Richard A. Levie (Ret.)
JAMS
Washington, DC

James R. Madison, Esq.
Independent Arbitrator and Mediator
Menlo Park, California

Bruce E. Meyerson, Esq.
Former Chair
American Bar Association Section of Dispute Resolution
Phoenix, Arizona

Carroll Neesemann, Esq.
Partner
Morrison & Foerster
New York, New York

Gerald F. Phillips, Esq.
Partner
Phillips, Salman & Stein
Los Angeles, California

Lucy F. Reed, Esq.
Partner
Freshfields Bruckhaus Deringer
New York, New York

Thomas D. Reese, Esq.
Independent Arbitrator & Mediator
Palo Alto, California

Hon. Kathleen A. Roberts (Ret.)
JAMS
New York, New York

Deborah Rothman, Esq.
Independent Arbitrator & Mediator
Los Angeles, California

John M. Seitman, Esq.
JAMS
Del Mar, California

Stanley P. Sklar, Esq.
Partner
Bell Boyd & Lloyd
Chicago, Illinois

Francis O. Spalding, Esq.
Independent Arbitrator and Mediator
San Francisco, California

David E. Wagoner, Esq.
Independent Arbitrator and Mediator
Seattle, Washington

CHAPTER 1

INTRODUCTION

The origins of arbitration in America date back to the colonial era when individuals involved in certain areas of commerce sought alternatives to judicial processes that were seen to be expensive, slow, and unpredictable in outcome. The arbitrator was usually a non-lawyer, experienced in the line of trade in which the dispute arose. Simple procedure was agreed on by the parties. Stakes were generally modest. Proceedings were informal and short. Judicial involvement was not significant.

On that simple foundation has been built the present elaborate structure of commercial arbitration in the United States, with its governing statutes and rules, complex disputes, high stakes, and occasional judicial intervention. Arbitration is now extensively employed in virtually every field of commerce, including financial services, real estate sales and development, construction projects, contracts for goods and services, public works and procurement, energy, health care, intellectual property, insurance and re-insurance, franchising, mergers and acquisitions, entertainment, telecommunications, and international business transactions. Moreover, the United States Supreme Court has held that arbitration may be used to decide private disputes involving such public policy areas as antitrust, securities, and racketeering, which, until recently, were foreclosed to arbitration.

Disputes that a few years ago would have been resolved in court proceedings after protracted litigation are increasingly being determined by private arbitrators selected and paid by the parties. Since commercial arbitration is normally the product of freely-negotiated agreements, legislatures and the courts generally have been very supportive of such arbitration, giving arbitrators wide latitude in managing the process and declining to second-guess arbitral decisions absent extreme aberrations. Indeed, the durability of the Federal

Arbitration Act ("FAA") and the versatility of the recently revised Uniform Arbitration Act ("RUAA") both testify to the fact that commercial arbitration in the United States has become a widely accepted means of resolving business disputes.

There are, of course, many reasons for the popularity of commercial arbitration. Parties to commercial contracts often prefer to have their disputes resolved by arbitration because of the opportunity to select the decision-maker and the time and place of hearing, to obtain expedited consideration of their claims and defenses in a private forum, and to bring finality to the dispute once all sides have had a full and fair hearing. Nevertheless, because of the magnitude of the claims involved, many of these parties increasingly demand an arbitration process that provides for much of the discovery, motion, hearing, and briefing procedures that are typically available in litigation. In light of this trend, some arbitrators fear that arbitration is coming more and more to resemble litigation. Others regard this development as a tribute to the respect that experienced commercial arbitrators have earned for their expertise, judgment, and creativity in managing the resolution of complex controversies.

While experienced arbitrators maintain differing opinions regarding the desirability of litigation-like processes in arbitration, most would agree that the growing complexity of commercial arbitration requires arbitrators to actively address a multitude of procedural issues at virtually every stage of the arbitration process. For example, arbitrators are often confronted as soon as the arbitration commences with questions relating to the existence and/or scope of the arbitrators' authority or the alleged failure to satisfy a condition precedent to the arbitration. Arbitrators must skillfully manage the discovery and motions process and craft pre-hearing and hearing procedures that maximize efficiency and cost savings while still taking into account sophisticated expert testimony, the needs of advocates, and the parties' right to a fair process and a proper resolution of their dispute. Arbitrators must also take due care in drafting and issuing a final arbitration award that will not be vulnerable to challenge in state or federal court.

Given these circumstances, a guide to practices that have been found efficacious by experienced and respected arbitrators would seem to be a valuable tool for those charged with managing such arbitrations. In 2001, the American College of Construction Lawyers undertook preparation of such a guide for construction arbitrations. In 2003, the College of Commercial Arbitrators began a similar effort regarding commercial arbitration in general. It was soon recognized that duplicative guides were not needed, and the former college graciously furnished its very useful work product to the latter, providing a solid and greatly appreciated foundation for this Guide. Thus, the present Guide brings together the experience and learning of the Fellows of both Colleges.

The aim of this Guide is to identify "best practices" that arbitrators can employ to provide users of arbitration with the highest possible standards of economy and fairness in the disposition of business disputes. In pursuing that aim, the many contributors to the Guide confirmed what most had expected, namely, that there are significant differences in the ways in which arbitrations are conducted in different substantive fields of commerce and among different arbitrators in the same field. Some techniques are favored by certain very able arbitrators and not by others. Moreover, most arbitrators recognize that techniques that are appropriate and useful in one case may be quite unsuited to another.

For this reason, it is not possible to prescribe a single set of best practices that commercial arbitrators should invariably follow in every case. Rather, this Guide attempts to identify the principal issues that typically arise in each successive stage of an arbitration and to explain the pros and cons of various preferred ways of handling each issue. From this perspective, the "best practice" for the arbitrator is to carefully consider the merits of the alternative techniques available for dealing with a particular issue and to then select the technique best suited to the pertinent situation. Additionally, while the Guide attempts to identify the full array of practices available for use in complex arbitrations, arbitrators in simpler cases will probably prefer a more streamlined approach that adopts, and perhaps simplifies, only those practices that are suited to such cases.

It is also worth recalling that, in designing and managing the arbitration process, the arbitrator does not have an unfettered hand. Commercial arbitration is a product of the parties' agreement, and parties can, and sometimes do, prescribe in detail how the arbitration will be conducted. Legally, an arbitrator is bound to adhere to the parties' agreement. However, most parties look to the arbitrator as an expert in the arbitration process. The best arbitrators are those who know how commercial arbitrations, whether simple or complex, can be managed most fairly and efficiently and who share that knowledge and wisdom with the parties, thereby making them partners in a joint effort to devise an appropriate and workable process for each case. Accordingly, while this Guide is addressed chiefly to arbitrators, it may also prove useful to those who serve primarily as advocates in arbitration.

The subject of this Guide is "commercial arbitration," *i.e.*, arbitration that results from an agreement negotiated by the parties, either before or after the dispute arises, that pertains to the parties' rights and obligations in some business matter. Except with respect to class arbitrations, the Guide does not attempt to address the unique considerations that apply to arbitrations mandated by consumer or employment contracts of adhesion, or to the highly specialized field of labor-management arbitration. The Guide principally focuses on matters relating to neutral arbitrators who serve as the sole arbitrator or as a member of a tripartite tribunal in domestic commercial arbitrations. (Thus, in this work, the term "arbitrators" includes both the three members of such a tribunal as well as persons serving as sole arbitrators.) However, in order to provide at least some insight into the rather different world of non-neutral arbitrators and international arbitration, the Guide includes overview chapters on those subjects as well.

This Guide does not comprehensively address the variations of practice that might arise from the application of procedures mandated or permitted by state arbitration statutes, the FAA, various international treaties, or the rules of the American Arbitration Association ("AAA"), JAMS, the CPR International Institute for Conflict Prevention and Resolution ("CPR"), the National Arbitration Forum ("NAF"), or other service providers. Naturally, any arbitration must be conducted in accordance with the applicable law and rules and any special requirements of the parties' agreement. Moreover, it should be noted that this work is a practice guide, not a treatise. No attempt has been made to provide a complete discussion of the rapidly expanding common law of arbitration. Many other publications provide that sort of information, and a rudimentary familiarity with that law is presumed on the part of the reader. While the Guide occasionally distinguishes the permissible from the impermissible, the primary objective of the Guide is to make clear the advantages and disadvantages of various permissible practices and to thus help the reader select the best practice for any particular arbitration.

The College of Commercial Arbitrators Guide to Best Practices in Commercial Arbitration is intended to be the starting point for a dialogue between the College and those involved in commercial arbitration. The College welcomes comments and suggestions concerning the Guide. It is likely that such responses, and the continuing study and experience of the College's Fellows, will result in the production of subsequent editions of the Guide in years to come.

CHAPTER 2

APPOINTMENT, DISCLOSURES, AND DISQUALIFICATION OF NEUTRAL ARBITRATORS

In addressing appointment and disclosure issues, the goals of arbitrators are (1) to comply with applicable law, institutional rules, and party agreements, and (2) to ensure that they are, and reasonably appear to be, impartial and independent.

I. INTRODUCTION

To ensure a fair arbitration process, neutral arbitrators must be impartial and independent. An effective disclosure and appointment process, in compliance with applicable law, institutional rules, and the parties' agreement, is essential for public confidence in the arbitral process and to ensure the enforceability of arbitration awards. Moreover, the AAA/ABA Code of Ethics for Arbitrators in Commercial Disputes, revised in March 2004, ("AAA/ABA Code") sets forth generally accepted standards of ethical conduct for commercial arbitrators, including standards relating to appointment, disclosures, and disqualification of arbitrators. This chapter examines those subjects in relation to neutral arbitrators. Chapter 3, *infra*, discusses appointment, disclosures, and disqualification of arbitrators who are not expected to act as neutrals.

II. APPOINTMENT OF ARBITRATORS

The parties' agreement to arbitrate ordinarily sets out the process to be used in selecting and appointing arbitrators, either specifically or by reference to the procedures of an arbitral institution. In the absence of such direction, the appointment process is derived from applicable state or federal law. Often, prospective arbitrators will initially receive an inquiry concerning their suitability and availability to serve. They should immediately conduct an appropriate investigation into all matters bearing upon their ability to serve as neutrals and respond to such inquiries in accordance with applicable law, institutional rules, and party agreements.

A.   Initial Communications

If not prohibited by the arbitration clause or applicable institutional rules, prospective arbitrators may have limited *ex parte* contact relevant to the appointment process.

Persons contacted to discuss availability to serve as neutral arbitrators should initially determine whether the arbitration clause or applicable institutional rules establish the manner or content of allowable communications between arbitrators and parties and, if so, should follow those procedures. If not prohibited by the clause or rules, prospective neutral arbitrators may have limited *ex parte* contact relevant to the appointment process. Prospective neutral arbitrators may talk with the representative of a party considering appointment and may ask about the identities of the parties, counsel, and witnesses. They may listen to an explanation of the general nature of the dispute and may respond to inquiries from a party or counsel designed to determine the arbitrator's suitability and availability for the appointment; but such dialogue should avoid discussion of the merits of the case. *See* AAA/ABA Code, Canon III.

B.   Determining Impartiality and Independence

Upon being asked to serve in an arbitration, prospective arbitrators should immediately conduct an analysis designed to determine whether they are capable of serving impartially and independently.

Persons contacted to discuss availability to serve as neutral arbitrators should accept appointment only if fully satisfied that they can serve impartially and independently. AAA/ABA Code, Canon I(B). Generally, an "impartial" arbitrator is one who is open-minded and not biased in favor of, or prejudiced against, a particular party or its case. An "independent" arbitrator is one who has no close financial, personal, or professional relationship with a party and will not profit from the arbitration's resolution. *See generally,* International Bar Association Rules of Ethics for International Arbitrators, Art. 3(1) (1987). While recently revised codes and statutes such as the AAA/ABA Code and the RUAA fail to clearly delineate the differences between these two concepts, they do succeed in identifying the general factors that arbitrators should consider in determining whether they are impartial and independent. In particular, both the AAA/ABA Code and the RUAA emphasize that in making those determinations, arbitrators should consider any financial or personal interest in the outcome of the arbitration, and any past or existing relationship with any of the parties, their lawyers, witnesses, or the other arbitrators. AAA/ABA Code, Canon II(A); RUAA §§ 11(b) and 12(a).

In order to avoid difficult complications that might arise after they are appointed, arbitrators should attempt to fully evaluate issues relating to impartiality and independence prior to the time they accept an appointment to serve. Names of at least the parties, their lawyers, and any other arbitrators already appointed should be determined in the first contact. It is equally important to obtain the names of affiliates of corporate parties. Once that information is made available to prospective arbitrators, they should conduct an immediate investigation designed to identify the existence of any of the types of relationships described above. The nature of that investigation will depend on the prospective arbitrators' practice setting. If arbitrators are members of a law firm, they should include a review of past matters on which other lawyers in the firm have worked. If arbitrators are not members of firms, they should undertake a review of records and recollection regarding prior or ongoing relationships with the parties, their lawyers, and other arbitrators. At the earliest reasonable time, arbitrators should also seek an identification of any individuals who might be called as witnesses in the arbitration, and should conduct the same form of investigation as pertains to the parties, their lawyers, and the other arbitrators.

Arbitrators should be aware that the existence of a present or past "relationship" with another person involved in the arbitration does not always dictate that the arbitrator cannot serve impartially or independently. For example, as is recognized by the International Bar Association Guidelines on Conflicts of Interest in International Arbitration, an arbitrator and counsel might have a "relationship" that arises through membership in the same professional association. Such a relationship might, or might not, be of such significance as to suggest that the arbitrator cannot serve impartially or independently. Consequently, while such relationships should be disclosed to the parties (see Section III, infra), arbitrators should not automatically presume that the existence of any such relationship disqualifies them from serving. Moreover, at least under some statutes, the parties are free to waive objections to an arbitrator serving due to the existence of certain relationships. See, e.g., RUAA § 11, Comment 1. On the other hand, once arbitrators determine that they cannot serve impartially or independently, they are obligated to decline the appointment. AAA/ABA Code, Canon I(B)(1) and (2).

C.   Determining Fitness to Serve

Arbitrators should determine their willingness, fitness, and availability to serve.

Arbitrators should determine whether they are competent to serve in the particular case. AAA/ABA Code, Canon I(B)(3). After learning the general nature of the dispute, they must ascertain whether they can ensure a fair and efficient resolution of the dispute by providing impartiality, independence, and in some cases, subject matter expertise. Some arbitration clauses prescribe the qualifications of those who may serve as arbitrators. Clauses may, for example, require arbitrators to be experts in the line of trade in which the dispute arose, attorneys with a certain number of years of practice experience, or retired state or federal judges. Prospective arbitrators should determine whether they meet any applicable contractual requirements, unless waived by all parties.

Prospective arbitrators should also determine whether they can be available to "commence the arbitration in accordance with the requirements of the proceeding and thereafter to devote the time and attention to its completion that the parties are reasonably entitled to expect." AAA/ABA Code, Canon I(B)(4).

D.   Establishing Terms of Appointment

Before finally accepting appointments, arbitrators should establish all material terms of the appointment and inform the parties in writing of those terms.

Like other professionals, arbitrators are free to set the terms on which they will render their professional services. AAA/ABA Code, Canon VII(B)(1) provides that, before finally accepting any appointment, an arbitrator should establish, and communicate to the parties in writing, all terms relating to compensation. Some arbitral institutions provide the parties with such information concerning arbitrator candidates before the arbitrators are selected; when this procedure is followed, the parties may take account of that information in agreeing on an arbitrator or exercising any rights they have to strike and rank candidates. Other institutions provide such information about appointed arbitrators immediately upon appointment. When the information is provided in this fashion, parties should be required to promptly raise any objections they may have to the arbitrator's terms. If such objections cannot be resolved to the mutual satisfaction of the arbitrator and the parties, the arbitrator should withdraw so that another arbitrator may be appointed.

Rates and terms of compensation vary considerably among arbitrators. Some charge an hourly rate for all work performed in the matter. Some charge a daily rate for hearings and an hourly rate for other work, such as reviewing briefs and motions, conducting telephone conferences, and preparing awards. Some arbitrators charge for time spent in traveling to the hearing site; others do not. Nearly all arbitrators require that the parties reimburse reasonable and necessary expenses incurred in serving as arbitrators, including plane, train, or taxi fare, hotel charges, and other similar expenses. Some arbitrators will only travel in business class.

Most arbitrators require that the parties deposit their respective share of the arbitrator's expected compensation and expenses. Some arbitral institutions also require advance deposit of administrative or case management fees or charges for use of conference rooms and other facilities.

One compensation matter that should be clearly communicated to the parties at the commencement of the arbitration is the terms under which the arbitrator may charge a fee if a hearing is cancelled or continued. When a continuance or cancellation is effected through the joint agreement of the parties or the arbitrators' grant of a contested request, arbitrators may suddenly find themselves with empty time on their calendar that was reserved for the now-cancelled hearing. If the case has been pending for some time, arbitrators may have already declined requests by other parties to schedule hearings at that time. Because arbitrators' time (and wisdom) is their stock in trade, it is entirely permissible for arbitrators to require that, when hearings are cancelled within a certain number of days prior to the scheduled commencement of the hearings, the party or parties responsible for the cancellation be charged a specified fee for any of the reserved time that the arbitrators are unable to fill with other hearings. Similarly, charging a fee in the event of arbitrator withdrawal may be permissible, depending on the circumstances giving rise to the withdrawal.

All of the foregoing terms of compensation and expenses reimbursement should be fully disclosed to the parties before the arbitrator commences work on the arbitration. Absent extraordinary circumstances, arbitrators should not request increases in the basis of their compensation during the course of a proceeding. AAA/ABA Code, Cannon VII (B)(3).

In proceedings conducted under the rules or administration of an institution that is available to assist in making payment arrangements, arbitrators generally should communicate about fees only through the institution. In ad hoc arbitrations, *i.e.*, arbitration conducted in the absence of an administering arbitral institution (*see* Section F, *infra*), arbitrators may avoid *ex parte* communications by determining at the outset that all arbitrators' fees will be paid from a common fund administered by the chairperson or the sole arbitrator. If arbitrators wish to propose to the parties that a secretary be retained to handle administrative matters, approval of such arrangements should be obtained at the time of arbitrator appointment.

Party-appointed neutral arbitrators (*see* Section G, *infra*) may consult with representatives of the appointing party concerning compensation and may, if consistent with any applicable institutional rules, accept payment directly from the party or its counsel. If *ex parte* compensation arrangements are made, the subsequent compensation communications should be limited to routine written fee requests. AAA/ABA Code, Canon III(B)(3).

In addition to compensation, some arbitrators may place particular conditions on their service. Some may be unwilling to accept appointment unless the parties agree to have the hearing recorded and transcribed. Others may have a firm prohibition on performing any professional services during certain times of the year that are strictly reserved for family vacations or other functions. Some may insist that they be permitted to employ a law clerk for legal research at a particular compensation rate to be paid by the parties. Others may insist that the parties bear the expense of their traveling home on weekends during extended hearings. All such terms should be communicated to the parties at or before the arbitrator's appointment.

E.   Appointments Made through Arbitral Institutions

Arbitrators should be aware of procedures regarding appointments made through arbitral institutions.

A reference in an arbitration clause to an arbitral institution or its rules is sufficient to invoke that institution's selection process.

Arbitral institutions use different methods to select arbitrators, including (1) a list-selection method, allowing parties to strike or rank arbitrators, (2) unilateral selection by an arbitral institution, or (3) enforcement of arbitration agreements that provide for the two party-appointed arbitrators to select the third arbitrator. Most arbitral rules also permit the parties to agree to their own arbitrator selection process. *See, e.g.,* AAA Rule 12(a); JAMS Rule 2. Since institutions often make appointments based on biographical information maintained in their files, arbitrators should make sure their information is accurate and current.

F.   Appointments in Ad Hoc Arbitrations

Arbitrators should be aware of special considerations concerning appointments in ad hoc arbitrations.

The process for appointing arbitrators in ad hoc arbitrations is determined by reference to the arbitration agreement. The arbitration clause may provide that the parties either shall jointly select a single neutral arbitrator, or that each party will appoint an arbitrator (either neutral or non-neutral) and that the party-appointed arbitrators will then select a third arbitrator. The primary distinction between ad hoc and administered arbitrations arises when the parties or the party-appointed arbitrators fail to agree upon the selection of the sole or third arbitrator or when, for whatever reason, a party fails to appoint a party-arbitrator when required to do so under the arbitration agreement.

Under such circumstances, and because the parties in an ad hoc arbitration usually have not agreed to enlist the services of an arbitral institution with respect to the selection of arbitrators, the parties necessarily must seek judicial assistance in the appointment of the arbitrator. Section 5 of the FAA and Section 11 of the RUAA clearly accord to the court the authority to grant such relief. 9 U.S.C. § 5; RUAA § 11. Arbitrators appointed under these statutes have precisely the same authority as if they had been appointed by agreement of the parties pursuant to the applicable arbitration clause.

It should be noted that some arbitration agreements providing for ad hoc arbitrations do provide for a means of avoiding judicial intervention when one or both of the parties, or the party-appointed arbitrators, fail to appoint an arbitrator under the contractually agreed process. For example, in ad hoc arbitrations governed by the CPR Rules, when a party or the party-appointed arbitrators fail to appoint an arbitrator in accord with the parties' arbitration agreement, the CPR will serve as the appointing authority. CPR Rule 6. When a party fails to appoint its own arbitrator, the CPR Rules grant to the CPR the unilateral authority to appoint a person "whom it deems qualified to serve." *Id.* Rule 6.5. In instances in which the parties or the party-appointed arbitrators have jointly failed to select an arbitrator, the rules provide for the use of a list-selection process. *Id.* Rule 6.4.

G.   Party-Appointed Neutral Arbitrators

Arbitrators should be aware of special considerations concerning appointments as party-appointed neutral arbitrators.

As noted above, an arbitration clause may provide that each party will appoint a neutral party-appointed arbitrator, and that the two party-appointed arbitrators will then select a third arbitrator. When contacted to discuss availability to serve as party-appointed neutrals, arbitrators should be aware of special considerations concerning the manner and content of allowable communications between such arbitrators and parties.

As is the case with neutral arbitrators generally, party-appointed neutral arbitrators may have limited *ex parte* contact relevant to the appointment process, unless prohibited by the clause or applicable rules. *See* Section A, *supra*. Thus, party-appointed neutral arbitrators should conduct the same kind of initial inquiry as is appropriate for other neutral arbitrators concerning the identities of the parties and nature of the case. They may ask about the identities of the parties and other persons involved in the arbitration, may listen to an explanation of the general nature of the dispute, and may respond to inquiries designed to determine the arbitrator's suitability and availability for the appointment.

Party-appointed neutral arbitrators who are expected to participate in selection of a third arbitrator may also consult with the representatives of the appointing party about the suitability of candidates for that position. AAA/ABA Code, Canon III(B)(2).

As noted above, party-appointed neutral arbitrators may consult with representatives of the appointing party concerning compensation and may, if consistent with any applicable institutional rules, accept payment directly from the party or its counsel. AAA/ABA Code, Canon III(B)(3).

In an arbitration involving party-appointed arbitrators, each party-appointed arbitrator may also consult with the appointing party concerning the arbitrator's status as neutral or non-neutral. AAA/ABA Code, Canon III(B)(4). The use of "non-neutral" party-appointed arbitrators continues to be a permitted practice in U.S. domestic arbitrations. Some institutional rules thus permit the parties to agree that the party-appointed arbitrators will be non-neutral. Because non-neutral arbitrators are not expected to satisfy the same standards of impartiality and independence that are required of neutral arbitrators, and in light of the fact that non-neutral arbitrators are typically permitted to communicate on an *ex parte* basis with the party that appointed them, it is essential that the neutral or non-neutral status of a party appointee be understood from the beginning. Arbitrators who are appointed by a party should presume they are to serve as neutral arbitrators unless and until it is determined that the intent of the arbitration agreement is that the party-appointed arbitrators are to be non-neutral. For a detailed discussion of non-neutral arbitrators, see Chapter 3, *infra*.

H.   *Ex Parte* Communications

> **During the appointment process, arbitrators should avoid all *ex parte* communication with parties except as expressly permitted by applicable rules, law, and ethical codes.**

In order to avoid an appearance of partiality, and except as otherwise specifically provided for in this chapter, arbitrators should avoid any *ex parte* communication with the parties or lawyers for the parties throughout the appointment process (and thereafter). AAA/ABA Code, Canon III.

III. DISCLOSURES

Arbitrators must make appropriate disclosures as required by applicable law, institutional rules, and ethical guidelines.

Ethical rules require arbitrators to make, at the time of appointment and throughout the arbitration, disclosures about any interest or relationship likely to affect impartiality, or that might create an appearance of partiality. In determining what disclosures to make, arbitrators are expected to exercise due diligence by reviewing records, and making reasonable inquiries about past or on-going relationships with parties, witnesses, attorneys, and other arbitrators, and any advantage they may personally gain that is dependent on the outcome of the arbitration. The particular standard for detail of disclosure depends on applicable law, institutional rules, and ethical guidelines.

A.   FAA

The FAA does not specifically address the matter of disclosure by arbitrators.

The FAA does not prescribe what disclosures must be made by arbitrators, nor specify grounds to vacate an arbitration award for specific non-disclosures. However, an award may be vacated when an arbitrator demonstrates evident partiality, corruption, fraud, or misconduct. 9 U.S.C. §10(a)(1), (2), and (3). Ever since the United States Supreme Court's decision in *Commonwealth Coatings Corp. v. Continental Casualty Co.*, 393 U.S. 145 (1968), courts have struggled with the question of whether the ground for vacating an award due to arbitrator non-disclosure is the failure to disclose (1) "any dealings that might create an impression of possible bias," or (2) dealings of a substantial interest or relationship that create an impression of partiality (a narrower position taken by Justice White in his concurring opinion). As a result, courts have conducted their own case-by-case factual analysis of whether an arbitrator's failure to disclose reached a standard of evident partiality.

B.   RUAA

The RUAA uses a "reasonable person" standard.

The RUAA, adopted by ten states and currently under active consideration by several more, requires that, before accepting appointment, an arbitrator must disclose any known facts a reasonable person would consider likely to affect the impartiality of the arbitrator, including (1) a financial or personal interest in the outcome of the arbitration proceeding, or (2) an existing or past relationship with any of the parties, counsel, witnesses, or other arbitrators. RUAA § 12 (a).

C.   AAA/ABA Code

Under the newly revised AAA/ABA Code, arbitrators have a continuing duty to disclose any interest or relationship likely to affect, or any information that might create an appearance of, partiality.

Under the newly revised AAA/ABA Code, arbitrators have a duty to disclose (1) any known direct or indirect financial or personal interest in the outcome of the arbitration, (2) any existing or past financial, business, professional, family, or social relationships that might create an appearance of bias, (3) the nature and extent of any prior knowledge they may have of the dispute, and (4) any other matters, relationships, or interests that they are obligated to disclose by the agreement of the parties, the rules or practices of an institution, or applicable law. AAA/ABA Code, Canon II(A). The obligation is a continuing duty that requires disclosure, as soon as practicable, at any stage of the arbitration, of any such interests or relationships that are recalled, discovered or subsequently arise. AAA/ABA Code, Canon II(C).

D.   Other Ethical Standards

Certain arbitral institutions or institutional rules require the application of ethical standards other than those established by the AAA/ABA Code, and arbitrators, therefore, must be familiar with, and comply with, the standards that apply to the arbitration in which they are serving.

While the AAA/ABA Code was designed to reflect ethical principles presumed to be generally applicable, particular arbitral institutions or institutional rules will sometimes differ. The CPR recently endorsed the AAA/ABA Code to the extent it complemented and was not inconsistent with its general rule requiring disclosure of "any circumstances that might give rise to justifiable doubt regarding the arbitrator's independence and impartiality," a standard that is not inconsistent with the Code. CPR Rule 7. Conversely, the NAF has established its own Code of Conduct for Arbitrators, which only partially adopts the AAA/ABA Code. Other arbitral rules may not contemplate or provide for "non-neutral" arbitrators. Because such standards and rules may differ from the AAA/ABA Code in a variety of respects, arbitrators serving in such circumstances should not only be familiar with such standards and rules, but should make their disclosures in accordance with them, subject, of course, to any other applicable statutory or contractual considerations.

E.   California Requirements

California has enumerated specific disclosure and ethics requirements for neutral arbitrators conducting contractual arbitrations in that state.

The California Arbitration Act (Cal. Civ. Proc. Code §§ 1280 *et seq.*) ("CAA") and the Ethics Standards for Neutral Arbitrators in Contractual Arbitrations, (Division VI, California Rules of Court

Appendix, rev. 2003) ("California Ethics Standards") contain enumerated ethical and disclosure obligations for arbitrators. They substantially expand disclosure requirements, regulate arbitrator conduct, and afford parties an absolute right to disqualify arbitrators within fifteen days of the arbitrators' disclosures. Failure to comply with the standards constitutes grounds for disqualification or vacatur of the arbitration award. *See* Section IV, *infra*.

The CAA requires neutral arbitrators conducting arbitrations in the state to disclose, within ten days of notice of the proposed appointment, "all matters that could cause a person aware of the facts to reasonably entertain a doubt that the proposed neutral arbitrator would be able to be impartial," including service as a neutral or non-neutral arbitrator for a party or lawyer for a party for the preceding five years. Cal. Civ. Proc. Code § 1281.9. The California Ethics Standards require arbitrators to disclose any existing or prior matters concluded within the past two years in which the arbitrator served as a dispute resolution neutral other than an arbitrator and in which any of the parties and/or counsel in the pending arbitration were involved. California Ethics Standards 7(d)(5) and (6).

Arbitrators must also disclose financial or other relationships between their immediate family members (spouses, domestic partners, or minor children) and the parties, lawyers, or lawyers associated in the practice of law with the lawyers in the arbitration. Cal. Civ. Proc. Code § 1281.9(a)(6); California Ethics Standards 2(n) and 7(d). Certain close relationships between parties and arbitrators' extended family members ("parents, grandparents, great-grandparents, children, grandchildren, great-grandchildren, siblings, uncles, aunts, nephews and nieces of the arbitrator or the arbitrator's spouse or domestic partner or the spouse of such person") must be disclosed, including whether such persons have knowledge of disputed evidentiary facts. California Ethics Standards 2(o) and 7(d). Arbitrators may fulfill their disclosure obligations regarding the relationships of their extended family by seeking such information from family members living in the arbitrator's household, and by declaring in writing that they have done so. California Ethics Standards 9(b). They may fulfill their disclosure obligation regarding relationships with lawyers and associates of lawyers in the arbitration by first disclosing all such relationships known to the arbitrator, then making a written inquiry of the lawyers in the arbitration regarding whether they are aware of any such relationships, and by declaring in writing that they have done so. California Ethics Standards 9(c).

Arbitrators must also disclose in writing whether they will entertain additional offers of employment from the parties or attorneys while the current arbitration is pending. Arbitrators who indicate that they will do so may be disqualified on that basis. However, if not so disqualified, they may later accept such additional employment without disclosure to the parties in the pending case. California Ethics Standards 12(b) and 7(b)(2). *See* Section V, *infra*. While there is no definite authority on the point to date, acceptance of subsequent employment that raises a reasonable appearance of partiality or lack of independence in the pending case would presumably be a proper ground for a party in that case to demand that the arbitrator withdraw.

If the arbitration involves a consumer, arbitrators are obligated to further disclose any relationship between the arbitral institution and parties or lawyers of the parties, and may rely on information provided by the arbitral institution. California Ethics Standard 8.

The California Ethics Standards also regulate conduct by prohibiting gifts, favors, and *ex parte* communications. Arbitrators must also provide truth in marketing and advertising, give notice of membership in an organization that practices discrimination, and conduct the proceeding fairly, promptly, and diligently. California Ethics Standards 11, 14, 17.

IV. DISQUALIFICATION

When requested to withdraw by all parties, arbitrators must comply; when requested by only one party, arbitrators should refer to the arbitration agreement, applicable law, or institutional rules for guidance.

Since arbitration is a matter of agreement between the parties, an arbitrator must withdraw if all parties request the arbitrator to do so. AAA/ABA Code, Canon II(G). If only one party moves to disqualify an arbitrator in an administered arbitration, and the parties' agreement or institutional rules set forth procedures for determining challenges to arbitrators (*see, e.g.*, AAA Rule 17, CPR Rule 7), then the parties' agreement, applicable rules, or governing law should be followed. AAA/ABA Code, Canon II(G)(1). In ad hoc arbitrations in which no specific institutional rules apply, and one party moves to disqualify the arbitrator because of alleged partiality, Canon II(G)(2) of the AAA/ABA Code provides that the arbitrator should withdraw unless the arbitrator determines after careful consideration that the "reason for the challenge is not substantial, and that he or she can nevertheless act and decide the case impartially and fairly."

Neither the FAA nor the RUAA provides for disqualification. As is discussed above, case law under the FAA does provide a potential ground for vacatur based on arbitrators' failures to disclose. The RUAA provides that if a party timely objects to an arbitrator's continued service after receiving the arbitrator's required disclosures, and the matter nevertheless proceeds to an award, the objection may be a ground for vacatur. RUAA § 12 (c). Likewise, failure to disclose required facts serves as grounds for vacatur of an award. RUAA § 12 (d).

Canon II(F) of the AAA/ABA Code provides: "When parties, with knowledge of a person's interests and relationships, nevertheless desire that person to serve as an arbitrator, that person may properly serve." Arbitrators may want to inquire at the preliminary conference whether the parties believe any grounds for arbitrator disqualification exist, and to memorialize in writing that the parties have advised that they are aware of none and are satisfied that the arbitrators may properly serve. This approach may substantially reduce the risk that a losing party may later object that the arbitrator failed to make a required disclosure. However, there is a split in authority among the circuits regarding whether parties waive the right to challenge an arbitrator when the party has constructive knowledge of potential bias but fails to timely challenge the arbitrator. *See Fidelity Fed. Bank FSB v. Durga Ma Corp.*, 386 F.3d 1306, 1313 (9th Cir. 2004).

Parties may also only be able to assert objections based on disclosed conflicts within a certain period if statutes or applicable rules so dictate. For example, under California law, parties have an absolute right to disqualify arbitrators within fifteen days of arbitrators' disclosures (and, presumably, not thereafter). Cal. Civ. Proc. Code §1281.91. If an arbitrator fails to disqualify himself or herself after receipt of a timely filed notice, the court "shall vacate the award." *Id.* § 1286.2(a)(6)(B); *Azteca Construction., Inc. v. ADR Consulting, Inc.*, 121 Cal. App. 4th 1156 (2004) (holding (1) that the CAA "confers on both parties the unqualified right to remove a proposed arbitrator based on any disclosure required by law which could affect his or her neutrality," and the further right to seek vacatur when the arbitrator fails to make such disclosures, and (2) that such rights were not waived when the parties agreed to the application of certain institutional rules that conferred on AAA the final authority to determine challenges to arbitrators). Proposed arbitrators may also be disqualified by a party based on their disclosures that they will accept offers of employment as dispute resolution neutrals from the lawyers or parties in the arbitration while the arbitration is pending. California Ethics Standard 12(b). *See* Section V, *infra*.

The disqualification provisions of California law present unique issues relating to continuing or subsequent disclosures, which are required both by AAA/ABA Code, Canon II(C), and by California Ethics Standard 7(c). A currently unresolved question is whether *Azteca*'s rule (that arbitral institutions' discretion over disqualification is trumped by the parties' rights under California law) applies to the situation in which a new disclosure is made subsequent to the original appointment because of new information or a later occurring event. If *Azteca* were so read, it would eviscerate institutional rules that protect the parties in such circumstances against undue prejudice when removal of an arbitrator would occasion much expense or other hardship and in which the disclosure is not material. *See* JAMS Rule 15(i) (party may challenge the continued service of an arbitrator based on information not known at the time of appointment; final determination shall be made by JAMS and shall take into account the materiality of the facts and any prejudice to the parties).

V. CONTINUING DISCLOSURES AND LIMITATIONS ON ACTIVITIES DURING PENDENCY OF A CASE

Arbitrators should comply with applicable law, institutional rules, and party agreements regarding continuing disclosure obligations and should recognize that the appointment will limit their activities while the case continues and for a reasonable time thereafter.

While serving, arbitrators should avoid entering into any business, professional, or personal relationship, or acquiring any financial or personal interest, that is likely to affect independence or which might reasonably create the appearance of partiality. If changes in relationships with parties, counsel, co-arbitrators or witnesses do occur while the arbitration is pending, arbitrators should disclose to the parties anything that could give rise to justifiable doubts of their impartiality and independence. AAA/ABA Code, Canon II(C).

Arbitrators should also anticipate, and be prepared to accept, that some limitations will continue even after conclusion of the case. For a reasonable period of time after the decision of a case, arbitrators should avoid entering into any business, professional, or personal relationship, or acquiring any financial interest that might reasonably create the appearance that they had been influenced in the arbitration by the expectation of the creation of such a relationship or interest. AAA/ABA Code, Canon I(C).

Prospective arbitrators who are members of law firms should anticipate and avoid future conflicts that may arise from activities of others at their firms. As a precaution, arbitrators should insert the names of the arbitration parties and counsel in their firms' conflicts systems with the requirement that other attorneys in the firm should not represent or become adverse to them without consulting the arbitrator. Although service as an arbitrator does not constitute legal representation of any or all of the parties, it still may be a source of claims of conflicts if other members of an arbitrator's law firm undertake legal representation of a party or one of its affiliates while the arbitration is pending.

Sometimes, in the course of an arbitration, a party or counsel in the case seeks to appoint one or more of the same arbitrators in another arbitration. Such a request should generally not be accepted without disclosure to, and consent of, all parties and counsel in the pending and prospective cases. However, arbitrators should consider whether applicable rules, statutes, or ethics standards may create exceptions to this general rule. For example, under California law, arbitrators must declare, prior to being appointed, whether they will entertain future offers of employment as a neutral while the current arbitration is pending. Otherwise they are prohibited from accepting such appointments. *See* Section III E, *supra* and California Ethics Standards 12(b) and (c). In the event arbitrators have made such an initial disclosure, however, Standard 7(b)(2) provides a "safe harbor" provision that eliminates a continuing duty of disclosure of such offers or acceptance of employment.

There is no corresponding safe harbor provision under the FAA; instead, case law establishes a continuing duty to disclose. *See generally Commonwealth Coatings Corp. v. Continental Casualty Co.*, 393 U.S. 145 (1968); *Crow v. Jeffrey M. Brown Associates, Inc.*, 264 F. Supp. 2d 217 (E.D. Pa 2003). That obligation is also clearly stated in the AAA/ABA Code, Canon II(A) and (C), and Section 12(b) of the RUAA. Thus, if an arbitrator, relying on the California Ethics Standards in an arbitration being conducted in California, makes a proper safe harbor disclosure and subsequently does not disclose otherwise relevant offers or acceptance of employment, there is a risk a court would determine that (1) the case concerns a dispute involving interstate commerce and that the FAA therefore applies, (2) the FAA preempts the safe harbor aspects of California law, (3) there was a duty to disclose the subsequent matter and such duty was breached, (4) the disclosure was material to the parties, (5) the circumstances establish evident partiality on the part of the arbitrator and, therefore, (6) the award must be vacated. *See Crow, supra*, 264 F. Supp. 2d 217. Given all of the foregoing risks and uncertainties, it is clearly the better practice for arbitrators to always make disclosures in accordance with the AAA/ABA Code, which reflects a broad national consensus on arbitrator conduct, even in cases where disclosure is arguably not mandatory due to possibly applicable unique state statutes or rules.

If disclosure of prospective new appointments is required or advisable, arbitrators should also consider the manner in which to make such disclosure. It could be awkward for parties or counsel to be told by an arbitrator, at a hearing or conference, that the arbitrator has been asked to serve as arbitrator in a second matter involving one of them. In administered arbitrations, the best solution may be to have the arbitral institution or case manager make the disclosure and tell counsel that if any party objects the arbitrator will decline the second appointment and will not be informed of who objected. In non-administered arbitrations, arbitrators may consider advising the parties in writing of the pendency of the second matter and soliciting written objections. To avoid putting either of the parties "on the spot," arbitrators may specifically advise that, to the extent there is an objection, the objecting party ought not be identified. Thus, arbitrators may request that the parties send a joint communication that simply states either that the parties "do object" to the arbitrators serving in the second arbitration or that they "do not object."

CHAPTER 3

NON-NEUTRAL ARBITRATORS

Since "non-neutral" arbitrators continue to be used in domestic arbitrations, arbitrators should be familiar with the appointment process and other considerations relating to non-neutral conduct and disclosures.

I. ARBITRATOR SELECTION GENERALLY

A. Parties' Arbitration Agreement

The use of "non-neutral" arbitrators continues to be a permitted practice in domestic arbitrations in the United States. Thus, a well-drafted arbitration clause will not only specify the number of arbitrators and the process to be utilized in selecting and appointing them, but will also clearly state whether the party-appointed arbitrators on a tripartite arbitration panel will be neutral or "non-neutral." This observation is particularly important both because courts are obligated to enforce the selection process agreed upon by the parties (*see, e.g.,* FAA, 9 U.S.C. § 5; RUAA § 11(A); Cal. Code Civ. Proc. § 1281.6), and because an arbitration administrator exceeds its powers if the arbitration selection process is not in compliance with the parties' agreement. *Brook v. Peak International, Ltd.,* 294 F.3d 668, 673-674 (5th Cir. 2002) ("AAA's departure from the selection procedure . . . was utterly unwarranted").

B. Institutional Rules and AAA/ABA Code

A reference in an arbitration clause to an arbitral institution or its rules is sufficient to adopt that institution's selection process and, under some rules, provide for administration of the arbitration by that institution. While institutional arbitration rules provide that most disputes will be resolved by a single arbitrator, those same rules, with some exceptions, permit the parties to specify the number of arbitrators and to further provide for party-appointed arbitrators that are non-neutral.

In the past, it was generally customary in domestic U.S. arbitrations to presume that, in the absence of a clear indication to the contrary, the contracting parties intended that party-appointed arbitrators be non-neutral. This general presumption was reflected in the 1977 version of the AAA/ABA Code, which provided that, in arbitrations involving party-appointed arbitrators, "the two party-appointed arbitrators should be considered non-neutrals unless both parties inform the arbitrators that all three arbitrators are to be neutral or unless the contract, the applicable arbitration rules, or any governing law requires that all three arbitrators be neutral." AAA/ABA Code (1997 version), Introductory Note and Canon VII. *See Sunkist Soft Drinks, Inc. v. Sunkist Growers, Inc.*, 10 F.3d 753, 759 (11th Cir. 1993), *cert. denied*, 513 U.S. 869 (1994).

However, in 2004, the AAA/ABA Code was revised to provide that all arbitrators initially should presume that they are neutral, and that party-appointed arbitrators should continue to act as neutrals until such time as they form a "reasonable belief" that the contracting parties intended them to serve as non-neutral arbitrators. AAA/ABA Code, Canon IX(C)(3). This "presumption of neutrality" relates only to the initial conduct of the arbitrators and does not affect the determination of the parties' contractual intent concerning whether the party-appointed arbitrators are to be neutral or non-neutral. The revised Code provides that any "doubt or uncertainty" relating to the party-appointed arbitrators' status is to be resolved "in accordance with Canon IX." *See* AAA/ABA Code, Note on Neutrality. Canon IX states that, in making this determination of the parties' intent, the arbitrator should review the parties' agreement, any applicable rules, and the applicable law. Moreover, when appropriate, arbitrators may also "inquire into agreements that have not been expressly set forth, but which may be implied from an established course of dealings of the parties or well-recognized custom and usage in their trade or profession." *Id.* Determination of the contracting parties' intention in this regard, therefore, is to be based on normal contract construction principles without the application of any form of presumption. Of course, evidence that the drafters of the arbitration clause (1) were aware of either version of the Code, (2) concluded that its "presumption" regarding neutrality or non-neutrality would control in the absence of contrary language in the clause, and (3) thus relied on that "presumption" rather than inserting specific contractual language, could be relevant evidence of the parties' intent.

In contrast to the revised AAA/ABA Code, the recently revised rules of one arbitral institution, the AAA, do establish a rebuttable presumption of neutrality that lasts beyond the initial conduct of the arbitrators and governs arbitrators' status throughout the arbitration, unless the arbitration agreement expressly provides to the contrary. Thus, AAA Rule 12(b), as recently revised, provides that party-appointed arbitrators shall be neutral "unless the parties have specifically agreed pursuant to [Rule] 17(a) that the party-appointed arbitrators are to be non-neutral." In turn, Rule 17(a)(iii) states that the parties "may agree in writing" that the party-appointed arbitrators will be non-neutral. As a result, with respect to arbitrations conducted under the AAA rules, the "presumption of neutrality" established by those rules will be determinative of the parties' intent regarding the status of the party-appointed arbitrators absent a specific written agreement to appoint non-neutral arbitrators.

II.   LIMITATIONS ON CHOICE OF NON-NEUTRAL ARBITRATORS

A.   Parties' Arbitration Agreement

Before accepting an appointment to serve as a non-neutral arbitrator, the candidate should determine whether a specific provision in the parties' agreement precludes the appointment.

Depending on the applicable rules of ethics, non-neutral arbitrators generally are not subject to disqualification. *See* Section IV, *infra*.

That does not mean, however, that any person at all can be appointed to serve as a non-neutral arbitrator. In some instances, the parties' contract will place limitations on who may serve as a non-neutral. For example, the arbitration provision might require not only that the third arbitrator be neutral, but further that all three arbitrators, including the non-neutral arbitrators, be "independent." The concept of arbitrator "independence" differs from arbitrator "impartiality" and generally requires that an arbitrator must have no direct financial or business ties with the parties, counsel, witnesses, and perhaps the other arbitrators. *See* Chapter 2 § III, *supra*. *See generally* IBA Rules of Ethics for International Arbitrators, Art. 3(1) (1987). As was noted in Chapter 2, *supra*, the arbitration clause also might provide that prospective arbitrators also satisfy other qualification requirements. In contrast, the revised AAA Rules acknowledge that non-neutral arbitrators are not required to be independent. It is thus critical for arbitrators who are considering whether to accept an appointment as a non-neutral to determine the nature and extent of any qualifying limitations relating to non-neutrals.

B.   Applicable Law and Ethical Rules

Before accepting an appointment to serve as a non-neutral arbitrator, the candidate should determine whether unique considerations weigh in favor of declining the appointment.

Parties commonly select non-neutral arbitrators who have knowledge of the industry, the particular form of business transaction, or some other aspect of the dispute involved in the arbitration. Similarly, non-neutrals often have some relationship with the party or counsel. There are, nonetheless, some types of relationships that could raise concerns regarding the propriety of the non-neutral arbitrator serving on a tripartite panel. Regardless of an institutional rule that might not require a non-neutral to be independent, any potential financial interest in the outcome of the arbitration might cause a court to question even a non-neutral arbitrator's ability to ensure a fair hearing.

Arbitrators who are potential witnesses or partners of counsel or who have a present business relationship with the party possibly will be challenged. Because there is so little case law addressing this issue, the outcome of such a challenge is manifestly uncertain. Such conflicts potentially make the eventual award vulnerable to vacatur, however, and prudence thus dictates that a party, and the arbitrator, should consider refraining from appointing, or accepting appointment, under those circumstances.

III.   DETERMINING STATUS OF PARTY-APPOINTED ARBITRATORS

A.   Party-Appointed Arbitrators' Role in Determining Status of Arbitrators

In order to ensure an efficient dispute resolution process, party-appointed arbitrators should endeavor to determine their status at the earliest possible moment.

The revised AAA/ABA Code focuses on the parties' and the arbitrators' obligation to reach a common understanding of the role and status of the party-appointed arbitrators in each proceeding. Unfortunately, the arbitration clause often is silent or vague as to the parties' intent. The clause might simply state, "Each side shall select an arbitrator and they shall select the third arbitrator." Occasionally, the clause reflects a clearer expression of intent. For example, the clause might state, "Each side shall select an arbitrator and they shall select the neutral arbitrator." The use of such terms in different contexts can provide some guidance regarding the parties' understanding of whether the party-appointed arbitrators, or only the third arbitrator, are expected to be neutral.

Unless and until it is determined that the arbitrator is to be non-neutral, permissible communications between the appointee and the appointing party or its counsel are limited to questions concerning the arbitrators' status and other threshold issues. *Id.*, Canon III. *See also* AAA Rule 18.

At a minimum, the foregoing considerations require the following:

- Counsel should be familiar with the clause and applicable institutional rules and should promptly seek to determine the parties' intent as to the neutrality of the party-appointed arbitrators.

- Counsel should not appoint someone who is obviously predisposed or non-independent unless counsel knows or believes that the party-appointed arbitrator is expected to be non-neutral.

- Counsel should also consider consulting with opposing counsel on the subject of the meaning of the appointment clause.

- The arbitrator candidate must inquire about these matters upon first contact and should also read the clause and seek to ascertain the parties' understanding of contractual intent. The candidate, of course, would also be permitted to discuss any of the other narrowly defined topics—*e.g.,* availability, compensation, potential conflicts—that may be discussed by an individual who is being considered for appointment as a neutral arbitrator. *See* Chapter 2 § II, *supra.*

- Regardless of whether they are neutral or non-neutral, party-appointed arbitrators also may consult *ex parte* with their respective appointing party on the subject of the appointment of the third arbitrator. Those discussions may include such matters as the qualifications and suitability of particular candidates.

B.   Chairperson's Role in Determining Status of Party-Appointed Arbitrators

The neutral chairperson should take an active role in insisting that the status of the party-appointed arbitrators be clearly determined.

It is also the responsibility of the chairperson, once appointed, to attempt to ensure that the parties have a common understanding of the roles of their respective appointed arbitrators and the procedures that shall apply to them. When necessary, the chairperson therefore should insist that the parties resolve any issue regarding the neutrality of the party-appointed arbitrators. The status of the party-appointed arbitrators should be determined early in the process and documented in writing.

It is also possible that the neutral chairperson will be reluctant or unwilling to serve on a tripartite panel with non-neutral arbitrators. As a consequence, it is preferable to determine prior to the appointment of the chairperson whether that person is willing and able to serve with non-neutral arbitrators. In the instance in which a chairperson who is unwilling to serve with non-neutral arbitrators is inadvertently appointed, the parties will be left with only three alternatives: (1) replace the chairperson; (2) replace the non-neutral arbitrators with neutral party-appointed arbitrators; or (3) convert the non-neutral arbitrators to neutral arbitrators. As is discussed below, the third option of converting the non-neutral arbitrators to neutral arbitrators often presents potentially problematic issues.

IV. DISCLOSURES BY NON-NEUTRAL ARBITRATORS

A. General Practice of Disclosure

Non-neutral arbitrators are generally required to make disclosures. A non-neutral arbitrator should be guided by the AAA/ABA Code and any applicable statutes and institutional rules when determining what disclosures to make.

The AAA Rules require non-neutral arbitrators to make the same disclosures as neutral arbitrators. AAA Rule 16(a). Although the RUAA maintains the distinction between neutral and non-neutral arbitrators, *see* RUAA § 23(a), it also requires disclosures of all arbitrators, subject to the parties' waiver of that obligation directly or as a result of the selection of rules of an administering body. *Id.* § 12(f).

The FAA does not address what disclosures must be made by arbitrators. *See* Chapter 2 § III(A), *supra.* Case law under the FAA suggests, however, that arbitrators must disclose to the parties, (1) "any dealings that might create an impression of possible bias," or (2) a substantial interest or relationship that create an impression of partiality. *Id.* This disclosure requirement is probably equally applicable to neutral and non-neutral arbitrators. *See Sphere Drake Insurance Ltd. v. All American Life Ins. Co.,* 307 F.3d 617 (7th Cir. 2002), *cert denied,* 538 U.S. 961 (2003); *Delta Mine Holding Co. v. AFC Coal Properties, Inc.,* 280 F.3d 815, 822 (8th Cir. 2001); *Employers Insurance of Wausau v. National Union Fire Insurance Co.,* 933 F.2d 1481, 1488-90 (9th Cir. 1991).

In determining what disclosures to make, non-neutral arbitrators can reasonably look to the AAA/ABA Code—the leading national code of ethics—which requires the same disclosures by neutral and non-neutral arbitrators. AAA/ABA Code, Canons II(A), X(B). Thus, in the absence of controlling authority to the contrary, a non-neutral arbitrator should follow the AAA/ABA Code and make disclosures in compliance with that Code.

B.   Unique State Requirements Relating to Disclosures

Even when unique state statutes or rules establish less stringent requirements than those delineated in the AAA/ABA Code, non-neutral arbitrators will usually be well advised to make disclosures in accordance with that Code.

Prior to the development of statutory disqualification standards in California, it was understood that, since party-appointed arbitrators were expected to be predisposed, only neutral arbitrators were required to make disclosures. *Tate v. Saratoga Savings & Loan Ass'n,* 216 Cal. App. 3d 843, 858 (1989). However, the conduct of a party-appointed arbitrator might nonetheless give rise to the vacatur of an award for "corruption." *Id.* The adoption of new California disclosure standards for arbitrators did not change this rule. The California Ethics Standards thus expressly do not apply to non-neutral arbitrators. California Ethics Standards 2(a) and (q), 3(b)(1). As a result, disclosures of prior service as an arbitrator in California are only required of a neutral arbitrator. Cal. Civ. Proc. Code § 1281.9(a), (b), (c), and (d). These observations, however, should not be interpreted as meaning that a non-neutral arbitrator in a California arbitration should not make disclosures.

At a minimum, arbitrators should be aware that the conflict between state and federal standards concerning the existence of a legal obligation compelling non-neutral arbitrators to make disclosures creates confusion and risk for the arbitrator appointment process in California. Because California law and the California Ethics Standards suggest that disclosure obligations are only applicable to neutral arbitrators, there is a widespread belief that non-neutral arbitrators need not make any disclosures upon their appointment in California-based arbitrations. Unfortunately, it is not always clear at the outset of an arbitration whether California arbitration law or the FAA applies, and whether the party-appointed arbitrators are to be neutral or non-neutral. As noted above, the revised AAA/ABA Code addresses this latter uncertainty by providing that the party-appointed arbitrators have the duty to establish their status at the earliest possible moment. AAA/ABA Code, Canon IX.

If the party-appointed arbitrators elect not to make any disclosures because they conclude they are non-neutral and that the CAA and the California Ethics Standards apply, the question arises whether a party may subsequently seek to disqualify an arbitrator for failure to make disclosures or seek to vacate the award based on a claim that the FAA applies and that material information was not disclosed.

This dichotomy between federal and state standards presents potential risks for non-neutral arbitrators in California. Given the very broad reading that courts give to the preemptive effect of the FAA, *see, e.g., Allied-Bruce Terminix Companies, Inc. v. Dobson*, 513 U.S. 265 (1995), it is likely that in most large commercial cases there will be some basis for arguing that the dispute concerns an issue "involving commerce" and that the FAA therefore applies. It is possible that the California Standards and procedure thus would be subject to federal preemption. As is discussed in Chapter 2, *supra*, the "safe harbor" provisions of the California standards—relating to prospective offers of employment as an arbitrator or ADR neutral— also can potentially conflict with the FAA. These points are highly significant with respect to non-neutral arbitrators, since they illustrate why it can be extremely important for the parties and the arbitrators to determine promptly whether the FAA applies.

Given all of the foregoing risks and uncertainties, it is clearly the better practice for non-neutral arbitrators to always make disclosures in accordance with the AAA/ABA Code even in cases in which disclosure is arguably not mandatory for non-neutrals due to less demanding state statutes or rules.

C.   Changes in Status of Arbitrators

In the event the non-neutrals' status changes to "neutral," the formerly non-neutral arbitrators will be required to make the same disclosures that are required of neutral arbitrators.

If, for whatever reason, non-neutral arbitrators are later "converted" by the parties into neutral arbitrators, several considerations come into play. First, in jurisdictions such as California, previously non-neutral arbitrators who, in reliance on the California Ethics Standards, did not make disclosures would now be required to do so, and the parties then might be entitled to disqualify them through the same process that applies to neutral arbitrators. *See* Chapter 2 §§ III and IV, *supra*. Under these circumstances, a basis for disqualification will often be present, since parties frequently select non-neutral arbitrators because of their special knowledge of the dispute, the business of the party, or the arbitrator's relationship with the party or counsel. Moreover, the "converted" arbitrators must be aware that the various complicated issues that already relate to neutral arbitrators under the California rules would also apply to the former non-neutral arbitrators. Thus, as was generally discussed above, the "converted" arbitrators would potentially be required to make disclosures that are required in the absence of a prior "safe harbor" disclosure under California Ethics Standard 7(b)(2).

When non-neutral arbitrators are "converted" to neutral arbitrators in a California arbitration, the court's decision in *Azteca Construction, Inc. v. ADR Consulting, Inc.*, 121 Cal. App. 4th 1156, 1167 (2004) might also become relevant. *Azteca* confirmed the generally held view that, upon making any disclosure, arbitrators serving in California may be disqualified for any reason or for no reason and that the parties are entitled to exercise that same right with respect to proposed replacement arbitrators. As was discussed in Chapter 2 § III(E), *supra*, the *Azteca* decision gives rise to an issue regarding whether parties' right to disqualify an arbitrator is renewed when formerly non-neutral arbitrators make new disclosures due to their conversion to neutral arbitrators.

The complications that can potentially arise due to differing federal and state law on the question whether non-neutral arbitrators must make disclosures further illustrate why the best practice is for non-neutral arbitrators to make disclosures even when, in the first instance, it might appear that such disclosures are not legally required. As a practical matter, such disclosures enhance the viability of the arbitration process by helping to ensure that the parties and arbitrators are aware of all circumstances affecting the conduct of the arbitration and the resolution of the parties' dispute.

V. NON-NEUTRAL ARBITRATOR CONDUCT

A. Ensuring a Fundamentally Fair Hearing

Non-neutral arbitrators have the same obligation as the neutral arbitrator to provide the parties with a fundamentally fair hearing.

Non-neutral arbitrators are expected to comply with Canons I and V of the AAA/ABA Code and uphold the integrity and fairness of the arbitration process.   Thus, while non-neutral arbitrators may be predisposed to the side that appointed them, they must act in a fair and diligent manner.   For example, the non-neutral should not interfere with the arbitration process or in the presentation of a party's case, and should refrain from conducting unduly aggressive "cross-examination" of a party's witnesses, as distinguished from asking questions that were not answered in a witness' testimony.

B.   *Ex Parte* Communications

While non-neutral arbitrators typically are permitted to maintain *ex parte* communications with the party that appointed them, it is important that the rules relating to such a practice be clearly established at the earliest possible time.

The best practice is for non-neutral arbitrators and parties to confer and agree on the extent of permissible *ex parte* communications before or immediately after the appointment of the neutral chairperson.   It is common to permit such communications until the commencement of the hearing on the merits or the submission of a dispositive motion. Alternately, *ex parte* communications might cease immediately upon the appointment of the chairperson or might continue through the hearing.   Except in unique situations in which the neutral specifically requests or approves of such communications, non-neutral arbitrators should never share information with the party or counsel relating to the substantive deliberations of the panel.

The best practice is to document in the preliminary conference order any agreements by the parties relating to non-neutral arbitrators. Even without express agreement, however, courts usually permit non-neutral arbitrators to have *ex parte* communications with parties, counsel, and witnesses on matters of substance and further permit conduct that clearly reveals a predisposition to the position of the party that appointed them.   In *Employer's Insurance of Wausau, supra,* 933 F.2d 1481, the Ninth Circuit thus rejected a challenge to an award in an instance in which a non-neutral arbitrator had performed consulting services with counsel on the issues in dispute and *ex parte* communications had occurred throughout the matter (by both party-appointed arbitrators). *See also Delta Mine Holding Co. v. AFC Coal Properties, Inc.*, 280 F.3d 815, 822 (8th Cir. 2001) (when parties have agreed to non-neutral party-appointed arbitrators, the award should not be vacated "unless the objecting party proves that the party arbitrator's partiality prejudicially affected the award"); *Sphere Drake Insurance Ltd., supra*, 307 F.3d 617.

C.   Providing Assistance to the Parties

When a non-neutral arbitrator is permitted to maintain *ex parte* communications with the appointing party, the non-neutral arbitrator is permitted to assist that party in the preparation of its case.

Non-neutral arbitrators often are called upon to participate in the selection of the neutral arbitrator and, in this regard, typically focus on the qualifications of the neutral candidate and the rapport the non-neutral arbitrator can expect to have with that person. Non-neutral arbitrators usually communicate with their party and counsel in this process. Some non-neutral arbitrators regard the selection of the neutral to be their exclusive right but, in most instances, the party retains an effective veto of any arbitrator the non-neutral arbitrator might propose or otherwise be inclined to accept.

Non-neutral arbitrators may also be called upon to assist counsel in identifying and resolving procedural issues; assessing substantive issues and formulating approaches to those issues; vetting witnesses, including experts; reviewing briefs before filing; assessing strategy generally; advising on cross-examination of opposing witnesses; assessing the need for expert witnesses and formulating approaches to expert issues; reviewing issues with the other arbitrators, and particularly the neutral arbitrator; and assuring that the issues, evidence, and legal points are being fully understood and appreciated. The right to maintain *ex parte* communications is often an essential component of most of these tasks. *See Delta Mine, supra*, 280 F.3d at

820-21 (refusing to vacate an award when the evidence showed that the non-neutral arbitrator had (1) assisted the party that appointed him in the preparation for the arbitration hearing, (2) disclosed ongoing arbitrator deliberations for the purpose of showing Delta Mine's attorneys "how to sway arbitrators to rule in Delta Mine's favor," and (3) participated in a mock arbitration held days before the hearing); *Sunkist, supra,* 10 F.3d at 759 (observing that non-neutral arbitrator participation in witness preparation, the selection of consultants, and expert witness testimony preparation is "not only unobjectionable, but commonplace"); *Stef Shipping Corp. v. Norris Grain Co.,* 209 F. Supp. 249, 253-54 (S.D.N.Y. 1962) (stating that "the fact that [a non-neutral arbitrator] consulted with his nominating party prior to the arbitration hearing is not shocking [and] is not the type of irregularity which [the FAA] contemplates as being sufficient to vacate an otherwise valid arbitration award").

VI. VALUE OF NON-NEUTRAL ARBITRATORS IN COMMERCIAL ARBITRATIONS

Neutral and non-neutral arbitrators should honor the parties' contractual intent and maximize the benefits that can be derived from involvement of non-neutral arbitrators.

Properly identified and ethically performing non-neutral arbitrators can bring procedural and substantive reliability to a tripartite arbitration. Theoretically, awards rendered in arbitrations involving non-neutral arbitrators are less likely to reflect the extreme position of either side for several reasons, including the fact that the presence of non-neutral arbitrators makes it unlikely that the chairperson will entirely misunderstand the law or evidence. Non-neutral arbitrators also frequently have special expertise with the industry or the particular issues involved in the arbitration. For those reasons, neutrals often rely on non-neutral arbitrators to provide a "reality check" on the evidence being presented and to ensure that the neutral fully understands the issues.

On occasion, the chairperson will ask a non-neutral arbitrator with the knowledge and agreement of the other arbitrators, to communicate with the party that selected it in an effort to expedite the prehearing process. For example, the non-neutral arbitrator might be asked to attempt to informally persuade the party to stipulate to the use of a deposition in lieu of the live testimony of a reluctant witness, to meet and confer on the realistic resolution of objections to the admission of certain evidence, or to produce a witness not "technically" in its control in order to avoid unnecessary delays that would accompany the issuance of a formal subpoena.

Face-saving agreements can also be "mediated" through the non-neutral arbitrators, thereby avoiding contentious rulings that have no ultimate effect on the outcome of the proceeding.

CHAPTER 4

DETERMINING JURISDICTION
AND ARBITRABILITY

**Arbitrators should see that challenges to jurisdiction and
arbitrability are resolved correctly, promptly, and
efficiently by the appropriate decision maker.**

I.   INTRODUCTION

**Arbitrators should be aware that the question of
whether challenges to jurisdiction and arbitrability are
to be decided by courts or arbitrators is a subject of
complex and evolving case law.**

Arbitrators generally have power only over those persons who
have agreed to arbitrate and those disputes that fall within the terms
of the parties' written arbitration agreement. Arbitral power over
persons and disputes is referred to herein as the arbitrators'
"jurisdiction" over such persons and disputes. Disputes that are
subject to arbitral power are referred to herein as being "arbitrable."
Questions of whether persons or disputes are subject to arbitral
power are variously referred to in the literature and case law, and
accordingly in this chapter, as questions of "jurisdiction" and
"arbitrability." The term "arbitrability" may also refer to questions
of whether public policy bars arbitration of certain types of
substantive disputes, *e.g.*, claims for violations of statutory rights.
(The United States Supreme Court has held that disputes that arise
from federal statutes such as antitrust, securities, RICO, and
employment disputes, both statutory and otherwise, are arbitrable.)
When parties assert that the arbitrator lacks power over the persons
or the subject matter, the question naturally arises whether the

arbitrator, who arguably lacks power, is the proper entity to decide that issue. In certain circumstances, questions of jurisdiction and arbitrability are properly resolved only by a court. In many circumstances, however, such disputes can and should be resolved by arbitrators themselves. The line between which disputes are for courts and which are for arbitrators is not always clear. There is a significant body of complex and rapidly evolving case law in this area. The trend, however, is toward increasing the authority of arbitrators to decide questions of jurisdiction and arbitrability.

This chapter addresses the issues of jurisdiction and arbitrability in non-class arbitrations. Chapter 5, which deals with all aspects of class arbitration, addresses jurisdiction and arbitrability issues in such arbitrations.

II.   LEGAL BACKGROUND

A.   The *Prima Paint* "Separability" Doctrine

Challenges to the jurisdiction of arbitrators based on contract defenses such as fraud or duress must relate to the arbitration agreement itself; any such defenses directed to the underlying contract as a whole will not defeat arbitral jurisdiction.

In 1967, the United States Supreme Court applied the doctrine of "separability" to arbitration agreements, holding that an arbitration clause can be severed from the underlying contract in which it is embedded and treated as a separate agreement independent of the underlying contract. *Prima Paint Corp. v. Flood & Conklin Manufacturing Co.*, 388 U.S. 395, 402-06 (1967). Under this doctrine, when the validity of the entire contract is called into question, the arbitration provision should be deemed severable so that the dispute is nonetheless arbitrable. In contrast, when the defense to enforceability strictly relates to the arbitration provision (*e.g.*, an allegation that a party was fraudulently induced to enter into an arbitration provision), the question of the validity of the arbitration agreement is normally to be decided by the courts.

Prima Paint involved a claim of fraudulent inducement. In holding that the claim was for the arbitrators, the Court relied on the following language of the FAA: "The court . . . upon being satisfied that the making of the agreement for arbitration . . . is not in issue, . . . shall make an order directing the parties to proceed to arbitration in accordance with the terms of the agreement." 9 U.S.C. § 4. The Court held that the claim of fraudulent inducement of the entire contract did not implicate the "making of the agreement for arbitration," and therefore the statutory language did not permit courts to consider such claims.

The separability doctrine is designed to ensure that questions relating to the validity of the underlying contract do not call into doubt the parties' intent to arbitrate their disputes. AAA Rule 7(b), CPR Rule 8.2, and JAMS Rule 11(c) embody the separability doctrine, providing that an arbitration clause shall be treated as an agreement separate and independent from the remainder of the contract containing it.

B.   The *First Options* "Clear and Unmistakable Evidence" Doctrine

Under the Supreme Court decision in *First Options v. Kaplan*, questions of arbitrability are presumptively for the court. However, such questions are for the arbitrators to decide if the parties have "clearly and unmistakably" submitted them to the arbitrators.

In the case of *First Options of Chicago v. Kaplan*, 514 U.S. 938 (1995), the United States Supreme Court articulated a rule that, absent "clear and unmistakable evidence" of the parties' contrary intent, courts, and not arbitrators, have the power to determine questions of arbitrability. However, such questions are for arbitrators to decide if the parties have "clearly and unmistakably" submitted them to the arbitrators.

Most major domestic institutional arbitral rules now explicitly provide that the arbitrator shall have the power to rule on any challenges to jurisdiction and any objections with respect to the existence, scope, or validity of the arbitration agreement or the contract of which the arbitration agreement forms a part. *See* AAA Rule 7; CPR Rule 8; JAMS Rule 11(c). Most, but not all, courts that have addressed the issue have held that when parties agree to rules of an arbitral institution that expressly provide for the arbitrators to rule on issues of arbitrability, they have manifested their clear and unmistakable intention to have the arbitrators determine such issues. *Shaw Group, Inc. v. Triplefine Int'l Corp.*, 322 F.3d 115 (2d Cir. 2003). *Cf. China Minmetals Materials Import & Export Co. v. Chi Mei Corp.*, 334 F.3d 274 (3d Cir. 2003).

Thus, when any of these institutional rules apply, it is likely, but not certain, that the *First Options* presumption will have been rebutted, as the parties will be deemed to have clearly and unmistakably submitted questions of jurisdiction and arbitrability to the arbitrator.

However, courts, and not arbitrators, generally determine whether non-signatories can be bound by an arbitration clause, whether a non-signatory can take advantage of an arbitration clause signed by a predecessor (*but see Contec Corp. v. Remote Solutions*, 398 F.3d 205 (2d Cir. 2005)), or whether a contract containing an arbitration clause has been formed at all. *See* Section F, *infra*.

C.   "Gateway" (Procedural vs. Substantive) Jurisdictional Issues

Under legal developments after *First Options*, it is becoming clear that, even absent a statement of unmistakable intent by the parties, not all issues of "arbitrability" are presumptively for a court. Thus, while arbitrators should, of course, obey court orders staying the arbitration or directing the resolution of a particular issue in a specific manner, they otherwise should decide all jurisdictional and arbitrability issues presented by the parties unless the arbitrator determines that the issue is one that a court must decide.

Prior to *First Options*, there was a substantial body of state and federal law holding that issues of "substantive" arbitrability (*i.e.*, whether a dispute is encompassed by an agreement to arbitrate) are for a court to decide, whereas issues of "procedural" arbitrability (*i.e.*, whether prerequisites such as time limits, notice, laches, estoppel, and other conditions precedent to an obligation to arbitrate have been met) are for the arbitrators to decide. *See* RUAA, § 6 and cases collected under Comment 2.

Recent cases, including *Howsam v. Dean Witter Reynolds*, 537 U.S. 79, 83-84 (2002), have limited *First Options* and clarified that not *all* issues of "arbitrability" are presumptively for a court. Rather, a court is presumptively required to be the decision-maker only "where contracting parties would have expected a court to have decided the gateway matter." *Id.* According to *Howsam*, most procedural "gateway issues" are presumptively for an arbitrator to determine. These include "'procedural' questions that grow out of the dispute and bear on its final disposition," such as whether a statute of limitations bars a claim or whether there exists a particular defense to arbitrability, such as waiver. *Id. See* Section E, *infra*.

Howsam indicates that the distinction between "substantive" and "procedural" arbitrability is still alive, and that the *First Options* presumption that arbitrability is for courts to decide applies only to questions of "substantive" but not "procedural" arbitrability.

Accordingly, given the trend toward increasing arbitral power, arbitrators should decide all jurisdictional and arbitrability issues that are presented by the parties, absent a court order staying the arbitration or directing the resolution of a particular gateway issue in a specific manner, or a clear determination by the arbitrator that the issue must be decided by the court.

D. Conditions Precedent to Arbitration

Arbitrators normally should assume they have the power to resolve questions concerning whether a condition precedent to arbitration exists or has been satisfied.

Whether a provision of the parties' contract constitutes a condition precedent, and, if so, whether the condition has been satisfied, are questions that can be determined by arbitrators according to the principles of the applicable law for contract construction, a review of the contract provision in question, and relevant evidence. The RUAA, seeking to incorporate the holdings of the vast majority of state courts and the law that has developed under the FAA, provides in Section 6, "Validity of Agreement to Arbitrate," that "an arbitrator shall decide whether a condition precedent to arbitrability has been fulfilled." *See* RUAA, § 6 and cases collected under Comment 2.

E.   Waiver

When presented with a claim that the right to arbitrate has been waived, arbitrators should initially determine whether they have jurisdiction to determine such a claim; if arbitrators determine that the issue of waiver is properly before them, they should proceed to determine the issue in light of the presumption against a finding of waiver.

Because the right to arbitrate is dependent upon the agreement of the parties, it may be waived, but waiver of arbitration is not a favored finding. There is a presumption against it, and any doubts are to be resolved in favor of arbitration. Waiver may be express or implied, although implied waiver is not lightly inferred. Actions or omissions can result in a finding of waiver, but, generally, only when prejudice to the other party results. *See id.*

Typically, claims of waiver raised by one party are based upon an adverse party's decision to litigate rather than arbitrate. Factors that will be considered in determining whether a waiver of arbitration has occurred include the nature and extent of any litigation that may have taken place, the time elapsed between the commencement of litigation and the request for arbitration, whether discovery has been conducted, proof of prejudice, and proximity of a trial date at the time arbitration is sought.

In *Howsam, supra,* the Supreme Court clearly indicated that waiver is among those procedural "gateway issues" that are presumptively for an arbitrator to determine. Nevertheless, other authority continues to stand for the proposition that waiver is properly for courts to decide. "Waiver is one area where courts, rather than arbitrators, often make the decision as to enforceability of an arbitration clause. . . . Allowing the court to decide this issue of arbitrability may comport with the separability doctrine because in most instances waiver concerns only the arbitration clause itself and not an attack on the underlying contract." RUAA § 6, Comment 5.

It may be rare that an arbitrator will be asked to resolve the issue of a waiver alleged to arise out of a party's prior participation in litigation; when a party in litigation seeks to arbitrate, the other party, if it does not consent, will almost always move the court rather than the arbitrators for an order determining that the party seeking to arbitrate has waived its right to do so. However, arbitrators may occasionally be faced with such an assertion. Arbitrators must initially determine whether the issue of waiver is properly before them and should request briefing or argument on the jurisdictional issue, either prior to or concurrently with briefing and argument on the merits. If arbitrators determine that the issue of waiver is properly before them, they should proceed to determine the issue in light of the presumption against a finding of waiver.

F. Illegality and Other Defenses Arguably Going to the "Making" of the Contract

Arbitrators should be aware of recent Supreme Court authority holding that it is for arbitrators to determine whether contracts are void *ab initio* due to illegality or similar defenses.

As discussed in Section A above, *Prima Paint, supra,* involved a claim of fraudulent inducement of the contract generally (as opposed to the arbitration clause in particular) and held that such a claim did not implicate the "making of the agreement for arbitration" under Section 4 of the FAA. After *Prima Paint,* numerous courts struggled with the question of whether the "making of the agreement for arbitration" is implicated by other contract defenses, such as illegality, that arguably render the entire contract "void," and distinguished *Prima Paint* on the grounds that the defense at issue there, fraud in the inducement, merely rendered the contract "voidable" as opposed to "void *ab initio.*" *See, e.g.,* cases collected in R. Reuben, *First Options, Consent to Arbitration, and the Demise of Separability: Restoring Access to Justice for Contracts with Arbitration Provisions,* 56 SMU L. Rev. 819, 852-53 (2003); *Rosenthal v. Great Western Fin. Securities Corp.,* 14 Cal. 4th 394, 415-17 (1996) (fraud in the inception or execution); *Ericksen, Arbuthnot, McCarthy, Kearney & Walsh, Inc. v. 100 Oak Street,* 35 Cal. 3d 312, fn. 2 (1983) (discussing illegality).

The United States Supreme Court recently resolved this issue, deciding in *Buckeye Check Cashing, Inc. v. Cardegna,* - S.Ct. - (2006), 2006 WL 386362 (U.S. Feb. 21 2006), that it is for the arbitrator, not the court, to decide whether a contract containing an arbitration provision is void due to illegality. The Florida Supreme Court had upheld the trial court's denial of a motion to compel arbitration because of the alleged illegality (on grounds of usury) of the contract containing the arbitration clause. In reversing that holding, the U.S. Supreme Court reaffirmed the separability doctrine and clarified that it applies even when the challenge to the validity of the arbitration agreement is based on the illegality of the contract, because that challenge is directed to the contract as a whole rather than to the arbitration clause in particular. The Court rejected the argument that because illegal contracts are void *ab initio,* a claim of illegality goes to the "making of the agreement for arbitration" and is therefore for a court to decide under Section 4 of the FAA. The decision signals a broad rejection of the distinction that has been made in this context between void and voidable contracts, holding that the separability doctrine articulated in *Prima Paint* applies to both with equal force. The Court expressly distinguished cases which held that it is for courts, not arbitrators, to decide whether a contract was ever formed, such as, for example, when a putative obligor alleges that he never even signed the contract, or when a signor claims that a contract was never formed because he, as an agent, lacked authority to bind his principal, or when a signor alleges that he lacked the mental capacity to assent.

Thus, when faced with an argument that illegality or another contract defense renders a contract void *ab initio*, arbitrators should proceed to adjudicate that defense as they would any other defense presented in the normal course of the proceeding. However, it generally remains for courts and not arbitrators to determine whether a valid contract was formed at all. *See* Section B, *supra*.

III. DETERMINING JURISDICTIONAL AND ARBITRABILITY OBJECTIONS

Arbitrators should use the most expeditious and least expensive procedures for determining jurisdictional and arbitrability objections, consistent with the duty of treating all parties fairly.

In the preliminary conference, arbitrators should inquire whether there will be any objections to jurisdiction or arbitrability. If a party indicates that such an objection is likely, or if such an objection already has been asserted, arbitrators may properly inquire as to the practical consequences of sustaining such an objection and whether an alternative course, such as requiring a party to supplement a claim or defense, will obviate the issue and avoid unnecessary expense and delay. Arbitrators should not raise any jurisdictional or arbitrability issues not asserted by the parties, unless they conclude that such an unasserted issue is non-waivable.

Jurisdictional and arbitrability objections should normally be treated as a preliminary issue to be decided separately from the merits of the case as soon as reasonably possible and in the least expensive manner consistent with a full and fair development of the issues. AAA Rule 7 and JAMS Rule 11 expressly provide that arbitrators may rule on jurisdictional issues as a preliminary matter. However, such objections may, in the discretion of the arbitrators, be decided after the hearing on the merits when the objection appears on its face to be weak, when it is necessary to expedite the case, or when substantial evidence or briefing on the merits is necessary to decide the issue. A party is generally considered to have waived any challenge to arbitrators' jurisdiction unless made not later than the answer to the claim or counterclaim. *See* AAA Rule 7(c); CPR Rule 8.2.

Full briefing by all parties should be requested on any jurisdictional and arbitrability issues unless the proper decision is obvious. The briefing may include the attachment of supporting witness statements or affidavits. Following the submission of any briefs on the jurisdictional and arbitrability issues, arbitrators should consider holding an oral argument to allow the parties a full opportunity to explicate the issues. In unusual situations, it may be helpful at the hearing to allow limited witness testimony on specified disputed facts. A merits hearing, for example, may well be required if a laches or waiver defense is presented. Expert testimony is rarely necessary or helpful in deciding jurisdictional and arbitrability issues.

CHAPTER 5

CLASS ARBITRATION

Arbitrators who serve in class arbitrations should seek to achieve the procedural and substantive objectives underlying the concept of class actions while, at the same time, providing for the efficiencies that are meant to accompany arbitration proceedings.

I. ACCEPTING AN APPOINTMENT TO SERVE AS AN ARBITRATOR IN A CLASS ARBITRATION

Because of the specialized nature of class arbitration, arbitrators should not accept an appointment to serve as an arbitrator in such proceedings unless they are sufficiently experienced and qualified to manage all of the procedural steps through the issuance of a final award.

Class arbitration is a new and rapidly evolving procedure. By the time this Guide goes to print, new court decisions may affect the institutional rules and general considerations discussed below. Arbitrators acting in a class arbitration context must not only be familiar with the evolving case law relating to class arbitrations, but must also be alert to changes in any institutional rules that might govern the arbitration or provide guidance on how the arbitration should be conducted.

Two major arbitral institutions—the AAA and JAMS—have established procedures that apply in class arbitrations conducted under their rules. *See* JAMS Class Action Procedures (the "JAMS Class Arbitration Rules"); AAA Supplementary Rules for Class Arbitrations (the "AAA Class Arbitration Rules"). Given the relative absence of guidance relating to the manner in which class arbitrations should be conducted, arbitrators serving in class arbitrations should be conversant with these procedures even if their arbitration is ad hoc or administered by other arbitral institutions.

Arbitrators serving in class arbitrations should also be familiar with Rule 23 of the Federal Rules of Civil Procedure ("Federal Rule 23" or "Rule 23"), which specifies procedures relating to class actions conducted in federal district courts. While Rule 23 does not directly address class arbitrations, it nonetheless provides guidance with respect to many procedural considerations that are likely to arise in the arbitration of class claims.

II. CLASS ARBITRATIONS AND DISCLOSURE

Arbitrators should carefully consider what disclosures are needed in the context of a class arbitration.

While there is no definitive case law or other authoritative discussion of the matter to date, the same general principles relating to disclosures that apply in typical commercial arbitrations between named parties also presumably apply in class arbitrations. Consequently, before accepting appointment to serve in a class arbitration, the candidate, as in any arbitration, should ascertain what rules, law, and ethical standards apply in the arbitration and should make disclosures in accordance therewith. *See* Chapter 2, *supra.* On the other hand, the unique nature of class arbitrations—which often involve a putative class that includes thousands of individuals but in which the value of independent claims is *de minimis*—might, in a particular instance, impact the question whether a remote connection to a potential class member or to the issues to be determined is of sufficient significance to require a disclosure under *Commonwealth Coatings Corp. v. Continental Casualty Co.*, 393 U.S. 145 (1968). *See* Chapter 2, *supra.* For example, if a putative class of credit card holders includes the arbitrator candidate, then disclosure should be made, even if the amount at issue on an individual basis is *de minimis*. There might not, however, be a need—as in a significant commercial arbitration that does not involve class claims—to ascertain whether family members carry the credit card at issue. Nevertheless, in accordance with the respected maxim that it is "better to err on the side of disclosure," arbitrator candidates should always make disclosures unless they are fully satisfied that the information is of such insignificance that no disclosure is required under the applicable rules and law.

III. THE APPLICABILITY OF GENERAL ARBITRATION PROCEDURES AND PRINCIPLES TO CLASS ARBITRATIONS

Except as otherwise required due to the unique nature of class arbitrations, the same procedural considerations and policy objectives relevant to commercial arbitrations also apply to class arbitrations.

Before discussing in detail the several unique procedural considerations that relate to class arbitrations, it is worthwhile to emphasize that class arbitrations generally warrant the same procedural protections and efficiency that arbitrators should strive to provide in arbitrations involving only a few parties. It is for that reason that the JAMS and AAA Class Arbitration Rules "supplement" the general procedural rules of those institutions. *See* JAMS Class Arbitration Rule 1(a); AAA Class Arbitration Rule 1(a) and (b). The many procedural devices discussed elsewhere in this Guide—including, for example, preliminary conferences, limited discovery and motion practice, the issuance of subpoenas, and means by which to ensure a more efficient and economical presentation of the evidence—all, therefore, have equal relevance to class arbitrations. Similarly, the same considerations relating to arbitrator ethics and disclosures as would otherwise apply in a general commercial arbitration proceeding are equally applicable to class arbitrations.

In order to avoid an unnecessary repetition of matters concerning such general arbitration procedures and arbitrator duties, this chapter will focus narrowly on those aspects of the arbitration process that are unique to class arbitrations. The following discussion assumes that arbitrators will conduct preliminary conferences and implement such other measures as are required by applicable rule and law, or that are otherwise appropriate under the given circumstances.

IV. JURISDICTION AND THE *BAZZLE* DECISION

Under the Supreme Court's decision in *Green Tree Financial Corp. v. Bazzle*, when an arbitration clause is silent on the availability of class arbitration, the arbitrator determines whether the case can proceed as a class arbitration.

In the landmark decision in *Green Tree Financial Corp. v. Bazzle*, 539 U.S. 444 (2003), the plurality opinion of the United States Supreme Court held that, in the instance in which an arbitration clause is "silent as to whether arbitration might take the form of class arbitration," that issue "is a matter for the arbitrator to decide." *Id.* at 447. This opinion is widely seen as not only establishing the arbitrator's authority to resolve that issue, but also as effectively putting arbitrators in the business of arbitrating class claims.

Arbitrators serving in arbitrations involving an alleged class should have a basic understanding of *Bazzle* for several reasons. First, the Court's decision does not reflect the opinion of a majority of the Court and, instead, is based on a plurality decision in which a fifth justice concurred on a limited basis. Second, the underlying facts of the case provide an enlightening illustration of the types of issues that can arise with respect to the question of how the arbitration clause should be construed. Finally, the decision serves to highlight additional, unresolved issues concerning the arbitrability of class claims. A familiarity with *Bazzle* should thus assist arbitrators in addressing jurisdictional issues that are likely to arise in the class arbitration setting.

Bazzle involved a circumstance in which a South Carolina state court had compelled arbitration *after* determining that the alleged class claims could be asserted in an arbitration proceeding. In the arbitration proceeding that followed, the arbitrator found in favor of the class and entered an award against Green Tree. In a parallel arbitration, the same arbitrator considered similar claims asserted against a different group of respondents. The arbitrator certified a class in that arbitration as well, and entered an award against those respondents. The South Carolina Supreme Court eventually affirmed the judgments entered on both awards. That court agreed that the cases were properly heard as class arbitrations because the arbitration clauses did not forbid the claimants from arbitrating as a class.

In the Supreme Court's plurality decision in *Bazzle*, four of the nine Justices voted to vacate and remand the South Carolina Supreme Court judgments on the ground that it was for an arbitrator, and not a court, to determine whether the arbitrations could be maintained as class arbitrations. Justice Stevens, who dissented in part, concurred in order to form a five-member block that ensured that the Court could issue a controlling judgment. The dissenting portion of Justice Stevens' opinion was based on his observation that the petitioner in the case before the United States Supreme Court had only challenged the merits of the decision by the South Carolina court, not the fact that it had arguably been rendered by the wrong decision-maker. Having found the state court's decision to be correct, Justice Stevens believed that the high court simply should have affirmed the judgments below. Thus, only four of the nine justices actually vacated the South Carolina judgments on the basis that it was for an arbitrator, and not a court, to decide whether a class arbitration may be maintained, *i.e.* that the state court was the wrong decision-maker. Justice Stevens did not concur on that basis. As a result, a majority of the Supreme Court has not yet held that an arbitrator has the sole authority to determine whether a class arbitration may be maintained when the arbitration clause is silent on that issue.

V.   THE EFFECT OF A CLASS ACTION PRECLUSION CLAUSE ON ARBITRAL JURISDICTION

Arbitrators serving in arbitrations involving an alleged class should be aware (1) that there is a split in authority regarding whether class action preclusion clauses are enforceable, with most courts upholding the validity of such clauses, and (2) that the majority of courts that have addressed the issue have held that it is the province of a court to determine the validity of such clauses.

A class action preclusion clause, sometimes called a "class action waiver clause" or a "no-class-action provision," typically appears in a credit card, retail, or other consumer contract. The preclusion clause, which is usually found in the agreement's arbitration provision, provides that the consumer or credit card holder may not maintain or participate in any legal action or arbitration as a member of a class. Most courts, with the notable exception of courts applying California law, have determined that these preclusion clauses are enforceable, although the opinions in such cases often discuss other factors that suggest that the consumer is adequately protected, even without the ability to participate in a class arbitration. *Compare, e.g., Ingle v. Circuit City Stores, Inc.*, 328 F.3d 1165, 1175-76 (9th Cir. 2003) and *Discover Bank v. Superior Court*, 36 Cal. 4th 148 (2005) *with Strand v. U.S. Bank National Assoc. ND*, 693 N.W.2d 918, 925 (N.D. 2005). These factors may include the consumer's ability to rely on a local small claims court procedure to adjudicate a claim, the manufacturer's or the credit card company's willingness to pay all arbitration costs, and the relative convenience of the arbitration forum in terms of its proximity to the consumer's place of residence.

The clear weight of authority also holds that it is for a court to determine whether a particular class action preclusion clause is unenforceable by reason of unconscionability. Thus, it is likely that an arbitrator will not be given the task of determining the enforceability of a class action preclusion clause. Instead, the case will usually be referred to arbitration after a determination on the issue has already been made, either because the consumer originally commenced a court action claiming that the arbitration clause was unconscionable and therefore unenforceable (and the respondent company countered with a motion to compel arbitration), or because the respondent company moved to stay a putative class arbitration filed by a consumer under an arbitration provision that contained a class action waiver. Nevertheless, issues concerning the enforceability of class preclusion clauses occasionally are presented to an arbitrator. In such an instance, full briefing and argument on the issues should precede any decision by the arbitrator. Limited discovery on the narrow issues presented by an unconscionability defense should also be permitted if discovery is required in order to ensure a sufficient development of the facts.

VI. DETERMINING WHETHER A CLASS ARBITRATION MAY BE MAINTAINED WHEN THE ARBITRATION CLAUSE IS SILENT ON THAT QUESTION

Arbitrators serving in an arbitration involving an alleged class should first decide whether a class arbitration can be maintained.

After being appointed to serve in a proceeding in which one or more claimants seek to assert claims on behalf of a class (and in which a court has not upheld the validity of a class preclusion clause), arbitrators, in accordance with *Bazzle*, should first determine whether a class arbitration may be maintained under the arbitration clause. This phase of the proceeding is generally known as "clause construction."

It is notable that even the nature of the arbitrators' determination regarding the force and effect of the arbitration clause in this respect is subject to varied characterizations by different courts and arbitral institutions. In *Bazzle,* the plurality opinion described the issue under South Carolina law as concerning "whether the agreement *forbids* class action." 539 U.S. at 451 (emphasis added). Other courts have described the issue in the same fashion. *See, e.g., Pedcor Management Company, Inc. v. Nations Personnel of Texas, Inc.,* 343 F.3d 355, 362 (5th Cir, 2003); *Garcia v. DIRECTV, Inc.,* 115 Cal. App. 4th 297, 302-03, 9 Cal. Rptr. 3d 190 (2004) ("it is for the arbitrator to decide whether DIRECTV's arbitration provision forbids class arbitrations"). In contrast, yet other courts that have addressed the issue have stated the issue in terms of whether the arbitration provision "permits" class arbitration. *See, e.g., In re John M. O'Quinn, P.C.,* 155 S.W.3d 195, 201 n. 2 (Tex. App. 2003). Similarly, the pertinent JAMS and AAA rules both describe the issue as being whether the arbitration clause "permits" the arbitration to proceed on a class basis. JAMS Class Arbitration Rules 2 and 3(a)(i); AAA Class Arbitration Rules 3 and 4(a). While it is not clear if the distinction between determining whether the arbitration provision "forbids" or "permits" class arbitration is merely semantic, arbitrators nevertheless should be aware that the cases and institutional rules are not necessarily uniform in this respect.

Indeed, prior to the United States Supreme Court's pronouncement in *Bazzle,* a split in authority had arisen concerning the question whether class arbitration was permissible under an arbitration clause that was silent on the topic of class arbitration. In ruling that, under South Carolina law, such a clause must be deemed to allow class arbitration, the South Carolina Supreme Court in *Bazzle v. Green Tree Financial Corp.,* 569 S.E.2d 349 (S.C. 2002) had relied on California case law that held that an arbitration clause that is silent on the topic of class arbitration is presumed to permit class arbitration unless it can be shown that, for some reason, the clause "forbids" such arbitrations. 569 S.E.2d at 355-58 (*citing Keating v. Superior Court,* 31 Cal. 3d 584 (1982), *rev'd in part on other grounds, Southland Corp. v. Keating,* 465 U.S. 1 (1984)). This principle is based on the existence of a pro-arbitration public policy that is reinforced by a presumption in favor of arbitrability.

In contrast, after analogizing to the issue concerning whether multiple arbitrations could be consolidated by an arbitrator, several federal courts had held that the FAA did not permit the maintenance of class-wide arbitration when the arbitration agreement is silent on the topic. *See, e.g., Champ v. Siegel Trading Co., Inc.*, 55 F.3d 269 (7th Cir. 1995). Given that the *Bazzle* decision does not reflect an opinion of the majority of the Court, and in light of the further fact that the Court remanded the case to the arbitrator so that, in keeping with the principles established in *First Options* (*see* Chapter 4, *supra*), the arbitrator could resolve the issue by applying South Carolina law, it is clear that no single governing standard exists regarding how to analyze the question whether a class arbitration may be maintained under an arbitration clause that is silent on the topic of class arbitration. Arbitrators, therefore, must construe the arbitration clause on a case-by-case basis in light of the applicable state law relating to the interpretation of the clause.

Finally, with respect to clause construction, arbitrators should be aware that institutional rules differ regarding the question whether the arbitrator should issue a partial final award on the clause construction issue. Under the AAA Class Arbitration Rules, the arbitrator must render a reasoned partial final award on clause construction and then wait at least thirty days before taking any further action in order "to permit any party to move a court . . . to confirm or vacate" the award. AAA Class Arbitration Rule 3. The issuance of a partial final award on the construction issue in proceedings conducted under the AAA Class Arbitration Rules thus can be followed by significant delays resulting from a district court confirmation or vacatur proceeding. Furthermore, as is discussed in more detail in Section VI, *infra*, upon the issuance of a partial final award, the arbitrator normally is *functus officio* with respect to the issues determined in that award and, as a result, the arbitrator will not be subsequently permitted to reconsider the merits of the determination reflected by the award. Arbitrators conducting class arbitrations under the AAA rules must, therefore, be aware of the possibility that they will not be legally authorized to reconsider clause construction determinations that are embodied in a partial final award.

Under the JAMS rules, the issuance of such an award is discretionary. When arbitrators are not proceeding under the AAA rules, they should thus consider whether the goals of arbitration—efficient and cost-effective adjudication—would best be served by issuing a partial final award on the single issue of clause construction or by refraining from the issuance of such an award and, instead, immediately moving forward to the next stage of the class arbitration proceeding.

In all cases, arbitrators should be alert to the possible need for discovery on the sole issue of clause construction, and should permit targeted and limited discovery on that issue if requested by a party and if warranted by the facts and circumstances.

VII. CLASS CERTIFICATION

> **Assuming that the arbitrators determine that a class arbitration may be maintained, they should then determine whether a class should be certified such that the arbitration may proceed as a class arbitration.**

The determination of whether, and if so how, to certify a class and allow an arbitration to proceed as a class arbitration involves a multitude of issues, and is arguably the most complicated procedural stage of a class arbitration. This determination requires great care and, if necessary, should be preceded by limited discovery relating to issues relevant to the determination.

The JAMS and AAA Class Arbitration Rules both generally identify certain "prerequisites" that must be satisfied before a class may be certified—including traditional class action considerations relating to numerosity, commonality, typicality, and the question whether the representative parties will fairly and adequately protect the interests of the alleged class. JAMS Class Arbitration Rule 3(a); AAA Class Arbitration Rule 4(a). These principles flow directly from Federal Rule 23, and a substantial amount of case law and commentary is therefore available to assist the arbitrators in evaluating each factor. The JAMS and AAA rules, as well as Rule 23, all require that any class certification be accompanied by a determination to the effect that designated class counsel will adequately represent the interests of the class.

The AAA and JAMS rules then provide that, if the foregoing "prerequisites" are satisfied, class arbitration may be maintained if the arbitrator further finds that common questions of fact and law predominate over questions affecting only individual members of the class, and that class arbitration is superior to other methods in ensuring a fair and efficient adjudication of the controversy. AAA Class Arbitration Rule 4(b); JAMS Class Arbitration Rule 3(b). A close examination of AAA Rule 4(b), JAMS Rule 3(b), and Federal Rule 23 reflects that the three rules do vary to some extent with respect to the specific factors that are to be considered in making these determinations and the specific findings that must be made. These distinctions should be noted by arbitrators since, in cases in which the AAA or JAMS rules apply, arbitrators are presumably obligated to consider specifically each of the relevant factors cited in the applicable rules so that any necessary findings can be made in connection with the class certification determination.

In evaluating the merits of certifying an alleged class, arbitrators should give due consideration to issues that might be unique to the fact that the class claims would be asserted in an arbitration context. For example, in class arbitrations involving class members from multiple states, varying state or federal law might apply with respect to the arbitrators' authority to issue discovery subpoenas relating to evidence that is critical to a resolution of the issues. *See* Chapter 8 § VI, *infra*. In such an instance, arbitrators presumably have the authority to mitigate such concerns through the implementation of traditional arbitration procedures, provided they have determined at the class certification stage that it is desirable to "concentrat[e] the arbitration of the claims in a single forum." JAMS Class Arbitration Rule 3(b)(3)(C); AAA Class Arbitration Rule 4(b)(3). Moreover, while it is not clear under the AAA and JAMS rules whether arbitrators have the authority to designate the type of "subclasses" that are contemplated under Federal Rule 23(c)(4), the designation of such subclasses would, at times, logically be consistent with the arbitrators' discretion in certifying a class. Some examples of other considerations that could be relevant in determining the efficacy of adjudicating the claims in a class arbitration context include questions relating to any legal or practical limitations on the issuance of hearing subpoenas (*see* Chapter 6, *infra)* and the geographical location of key witnesses and documents. In view of considerations such as these, the arbitrator cannot simply assume that if class claims are suitable for court determination they should also be deemed equally suitable for determination in an arbitration forum.

VIII. PARTIAL FINAL AWARDS ON THE CLASS CERTIFICATION ISSUE

Arbitrators must issue a partial final award on the class certification issue when the applicable rules so require and, otherwise, should exercise discretion in determining whether to issue such an award.

After arbitrators have determined whether a class should be certified, they should then decide whether to issue a partial final award on this discrete issue. As is the case with respect to determinations relating to "clause construction," the AAA rules state that the arbitrator shall render a reasoned "partial final award" on any class certification determination and then wait at least thirty days before taking any further action in the arbitration proceeding. AAA Class Arbitration Rule 5(a). Under the JAMS procedures, the issuance of such an award is discretionary. JAMS Class Arbitration Rule 4(c). If not operating under the AAA procedures, the goals of arbitration may be better served by refraining from issuing a partial final award on the single issue of class certification and, instead, by immediately proceeding to the next stage of the class arbitration.

In this regard, it is important to remember that, at least under the FAA, a party is entitled to seek confirmation or vacatur of a partial final award within the time periods respectively set forth in Sections 9 and 12 of the FAA. Some courts have held that when a party fails to seek vacatur of a partial final award within the time period specified in the FAA, that party forever waives its right to seek vacatur of the relevant determination. *See, e.g., Hart Surgical, Inc. v. Ultracision, Inc.*, 244 F.3d 231, 235 (1ˢᵗ Cir. 2001); *Nationwide Mutual Ins. v. First St. Ins. Co.*, 213 F. Supp. 2d 10, 16 (D. Mass. 2002). Indeed, some courts have suggested that the same rule applies to applications to confirm a partial final award under the FAA. *See, e.g., Hart Surgical, supra*, at 235; *Kerr-McGee Refining Corp. v. M/T Triumph*, 924 F.2d 467, 471 (2d Cir. 1991). The issuance of partial final awards thus can have far-reaching implications for the parties and arbitrators. This point is further underscored by the related principle that, once arbitrators issue a partial final award relating to certain issues, they normally are *functus officio* with respect to those issues and will have no further authority to reconsider their determination. *See Trade & Transport, Inc. v. Natural Petroleum Charterers, Inc.*, 931 F.2d 191, 195 (2d Cir. 1991).

The AAA rules appear to attempt to take this latter consideration into account by providing that, "A Class Determination Award may be altered or amended by the arbitrator before a final award is rendered." AAA Class Arbitration Rule 5(e). This rule raises its own issues, since many cases hold that, under the FAA, a court may not confirm or vacate an award that is not final in nature. Since the AAA rule plainly provides that a "partial final award" on the class determination issue is not final under traditional notions of *functus officio*, it is possible that the courts will hold that they have no jurisdiction to consider the type of award contemplated under the AAA Rules. Interestingly, the AAA rules do not contain a similar provision relating to the mandatory issuance of a partial final award on the issue of clause construction. For a further discussion of general considerations relating to the issuance of interim or partial awards that are final in nature, see Chapters 10 and 11, *infra*.

IX. NOTICE OF CLASS DETERMINATION

In the event arbitrators certify a class, they must make provision for the issuance of a detailed Notice of Class Determination that provides prospective class members with adequate notice and information relating to the pending class arbitration.

Under both the JAMS and AAA Class Arbitration Rules, once arbitrators determine to certify a class, they are required to issue a detailed Notice of Class Determination. JAMS Class Arbitration Rule 4; AAA Class Arbitration Rule 6. These rules, which generally are patterned after Federal Rule 23(c)(2)(B), are intended to ensure that prospective class members are provided with sufficient information—pertaining to such matters as the nature of the action, the definition of the class, the substantive issues, and counsel—to allow the potential class member to make an informed decision concerning whether to be excluded from the class.

JAMS Rule 4 and AAA Rule 6 additionally require that the notice contain biographical information about the arbitrator. As was discussed in Chapter 2, *supra*, arbitrators should ensure that any such biographical information is current and accurate. In order to give prospective class members adequate notice of all factors that might be relevant to a determination of whether to "opt out" of the class, arbitrators should further consider including in the notice a restatement of any disclosures that were made by them prior or subsequent to being appointed to serve in the arbitration.

X. MANAGEMENT OF THE PRE-HEARING AND HEARING PROCESS

In determining how to manage the pre-hearing process and the hearing on the merits of class claims, arbitrators should consider the full range of techniques and procedural options that would otherwise be available in a typical commercial arbitration.

As was briefly mentioned above, in conducting the actual hearing on the merits of class claims, arbitrators generally may employ the full range of procedural techniques and principles available in a typical commercial arbitration. In that regard, arbitrators should thus consider the guidance set forth in other chapters of this Guide relating to preliminary conferences and pre-hearing management, discovery, motions, and the conduct of the hearing on the merits. *See* Chapters 6-9, *infra*. Nevertheless, in determining what procedures to employ, arbitrators must always be mindful of the fact that arbitrators in a class arbitration play a unique role in attempting to ensure that the due process rights of the absent class members are adequately protected by the arbitration process.

XI.   ATTORNEYS' FEES AWARDS

Prior to awarding attorneys' fees in a class arbitration, arbitrators should (1) verify they have authority to enter such an award, (2) ascertain whether the applicable rules, law, and/or arbitration provision impose limits on the amount that can be awarded, (3) seek guidance from established legal principles that apply in court class actions, and (4) attempt to determine whether unique circumstances associated with the arbitration proceeding influence the amount of fees, if any, to be awarded.

Generally, the same principles that apply with respect to an award of attorneys' fees in a typical commercial arbitration also apply in class arbitrations. Upon receipt of a request for an award of attorneys' fees in a class arbitration, arbitrators must first examine the pertinent arbitration provision, any applicable rules, and the applicable law for the purpose of determining whether they have authority to grant such a request. *See* Chapter 10, *supra*.

In the instance in which the arbitrators do have the authority to award attorneys' fees, they will find that little direct guidance exists concerning the appropriate means of determining the amount of fees to be awarded in the specific context of a class arbitration. The AAA and JAMS rules do not address the topic and little other authority exists concerning the appropriate method for determining class arbitration attorneys' fee awards. Thus, arbitrators should seek guidance from related case law concerning the various methods currently approved by courts for the purpose of determining attorneys' fees awards in class litigation. *See, e.g., In re Cendant Corp. Securities Litigation*, 404 F.3d 173, 187-91 (3rd Cir. 2005) (discussing a variety of approaches and considerations for determining the appropriate amount of a class action attorneys' fee award, including the "common fund doctrine," the "lodestar method," "the percentage-of-recovery approach," and the "auction approach to setting class counsel's fees in advance of litigation").

Of course, in determining what method to apply in issuing an attorneys' fee award, arbitrators must take into account any substantive law or institutional rules that might govern a party's right to recover attorneys' fees in the proceeding. Arbitrators should also consider whether the expedited and simplified nature of the arbitration proceeding itself is relevant in assessing traditional class action attorneys' fees criteria such as the efficiency of class counsel or the complexity and duration of the arbitration. *Cf. Gunter v. Ridgewood Energy Corp.*, 223 F.3d 190, 195 n. 1 (3rd Cir. 2000) (discussing the seven-factor test under the percentage-of-recovery approach). Finally, arbitrators should address whether other factors unique to arbitrations give rise to reasons why an altogether different approach to an award of attorneys' fees might be reasonable.

XII. THE FINAL AWARD

Final awards in class arbitrations should contain a statement of reasons and should provide additional information that serves to identify not only the class members, but also those class members that opted out of the arbitration.

The JAMS and AAA Class Arbitration Rules contain virtually identical rules requiring that the arbitrator issue a reasoned final award in class arbitrations. Regardless of whether a particular set of institutional rules applies in a particular class arbitration, arbitrators should always comply with this principle, since the existence of a reasoned award in a class arbitration helps ensure that a reviewing court will have the information that it may need to confirm that the procedural and substantive rights of class members have been adequately protected.

The JAMS and AAA Rules provide further guidance regarding certain findings that should be included in any final award in a class arbitration, including (1) a specific identification of the class, (2) an identification of the parties to whom the Notice of Class Determination was provided, (3) an identification of the parties found to be members of the class, and (4) an identification of those parties who elected to opt out of the class. JAMS Class Arbitration Rule 5; AAA Class Arbitration Rule 7. Once again, these elements of a final award in a class arbitration are consistent with the requirements of Federal Rule 23, and arbitrators should thus include all such information in a final award in a class arbitration regardless of whether a particular set of institutional rules applies. In drafting the final award, arbitrators, of course, should also include such other information as is normally included in final awards. *See* Chapter 10, *infra.*

XIII. SETTLEMENT, VOLUNTARY DISMISSAL, OR COMPROMISE

Arbitrators must strictly comply with the requirements of any applicable rules relating to the approval of settlements, dismissals, or compromises and, in the absence of such rules, should seek guidance from the JAMS and AAA Class Arbitration Rules and from Federal Rule 23.

No direct legal authority exists regarding the nature and extent of arbitrators' authority and duties when the parties in a class arbitration jointly propose to settle or compromise the claims in the arbitration, or in which claimants seek to unilaterally dismiss the arbitration. Federal Rule 23 and the AAA and JAMS rules nevertheless provide adequate guidance; in the absence of better authority, arbitrators should refer to those rules when faced with formal proposals to compromise or dismiss the arbitration.

JAMS Rule 6 and AAA Rule 8 both require that the arbitrator formally approve any settlement, voluntary dismissal or compromise. JAMS Class Arbitration Rule 6; AAA Class Arbitration Rule 8. Those rules further provide that the arbitrator must conduct a hearing on the question of whether to approve the proposal, and that such approval should not be granted until after notice of the proposed settlement, dismissal, or compromise has been given to all interested parties. Moreover, the rules require that class members must be afforded an opportunity to object to the proposal and also a later opportunity to opt out if the proposal is approved. These rules serve to emphasize that, in approving any such proposal, arbitrators effectively are determining the rights of absent parties who are dependent on the arbitrators to ensure that those rights are adequately protected.

XIV. CONFIDENTIALITY

The usual rules governing confidentiality in arbitration are generally inapplicable to class arbitration proceedings.

The nature of class arbitrations, most particularly those aspects of class arbitration relating to the need to ensure adequate notice to class members, are such that traditional arbitration principles relating to confidentiality are largely unworkable in class arbitrations. Thus, the AAA Class Arbitration Rules explicitly provide that "[t]he presumption of privacy and confidentiality in arbitration proceedings shall not apply in class arbitrations." AAA Class Arbitration Rule 9(a). Indeed, the AAA maintains on its web site a Class Arbitration

Docket, which provides various information relating to class arbitrations conducted under the AAA rules. While the JAMS rules do not contain similar provisions, those rules relating to the various notices that must be issued in class arbitrations also serve to illustrate that confidentiality in class arbitrations often cannot be practically, or perhaps even legally, achieved. On the other hand, arbitrators can expect that, on occasion, narrow confidentiality issues might arise in a class arbitration concerning such matters as trade secrets or other proprietary information that arguably need to be protected through the imposition of a confidentiality or protective order. In such instances, arbitrators who are concerned about the confidentiality of such matters must always first ensure that any requirements relating to confidentiality do not impair the rights of all interested parties to adequate notice of the many procedural and substantive matters that have been, or will be, addressed by the arbitrators.

CHAPTER 6

PRELIMINARY CONFERENCES AND PRE-HEARING MANAGEMENT IN GENERAL

Arbitrators' goals in managing the pre-hearing process are (1) to work with counsel in devising fair and efficient procedures for the pre-hearing and hearing phases of the arbitration, (2) to monitor the parties' compliance with those procedures, and (3) to resolve promptly any disputes or problems that might delay the arbitration.

I. THE IMPORTANCE OF PRE-HEARING MANAGEMENT

From the time of appointment to the commencement of the hearing, arbitrators should take an active, hands-on approach to managing the pre-hearing process by working with counsel to establish and implement fair and efficient procedures and schedules that are appropriate to the particular case.

Like most things in life, getting an arbitration off on the right foot and keeping it on track are critical to a successful process. While responsibility for so managing arbitrations falls squarely on arbitrators, they should not attempt to perform this task without assistance. Counsel, who know far more about the case than the arbitrators and often have considerable arbitration experience and insight, are essential partners in the undertaking. From their first contact with counsel, arbitrators should set a tone of professionalism, cooperation, and mutual respect. They should make clear that, although the ultimate responsibility (and authority) for managing the arbitration rests with them, they intend to work with counsel in developing a process appropriate to the particular case and, in turn, expect counsel to act cooperatively and professionally with the arbitrators and with each other.

Whenever possible, arbitrators should endeavor to obtain agreement from all parties concerning the procedures and schedule that will govern any arbitration. The prospects for obtaining such agreement are greatly enhanced if arbitrators lead by example rather than rule by fiat. For example, arbitrators should be punctual and well-prepared for all arbitration proceedings (conference calls, conferences, and hearings) and make clear that they expect the same from counsel and parties.

In undertaking to devise procedures and schedules for the arbitration, arbitrators should be mindful of any particular requirements imposed by the arbitration agreement or applicable rules. Most arbitration agreements do not set forth in detail procedures that must be followed during the arbitration; when they do, the arbitrator can always ask the parties to agree to modify any such procedure that appears unworkable or unwise. While the rules of most arbitral institutions do contain some provisions applicable to the pre-hearing and hearing process, those rules typically authorize arbitrators to vary such provisions in their discretion. Certainly, arbitrators and parties can agree to whatever procedures they think best in any particular case, and arbitrators generally have authority, in the absence of party agreement, to decide what procedures will obtain.

Normally, the first opportunity that arbitrators have to appropriately shape the pre-hearing process is the preliminary conference. Thus, the arbitrators' actions in convening, conducting, and memorializing that conference will generally have a major impact on whether the arbitration runs smoothly and efficiently.

II.   CONVENING THE PRELIMINARY CONFERENCE

A.   Time of the Preliminary Conference

The preliminary conference should be held as soon after the arbitrators' appointment as possible, consistent with affording the parties adequate time to prepare for the conference.

Cases, like ships, should not be left adrift. When substantial time passes between arbitrator appointment and the arbitrators' next contact with counsel, the parties will assume that the arbitrators intend to proceed at a leisurely pace; they may also fill the void in active management with arguing about discovery, motions, or other matters. Thus, arbitrators should assure that the parties receive notice promptly, preferably within a week of their appointment, concerning the scheduling of a preliminary conference.

However, while notice of the preliminary conference should be issued quickly, that does not mean that the conference should be held immediately. First, it is preferable that, before the preliminary conference is held, respondents file a response to the demand for arbitration and claimants reply to any counterclaims asserted by respondents; if this has not been done, arbitrators should order that the necessary pleadings be filed by a date reasonably in advance of the conference. Second, the preliminary conference is a critical step in the arbitration process, and it is important that the parties have time to properly prepare for it. Depending on the complexity of the case, the number of parties, and other pertinent circumstances, it may be most appropriate to hold the preliminary conference approximately two to four weeks after notice of the conference is issued.

B.   Who Should Attend the Preliminary Conference

Arbitrators should require that each party be represented at the preliminary conference by the

> attorney who will serve as lead counsel at the hearing
> and, in appropriate cases, by senior client
> representatives as well.

It is essential to a meaningful preliminary conference that "trial counsel," with authority to make commitments for their respective clients, attend the preliminary conference rather than junior lawyers working on the case. In some cases, it may also be desirable to require that a senior representative of each party attend. This approach may be particularly advisable in cases in which some or all counsel are likely to engage in posturing or obstreperous behavior; having their clients present to witness such behavior, and the negative effect it has on the arbitrators, is likely to deter such counter-productive conduct. In cases that may be protracted and expensive, it can also be useful to have client representatives in attendance so they can fully appreciate what lies ahead and better understand the need for cooperation and expedition in order to contain the arbitration costs as much as possible.

C.   Location of the Preliminary Conference

> Arbitrators should determine whether the preliminary
> conference will be held via conference call or in-person
> and, if the latter, at what location.

Many preliminary conferences are conducted via conference call, and this arrangement can be perfectly workable in fairly uncomplicated cases, especially if arbitrators and counsel know one another. However, in complex cases that will involve extensive pre-hearing activities and prolonged hearings, it is often preferable to hold the conference in person. "Live" conferences afford the arbitrators and counsel an opportunity to get acquainted and develop personal rapport. They also increase the likelihood that mutually agreeable arbitration arrangements can be hammered out, since it is much harder to be obstinate and uncooperative in person than over the phone. If an in-person conference is to be held, arbitrators must determine where the conference will be held. Sometimes that location is prescribed by the arbitration agreement or applicable rules. If it is not, arbitrators should seek to secure party agreement on the matter, failing which the conference should usually be held in the location that is convenient to the largest number of participants.

D.   Giving Notice of the Preliminary Conference

Arbitrators should give notice of the preliminary conference via a letter or order signed by them, should include a conference agenda to be discussed by counsel in advance, and should require counsel to make a good faith effort to reach agreement on as many agenda items as possible.

In some administered arbitrations, the arbitral institution customarily issues notice of the preliminary conference. While there is nothing wrong with such an administrative notice being issued as well, the primary communication to the parties concerning the conference should come from the arbitrators. This practice sends the message that the arbitrators are on the job, attentive to the case, and personally involved in establishing the procedure to be followed at the conference. The arbitrators' order or letter should indicate the date, time, and location of the conference and who is required to attend. It should also include, or attach, an agenda of subjects to be addressed at the conference and direct that counsel confer in good faith, by phone or in person, concerning each subject. Counsel should be required to report at the conference the agreements they reached and their respective positions on any matters on which they could not agree. In complex cases, it is often helpful to require that counsel provide to the arbitrators, a few days before the conference, a joint letter or e-mail stating their agreements and disagreements concerning the agenda items and identifying any additional matters they wish to raise at the conference.

III. CONDUCTING THE PRELIMINARY CONFERENCE

A.   Arbitrators' Introductory Statement

At the outset of the conference, after all participants have identified themselves, arbitrators should remind those present that arbitration is a private, flexible process that can be tailored to the nature of the particular dispute and needs of the parties involved in order to achieve efficiency, economy, timeliness, and fairness. Arbitrators should make clear that the purpose of the preliminary conference is to enable the arbitrators and counsel to work together in designing such a customized process for the case.

Regardless of whether the parties and counsel have had prior arbitration experience, it is helpful for arbitrators to begin the conference by noting that arbitration procedures can be tailored to the demands of the particular case and that everyone has been invited to the preliminary conference to engage in a collaborative exercise to that effect. Assuming that counsel have conferred and presented a constructive joint report, noting many points of agreement, arbitrators should commend counsel and the parties for their cooperation to date and indicate that they expect such cooperation and professionalism to continue throughout the case. Some arbitrators like to say at this point that they are so pleased and relieved to get a case with experienced, sophisticated counsel who understand that being zealous advocates about the merits does not preclude being civil, cooperative professionals in dealing with each other (and the arbitrators) concerning procedure and process. Counsel who have been thus lauded for taking the "high road" in the arbitration are much less likely to depart from it as the arbitration unfolds.

B. Opening Statements by Counsel

Counsel for each party should be given a reasonable opportunity to briefly state their perspective on the case and to identify what they regard as the important issues to be resolved at the preliminary conference.

After the arbitrators' introduction, counsel should be afforded a reasonable opportunity, perhaps fifteen minutes per side, to summarize their perspectives on the case and to identify the chief issues they want to have resolved at the conference. Counsel should be told that this is not the occasion to argue the case, which will come at the close of the hearing, but is rather the time for them to describe the factual, legal, and procedural issues that they want the arbitrators to address at the preliminary conference. In cases in which such conduct may be expected, counsel should also be told to avoid inflammatory statements that will polarize the parties and make progress at the conference more difficult to achieve.

C. Determining the Issues on the Conference Agenda

After the opening statements, arbitrators should lead a discussion of each item on the conference agenda, noting those on which the parties have already agreed and determining the others, with agreement of all parties if possible.

After the opening statements are completed, arbitrators should methodically go through every item on the conference agenda (*see* Section V, *infra*), noting in each instance the points on which the parties have reached agreement. Unless those agreements are clearly unworkable or inadequate, arbitrators should adopt them, with any modifications or elaborations that may be warranted. With respect to matters on which the parties have not reached agreement, the arbitrators should attempt to forge an agreement if possible. Failing that, arbitrators should carefully consider the views of both sides and the agreements already reached by the parties and then determine the matter in the manner most appropriate to the case.

If any items cannot be fully resolved at the preliminary conference, arbitrators should set a definite schedule for whatever briefing or further action may be required in order to resolve that item. Nothing should be left open to be determined "at a later day." In some cases it may be necessary to hold multiple preliminary conferences in order to address various issues that arise successively or require further exploration before definitive rulings can be made.

In conducting the preliminary conference, arbitrators should take whatever amount of time is required to thoroughly and carefully address each agenda item. Time spent designing the arbitration process and schedule with care and good judgment can spare all concerned from dozens of hours of needless argument later on.

IV. MEMORIALIZING THE PRELIMINARY CONFERENCE

As promptly as possible following the preliminary conference, arbitrators should issue a comprehensive order that sets forth, accurately and completely, every determination made at the conference and the schedule, in chronological order, of all pre-hearing and hearing activities.

The preliminary hearing should result in a comprehensive and detailed preliminary conference order that will govern all further proceedings in the arbitration. All determinations made at the conference should be recited in the order. The order should also set forth, in chronological sequence, the schedule for all pre-hearing and hearing activities.

The schedule should not be restricted solely to activities required of counsel. When arbitrators must take certain action, *e.g.*, resolving discovery disputes or ruling on motions, the schedule should include deadlines for arbitrator action as well. This is important for two reasons. First, a case can be thrown badly off schedule if arbitrators "sit" on certain disputed matters for extended periods without ruling.

Second, it is helpful, in demanding timely performance from counsel, for arbitrators to set and meet deadlines for their own performance.

The preliminary conference order should be issued as promptly as possible (typically, within twenty-four to forty-eight hours) following the conference. Some arbitrators prefer to issue this and all other orders by e-mail, followed by a mailed or faxed paper copy. This order, and all other orders, should be written by arbitrators, not staff members of an arbitral institution. If there is only one arbitrator in the case, that individual will write the order. If there are three arbitrators, one (usually the chair) will draft the order and circulate it to the other arbitrators for review and approval. In cases where counsel are working well together, some arbitrators ask counsel if they would like to prepare and submit to the arbitrators a draft order memorializing the actions taken at the conference.

Arbitrators should endeavor to obtain the express agreement of all counsel to the entire preliminary conference order and, when that is obtained, recite it in the order; some arbitrators request that counsel sign the order to signify their consent. The order should state that its provisions will govern all further proceedings in the arbitration, unless good cause for a change is shown.

V.   MATTERS TO ADDRESS AT THE PRELIMINARY CONFERENCE

Arbitrators should address and resolve at the preliminary conference all matters that may affect the conduct of the arbitration.

A.   Identity of the Parties

Arbitrators should ascertain, and record in the caption of the preliminary conference order, the correct names of all persons and entities that are parties to the arbitration. Since orders and awards entered in the arbitration may have to be enforced by courts, such orders and awards should make clear exactly who is participating in the arbitration and should never resort to potentially unclear designations, such as "et al." If a party is later dismissed from the arbitration for some reason, that fact should be recorded in a subsequent order but the party's name should remain in the caption.

B.   Claims and Defenses Presented

The preliminary conference order should clearly specify exactly what claims and defenses are before the arbitrators. If those claims and defenses are stated with sufficient clarity in the demand for arbitration, respondent's response, and any filed counterclaims and replies thereto, then the order can simply identify those documents as the controlling statements of claims and defenses. If such prior statements are not sufficiently clear, arbitrators should require the parties to file, by a date certain, amended statements that amplify or clarify their claims and defenses as necessary. When feasible, arbitrators should also explore with the parties the possibility of narrowing and focusing the issues that really need to be determined.

C.   Applicable Arbitration Agreement, Law, and Rules

Arbitrators should confirm, and specify in the preliminary conference order, (1) what particular document (and section thereof) sets forth the parties' arbitration agreement, (2) what procedural law (*e.g.*, FAA, CAA) and what rules (*e.g.*, JAMS Comprehensive Arbitration Rules) govern the arbitration process, and (3) which jurisdiction's substantive law governs the merits of the claims and defenses. If the parties disagree about any of these matters, arbitrators should set a schedule for briefing and deciding them.

D.   Disputes Concerning Arbitrability

Arbitrators should confirm, and recite in the preliminary conference order, that there are no disputes concerning the arbitrability of any claims or defenses presented in the case or the arbitrators' authority to decide them. If any such disputes do exist, arbitrators should set a schedule for briefing and deciding them. *See* Chapter 4, *supra*.

E.   Information Required For Additional Disclosure

As noted in Chapter 2, *supra*, arbitrators have a continuing duty to provide to the parties information that comes to their attention and requires disclosure under applicable standards. However, arbitrators can only make disclosures when they are aware of the matter. If such information, *e.g.*, that one of the key witnesses in the case is a relative or close friend of an arbitrator, is not made known to the arbitrator until shortly before the hearing, the arbitration schedule may be seriously delayed if the arbitrator feels obliged to withdraw. Accordingly, arbitrators should fix a date, as early in the proceedings as possible, by which parties will advise the arbitrators of the names of all known witnesses, key actors in the events who may not testify, experts, lawyers, or any other facts (not theretofore disclosed) that may cause a party to have a concern about the neutrality of any arbitrator. Arbitrators should make any required disclosures in a timely manner thereafter.

Some arbitrators ask parties to acknowledge, by a specified date, that they have received the arbitrators' disclosures, that they know of no information beyond that reported which would possibly warrant the arbitrators' withdrawal, that they have no objection to the arbitrators continuing to serve, or that any objection they may have has been presented to the arbitral institution (in the case of administered arbitration) or to the arbitrators.

F.   Disqualification of Counsel

The law concerning whether arbitrators, or only courts, have the power to disqualify counsel from serving in an arbitration varies among different jurisdictions. Thus, if any party seeks to have an arbitrator disqualify counsel, arbitrators should require the parties to brief both the merits of the request and the arbitrators' authority to grant it.

G. Consolidation and Joinder

Arbitrators should only grant requests to consolidate separate arbitrations or join additional parties when they have determined (1) that they have authority to grant such relief, and (2) that such relief would serve to provide a fair and efficient hearing to all concerned parties. When motions for consolidation of arbitrations are brought to courts, arbitrators will generally be held to have the power to determine preliminary clause interpretation issues with respect to whether the arbitration clauses permit or prohibit consolidation.

Sometimes one or more counsel at the preliminary conference will express a desire that their arbitration be consolidated with another arbitration that involves related issues, since in many situations consolidation of separate arbitrations would serve the interests of efficiency and judicial economy. As stated in Comment 1 to Section 10 of the RUAA, "Multiparty disputes have long been problematic in the enforcement of agreements to arbitrate. When conflict erupts in complex transactions involving multiple contracts, it is rare for all parties to be signatories to a single arbitration agreement. In such cases, some parties may be bound to arbitrate while others are not; in other situations, there may be multiple arbitration agreements. Such realities raise the possibility that common issues of law or fact will be resolved in multiple fora, enhancing the overall expense of conflict resolution and leading to potentially inconsistent results."

Nevertheless, neither the FAA nor the RUAA expressly authorize arbitrators to consolidate separate arbitrations. Due to the fact that the very nature of an arbitrator's authority derives from having been contractually empowered by particular parties to arbitrate particular disputes between those parties, until recently it has been widely presumed by arbitrators that they lack the power to consolidate separate arbitrations. *See Yuen v. Superior Court*, 121 Cal. App. 4th 1133 (2004) (arbitrators ruled that, absent agreement or court order, AAA did not have jurisdiction to consolidate proceedings).

The RUAA and some state statutes do expressly authorize courts to consolidate separate arbitrations in appropriate circumstances. *See, e.g.,* RUAA § 10; Cal.   Code Civ. Proc. §. 1281.3. Under such statutes, when separate arbitration proceedings are pending or likely, a party may petition the court for an order consolidating the proceedings. The statutes are silent with respect to the question whether arbitrators have concurrent authority to order consolidation.

Recently, however, some courts have interpreted the United States Supreme Court's decisions in *Howsam v. Dean Witter Reynolds,* 537 U.S. 79 (2002) (*see generally* Chapter 4, *supra*) and *Green Tree Financial Corp. v. Bazzle,* 539 U.S. 444 (2003) (*see generally* Chapter 5, *supra*) as supporting the proposition that arbitrators may consolidate related claims into one proceeding.   *See, e.g., Shaw's Supermarket v. United Foods,* 321 F.3d 251 (1ˢᵗ Cir. 2003) (consolidation is a procedural matter for the arbitrator to determine under *Howsam*); *Birmingham News Co. v. Horn,* 901 So. 2d 27 (Ala., 2004) (also relying on *Howsam* in holding that arbitrators exercised their discretion in structuring arbitration procedures, and did not exceed their powers in consolidating multiple cases); *Yuen, supra,* 121 Cal. App. 4ᵗʰ 1133 (*Bazzle* mandates that consolidation is an issue to be submitted to arbitration under broad arbitration clause stating that "all disputes" relating to the contract shall be submitted to arbitration).   Thus, when presented with a request to consolidate separate arbitration proceedings, arbitrators should initially determine whether they have the authority to do so and should request briefing or argument on that issue prior to determining the merits of the request.

In the event that a party requests a stay of the arbitration to enable it to seek a court order compelling consolidation, the arbitrator must weigh the rights of the party who desires such judicial relief prior to proceeding with the arbitration against the rights of another party who may be prejudiced by delay.   Normally the presumption should be against delaying the arbitration.   Arbitrators should also be cognizant of the fact that, when a party seeks a court order compelling consolidation of multiple arbitrations, it may be for the arbitrator, rather than the court, to determine the preliminary question of whether an arbitration clause permits or prohibits consolidation.   *See*

Garcia v. DIRECTV, Inc., 115 Cal. App. 4th 297, 302-03 (2004) (following *Bazzle*).

For reasons similar to those supporting consolidation requests, counsel may express a desire that additional parties be required to be joined in the pending arbitration. Arbitrators, lacking contempt power, cannot force parties who are not before them to participate in the arbitration. If those parties signed the arbitration agreement, were named in the demand for arbitration, and received due notice of the arbitration proceedings, arbitrators may render an award determining the rights and obligations of such absent parties. When parties before the arbitrators contend that certain parties who did not sign the arbitration agreement should be added to the arbitration (*e.g.*, on a theory of alter ego, corporate affiliation, or otherwise), such relief is ordinarily available only from a court. *See* Chapter 4, *supra*.

Occasionally, parties who did not sign the arbitration agreement but nevertheless have some involvement in the dispute may wish to join in the arbitration in order to benefit from an anticipated award or avoid having to prosecute parallel litigation. In such circumstances, assuming the parties present do not object, arbitrators may include in the preliminary conference (or other) order procedures and a deadline for the non-parties to sign a stipulation to join in the pending arbitration and file a statement of their claims and/or defenses.

If it becomes clear that notice of the arbitration cannot be provided to a signatory to the arbitration agreement, or that a non-signatory with a vital interest in the dispute cannot be joined in the arbitration, arbitrators should require the parties who are present to brief the question of whether the arbitration should proceed or be dismissed and the arbitrators' authority, under applicable law, to order either course.

Finally, in considering any joinder issues, arbitrators should be mindful of the logistical and economic problems that a joined party with a minor involvement in a major case might have and should consider the adoption of procedures designed to ameliorate those problems.

H.   Discovery

Arbitrators should set procedures and a schedule for any discovery to be conducted and for expedited resolution of any discovery disputes that may arise. *See* Chapter 8, *infra*. Counsel should ordinarily be required to confer and seek resolution of any discovery dispute before presenting it to the arbitrators.

I.   Motions

Arbitrators should set procedures and a schedule for the submission, briefing, and determination of any motions that may be filed, including motions dealing with threshold issues, interim relief, and dispositive motions. *See* Chapter 7, *infra*. Counsel should ordinarily be required to confer and seek resolution of any procedural issues before submitting a motion on the matter.

J.   Providing Specialized Information to Arbitrators

If the hearing will involve specialized technical or scientific matters with which the arbitrators are not familiar, the arbitrators should consider asking counsel if they can agree to identify, and make available to the arbitrators reasonably in advance of the hearing, such treatises or other publications (or portions thereof) as will allow the arbitrators to better understand the issues and evidence.

K.   Appointment of Neutral Experts

The rules of some arbitral institutions explicitly recognize the arbitrators' authority to appoint one or more "neutral experts" to serve as witnesses. *See* CPR Rule 9.3(d). The power is undoubtedly included, implicitly, in other institutional rules that grant the arbitrators broad power to manage the arbitration and seek such evidence as is needed to properly decide the case. Nevertheless, this power is rarely exercised in most domestic commercial arbitrations. The evident reluctance of arbitrators to appoint neutral experts probably stems from two concerns: (1) a desire to avoid increased costs for parties that have already spent considerable money on their own retained experts, and (2) a recognition that, in selecting the neutral expert, the arbitrator is likely determining the outcome of the case and a concomitant concern that it may be nearly impossible for the arbitrator to ascertain whether a particular expert has predispositions or opinions that might bias his or her assessment of critical issues.

Accordingly, arbitrators should consider appointing neutral experts over party objection only in the most unusual circumstances. On the other hand, in cases in which cooperative counsel suggest that the arbitrators appoint a single expert, whose costs would be shared by all parties (either permanently or subject to reallocation in the final award) in lieu of each party retaining its own expert, arbitrators may wish to accept this invitation if the parties can agree on the identity of the neutral expert or at least on a list of acceptable candidates; the arbitrators could select from this list based on a review of curricula vitae, publications, and perhaps interviews. If a neutral expert is appointed, arbitrators should set forth in an order the issues on which the expert is being asked to opine; the materials he or she may consider in reaching those opinions; whether and under what circumstances contact with the parties, their counsel, and witnesses will be allowed; provisions for compensation; and other pertinent parameters of the appointment.

L.   Communication Ground Rules

Arbitrators should establish ground rules and procedures for the submission of materials directly to the arbitrators, opposing counsel, and the arbitral institution (to the extent it requires copies of such materials). For documents generated by word processing, e-mail may be the easiest mode of communication. Exhibits, photographs, judicial opinions, and similar documents can be e-mailed, faxed, mailed, or sent by overnight delivery service as appropriate.

M.   Location of the Hearing

In some cases, the location of the hearing will be specified in the arbitration agreement or arbitration rules, and that specification controls unless the parties agree to change it. If the hearing location was not previously specified, arbitrators should determine whether the parties are now in agreement on that matter, in which event that agreement should be followed. If the parties are not in agreement concerning the hearing location, the arbitrator will have to determine it. Generally, hearings should be held in the location most convenient to the largest number of participants (witnesses, counsel, and parties). If, as sometimes happens, claimant would like to hold the hearing in city X (which is most convenient to its witnesses) and respondent would like to hold it in city Y (which is most convenient to its witnesses), arbitrators should consider receiving the testimony of claimant's witnesses in X and then reconvening the hearing in Y to hear respondent's witnesses.

N.   Dates of the Hearing

After discussing all the matters identified in this chapter, arbitrators and counsel should be able to arrive at a reasonably accurate estimate for the number of hearing days that will be required. Arbitrators should emphasize to counsel, however, that underestimating the hearing time required is common and often greatly delays disposition of the case, since attempting to find, at the end of the hearing, a block of additional days available to busy arbitrators, counsel, parties, and witnesses is likely to result in a delay of many weeks or months. The better course is to apply a substantial increase to the time initially estimated by counsel for the hearing and reserve a generous amount of hearing time with the understanding that, shortly before the date when any applicable cancellation fee would become due, the parties can delete any days they are sure they will not need.

Normally, it is most efficient to schedule the hearing for consecutive business days. In cases in which hearings are going to run for multiple weeks, it is often advisable to schedule the hearing for Monday-Thursday or Tuesday-Friday so that all participants can have one office day per week to attend to other matters. It is also sometimes appropriate to schedule one or more weeks "off" from the hearing, either at the close of claimant's case or the close of respondent's case. Whatever hearing dates and locations are selected should be precisely recorded in the preliminary conference order and all parties and counsel should be clearly advised that the hearing will go forward on those days absent good cause shown.

O.   Hearing Subpoenas for Non-Party Witnesses

Rules of some arbitral institutions make explicit the obligation of parties to produce at the hearing, without necessity of a subpoena, witnesses they control if so requested by another party. JAMS Rule 21 ("At the written request of another Party, all other Parties shall produce for the Arbitration Hearing all specified witnesses in their employ or under their control without need of subpoena."). Even without such a rule, arbitrators have the power to order a party to produce such witnesses at the hearing. Other witnesses, who are not under the control of one of the parties and are unwilling to come to the hearing voluntarily, may be subpoenaed under the authority of the FAA or most state arbitration statues, and such subpoenas will be enforced by the appropriate federal or state courts.

Once the hearing dates have been determined, arbitrators should establish, and record in the preliminary conference order, a procedure and deadline for any requests for subpoenas. Usually, the requesting party will serve the request on the arbitrators and other counsel; opposing counsel will then be afforded a reasonable time to object. Sometimes the proposed witness or an opposing party may object that the subpoena (and usually, more particularly, the accompanying schedule of documents to be produced by the witness) imposes oppressive burdens on them. When such objections are raised, arbitrators will need to balance the requesting party's need for the documents against the burdens such production places on others and then strike the balance that is most appropriate to all the circumstances, including the nature and magnitude of the claims in the arbitration.

Certain jurisdictional issues sometimes arise when a party desires to issue a hearing subpoena to a witness that is located outside of the jurisdiction in which the main hearing is scheduled to be conducted. These issues are essentially the same as arise in the instance in which a party desires to issue a discovery subpoena to such a witness. For a more in-depth discussion of this topic, see Chapter 8 § VI, *infra.*

P.   Continuances and Cancellations

It is generally wise for arbitrators to indicate to counsel at the preliminary conference how continuances (referred to in some jurisdictions as "postponements" or "adjournments") and cancellations of hearings will be handled, should such a request be made later in the course of the arbitration. *See* Chapter 7, *infra.* In stating their practices with respect to these subjects, arbitrators should bear in mind several factors.

First, since the authority of arbitrators rests entirely on party agreement, it is clear that the parties can agree that the hearing will be continued to a new date convenient to the arbitrators and all parties and, further, that the parties have the power to jointly cancel a hearing indefinitely while they pursue settlement discussions or other matters. In the latter instance, the selected arbitrator is not obliged to remain available to the parties forever and may reasonably withdraw from the arbitration if the arbitrator so desires, leaving the parties with the choice of picking a replacement arbitrator or perhaps terminating this arbitration and beginning a new one.

Second, if one party seeks a continuance and other parties oppose it, arbitrators have discretion to grant or deny the request. However, in exercising that discretion, arbitrators should recall that one ground for vacatur under the FAA and various state arbitration statutes is the refusal to postpone a hearing upon sufficient cause shown. The implicit bargain courts have made with arbitrators is to say, in effect, "we will generally not second-guess your decisions, provided that you give every party a full and fair opportunity to be heard"; accordingly, courts are likely to find good cause for continuance of an arbitration hearing more readily than they might for continuance of a court trial. Absent strong evidence of prejudice to the opposing party, it is probably safest to grant a short continuance, even if the showing in support of the request is far from overwhelming.

Arbitrators whose policies require that parties pay a cancellation fee when a hearing is cancelled within a certain number of days before it is scheduled to begin, *see* Chapter 2, *supra,* should make sure at the preliminary conference that the parties are aware of, and have agreed to, those policies, preferably in writing.

Q.   Nature of Award

In accordance with the principle of party autonomy, the parties have the right to decide what type of award they want to receive. In making that decision, the parties may find it useful to consider the arbitrators' views and preferences. Thus, after generally discussing with the parties the various alternative approaches, arbitrators should confirm the type of award the parties want, *e.g.,* a "bare award" that simply states the disposition of each claim or a "reasoned award" that provides an explanation of the reasons underlying the arbitrators' decision. *See* Chapter 10, *infra.* If the latter, it is often helpful to get some sense of how extensive a statement of reasons the parties contemplate and whether they prefer a particular format, for example, an award containing findings of fact and conclusions of law. It is highly desirable that the arbitrators and parties leave the preliminary conference with a common understanding of what sort of award will follow the hearing.

R.   Time of Award

Arbitrators should confirm with the parties whether their arbitration agreement or the applicable rules prescribe a deadline for the issuance of an award and, if so, what that deadline is. If, because of the complexity of the case or the length of the expected hearing, arbitrators believe that preparation and issuance of an adequate award within that time is not feasible, they should request that the parties agree to a reasonable extension of time to prepare the award and should reflect that agreement in the order.

S.   Hearing Procedures Checklist

Arbitrators should discuss with counsel, and memorialize in the preliminary conference order, all arrangements and procedures for the submission of pre-hearing materials and the conduct of the hearing. Since such matters are fully discussed in Chapter 9, *infra*, they need not be addressed in detail here. The hearing topics that arbitrators should particularly consider during the pre-hearing stage, and the sections of Chapter 9 in which they are discussed, are as follows:

1. Designing the appropriate hearing process (§ I).
2. Standards for admission of evidence (§ III(A)).
3. Order of proof (§ III(B)).
4. Early submission of core exhibits (§ IV(A)).
5. Management of evidentiary exhibits (§ IV(B)).
6. Management of demonstrative exhibits (§ IV(C)).
7. Possible use of written testimony (§ V(A)).
8. Expert witness testimony (§ V(B)).
9. Lay witness testimony (§ V(C)).
10. Testimony from witnesses at other locations (§ V(D)).
11. Previously recorded testimony (§ V(E)).
12. Sequestration of witnesses (§ V(F)).
13. Counsel's communications with witnesses during testimony (§ V(G)).
14. Setting a realistic daily hearing schedule (§ VI(B)).
15. Monitoring compliance with the hearing schedule (§ VI(C)).
16. Possible requests for additional hearing time (§ VI(D)).
17. Use of technology during hearings (§ VII(A)).
18. Transcripts (§ VII(B)).
19. Hearing room logistics (§ VII(C)).
20. Any special needs of hearing participants (§ VII(D)).
21. Possible site visits during the hearing (§ VIII).
22. Determining awards of costs, attorneys' fees, and interest (§ X).
23. Pre-hearing and/or post-hearing briefs (XI(A) and (B)).
24. Counsel's opening statements and mini-summaries (XII(A) and (B)).
25. Closing arguments (§ XII(C)).

Use of the foregoing checklist should be helpful to arbitrators in making certain that important hearing matters are not overlooked in the preliminary conference agenda and order.

T.   Other Matters

Arbitrators should raise with counsel any additional matters that may be pertinent and should afford counsel an opportunity to do the same.

VI.   ENCOURAGING MEDIATION OR OTHER SETTLEMENT EFFORTS

Arbitrators should be cautious about encouraging parties in an arbitration to pursue mediation or other settlement efforts but may appropriately do so in cases in which the benefits of that course clearly outweigh the possible harms.

The question of whether arbitrators, at or before the preliminary conference, should suggest that the parties consider mediating their dispute, or structure the arbitration process in a particular way for the express purpose of facilitating settlement, is a matter of some disagreement among arbitrators. The issues involved are subtle and implicate competing considerations regarding the role of an arbitrator.

Many, perhaps most, experienced commercial arbitrators recognize that, while arbitration is often preferable to litigation as a mode of resolving disputes, a settlement agreement, whether achieved through direct negotiations or mediation, is even better. In a settlement, the parties can fashion their own mutually-acceptable resolution and thereby eliminate the risks and uncertainties inherent in turning the outcome over to outsiders, can sometimes employ creative remedies and business alternatives that judges and arbitrators could not decree, and can often save considerable time and money that would be consumed by a full-blown arbitration or litigation. Thus, commercial arbitrators, many of whom also serve as mediators, widely believe that arbitration should be initiated only after reasonable efforts at mediation have failed to bring about a resolution.

Consequently, when asked for advice in designing dispute resolution processes, many ADR neutrals, and sophisticated counsel as well, recommend that the parties include a so-called "med/arb" clause in their contract. Such a "step" or "tiered" clause (as it is sometimes termed) can provide, in varying ways, that when a dispute arises under the contract, the parties must devote a specified amount of time to mediating it before arbitration may be commenced or that mediation and arbitration be conducted simultaneously on independent tracks. The mediation/arbitration transition can be structured in various ways. The most common is for the parties to pick one neutral to serve as mediator and one or more others to serve as arbitrator(s). A second approach is to utilize the same neutral as both mediator and arbitrator. (When this approach is used, the parties must execute, either before the mediation or before proceeding to arbitration, a written agreement to waive any objection to the arbitration award based on the arbitrator's having had *ex parte* communications with each side during the mediation.). A third approach is the same as the second, except that, at the end of an unsuccessful mediation, any party may demand that a new neutral be selected to serve as arbitrator.

Most arbitral institutions, including JAMS, AAA, and the CPR, have sample med/arb clauses that parties can utilize, with appropriate adaptations, in their contracts. Some ADR providers and neutrals recommend that, in some circumstances, it is most advantageous to include in commercial contracts a three-tiered dispute resolution clause under which high-level business executives of both parties must engage in direct, face-to-face negotiations for a period of time before the dispute can be submitted to mediation and, if necessary, arbitration.

While it is surely proper for any professional with ADR expertise to acquaint parties who are designing a dispute resolution process with the kinds of alternatives discussed above, the situation is quite different when an arbitration proceeding has been commenced, a sole arbitrator or tripartite panel has been appointed, and the parties appear before the arbitrator(s) at a preliminary conference to set the procedures and schedules for the arbitration. In the latter setting, the arbitrators are not being consulted for general advice about dispute resolution alternatives but instead have been appointed to manage and decide a particular, live controversy (often, an intense one) in which the parties have typically hired counsel to advise them, formulated their legal positions, and developed their overall strategies. By the time of the preliminary conference, the parties may have devoted considerable time and money to preparing their arbitration pleadings and selecting the arbitrators who are to decide the case. For such arbitrators to now suggest   that the parties consider submitting their dispute to a different resolution process, for example, mediation, raises a number of serious issues.

First, it is the arbitrators' responsibility to manage fairly and efficiently the resolution process (arbitration) for which they were selected. The responsibility and ethical duty of advising the parties concerning their legal strategy and options, including other possible resolution processes, rests with their counsel. Thus, some experienced arbitrators believe that arbitrators are treading on dangerous ground when they undertake to perform both functions simultaneously. Moreover, counsel may strongly resent what they perceive to be an incursion by the arbitrators into counsel's role, and such incursions may damage the relationship between counsel and client in ways that can greatly complicate the arbitrators' management of the arbitration proceedings.

Second, although arbitrators will frequently not know it, a suggestion that the parties consider mediation could potentially benefit one party to the disadvantage of another. It is quite possible, for example, that by this stage of the dispute, one side is very eager to complete the arbitration as quickly as possible while the other is equally eager to delay the resolution for as long as possible. Initiating a mediation at this time may delay the arbitration to some extent, perhaps considerably. Moreover, there may well be other factors unknown to the arbitrators (*e.g.*, business exigencies, disputes among one party's management or shareholders, disputes with insurers, a desire to secure a favorable award so as to discourage other pending or anticipated claims) that make the mediation alternative quite unappealing to one of the parties. That party may have carefully weighed many considerations that cannot be shared with the arbitrators and concluded that its best strategy lies in pushing for an early and favorable arbitration award. The ability to pursue that strategy could be seriously impaired if arbitrators extol the virtues of mediation at the preliminary conference and urge the parties to give it a try. The party that has devised such a strategy is now confronted with the Hobson's choice of either (a) forsaking its chosen strategy in order to keep the arbitrators happy or (b) running the risk that, in declining to participate in mediation, it will displease the person or persons who have been appointed to decide its fate in the matter.

Third, the suggestion that the parties take their dispute to mediation may also be perceived as confirmation of the criticism of arbitration, voiced by some observers, that arbitrators try to avoid making the tough decisions that could alienate parties and deter return engagements. Thus, it is said, arbitrators will try to steer hard cases to mediators or will "split the baby" in their awards. While this criticism is largely unfounded, suggesting that the parties would do well to mediate may help perpetuate the myth.

Finally, suggesting mediation can cause considerable difficulty for a tripartite panel, especially if some arbitrators want to get on expeditiously with the task for which they were appointed and others want to put it off a while and see if the parties can settle the matter. This problem can be exacerbated if the arbitrator who suggested mediation is a well-known mediator and the other tribunal members perceive his suggestion as a pitch to get the mediation work for himself. Moreover, if all tribunal members have heavy calendars, a delay of months or even weeks to pursue mediation may mean putting off the arbitration for quite some time until all participants again have time available, or, alternatively, may require that one or more tribunal members withdraw and the parties engage in a second round of arbitrator selection activities.

On the other hand, there are experienced and well-respected arbitrators who consider that it is often useful and entirely proper for arbitrators to raise the possibility of mediation at the preliminary conference. Such arbitrators believe that the mediation option can be presented in a neutral, non-coercive manner in order to afford the parties a chance to make use of a mediation process (which is often available from the ADR provider that is administering the arbitration without affecting the arbitration timetable) if all parties so desire. Some arbitrators ask counsel, prior to the preliminary conference, to discuss with their clients and each other whether the parties want to pursue mediation and then to advise the arbitrators, without disclosing the respective position of any party, whether or not all parties wish to mediate the case. If the report is negative, the arbitrators can proceed with arbitration in the normal course, unaware of which, if any, of the parties favored mediation and which did not. However, say those who advocate this view, by raising the issue, the arbitrators have at least given all parties an opportunity to consider a potentially faster and more economical way of resolving their dispute.

The College of Commercial Arbitrators takes no position concerning which of the foregoing views represents the "best practice" on this subject. The answer probably depends on a host of factors which vary from case to case, including the extent of the parties' and counsel's familiarity with different ADR processes, the extent of the parties' resources and their relative bargaining power, whether or not there is an urgent need to complete the arbitration as quickly as possible, and similar considerations. Perhaps the best advice that can be given is that arbitrators should approach this matter with care, conscious of both the potential benefits and potential risks, and should tailor their actions to the circumstances of each case rather than adopting a uniform practice to be followed at all preliminary conferences.

VII. SUBSEQUENT PRE-HEARING MANAGEMENT

After the preliminary conference, arbitrators should maintain an active role in managing pre-hearing activities and monitoring the parties' progress to assure compliance with the preliminary conference order and timely completion of the arbitration.

Once the preliminary conference order is issued, arbitrators should remain actively involved in management of the case. Any issues that could not be resolved at the preliminary conference should be resolved as soon thereafter as possible and memorialized in a subsequent order. Many arbitrators find it helpful to sequentially number their orders, *e.g.*, Order No. 1, Order No. 2, so that later orders may readily refer back to issues addressed in earlier orders. Arbitrators should respond promptly and firmly to discovery disputes, rule promptly and clearly on motions presented, and move quickly to address any unexpected developments that arise after the preliminary conference.

If circumstances occur that make compliance with the dates in the preliminary conference order plainly unachievable, arbitrators should confer with counsel, adjust those dates as appropriate, and issue a revised order. However, whether dealing with an original or revised preliminary conference order, arbitrators should monitor the parties' compliance and progress with it and should act quickly if significant shortfalls begin to develop.

Monitoring progress can be accomplished in various ways. Some arbitrators prefer to have conference calls with counsel at regular intervals, for example, monthly, to ascertain the status of pre-hearing activities. This approach has the advantage of ease and informality but may encourage parties to save up their grievances and problems for the arbitrator to resolve in the monthly calls. Another acceptable approach is to require the parties to e-mail to the arbitrators joint status reports advising of their progress. In this way, parties are required to confer and will likely feel some incentive for demonstrating that, as the arbitrators requested at the preliminary conference, they are cooperating in working out process issues.

Even in cases in which the status report approach is used, it may be useful to have a conference call with counsel at an appropriate time, perhaps thirty to sixty days before the hearing, to make sure that they are entering the home stretch in good shape and ready to go into the hearing on time.

Whatever monitoring method may be selected, arbitrators should not attempt to micro-manage the case unless absolutely necessary. Counsel should be encouraged, and given reasonable latitude, to resolve problems between themselves as much as possible. If counsel's efforts in this regard start to lag, it is often effective for arbitrators to remind the parties that the arbitrators will be deciding the case and that they take a dim view of both "hiding the ball" and "fishing expeditions," each of which they recognize quite well from years of experience in litigation and arbitration.

CHAPTER 7

MOTIONS

Arbitrators' goals with respect to motion practice are (1) to
encourage motions that are likely to expedite or facilitate
the arbitration proceedings, (2) to discourage motions
that are not likely to be productive, and (3) to provide
a fair, efficient, cost-effective process for party
presentations and arbitrator decisions.

I.   INTRODUCTION

Procedures for managing motions in arbitration should reflect the
desire to be cost-effective and expeditious without sacrificing a full, fair
hearing. Certain motions should be identified and scheduled early in
the proceeding, such as motions related to jurisdiction and arbitrability
(*see* Chapter 4, *supra*) and provisional relief. This approach may also
be appropriate for certain dispositive motions, since it may be wasteful
to engage in discovery and a full evidentiary hearing if all or any
portion of a claim is subject to a valid defense, such as statute of
limitations, release, or statute of frauds.

The following procedural options regarding motion practice are
available to arbitrators:

1. Early identification of motions at the preliminary conference.
2. Imposition of a rule that no motions can be presented without
    first obtaining permission from the arbitrators.
3. Hearing oral argument on the substance of the motion without
    any written submissions.
4. Compelling counsel to confer regarding whether the motion is
    really necessary and/or to develop a schedule for written
    submissions.

5. Requiring either simultaneous or responsive written submissions.
6. Limiting the length of briefs and time for oral argument.
7. Permitting affidavits or live testimony regarding factual issues.

II. ARBITRAL AUTHORITY TO HEAR MOTIONS

Consistent with their broad authority to manage the arbitration and to grant relief not available in court, arbitrators have the power to grant any well-taken motion unless there is a specific prohibition in the agreement, rules, statute, or case law.

Arbitrators have the authority to consider any form of motion, and to grant any form of relief, subject to whatever specific limitations might be imposed by the applicable arbitration clause, law, or institutional rules. Thus, in allowing motions to be presented and in considering those motions, arbitrators must always remain diligent in ensuring that they do not violate legal requirements, such as those established under the FAA and RUAA relating to the failure to consider material evidence. 9 U.S.C. § 10(a)(3), RUAA § 23(a)(3). Similarly, arbitrators must ensure that the consideration of a particular motion will not serve to deny a party a fundamentally fair hearing. In the absence of a contractual provision, legal principle, or rule prohibiting the granting of a particular motion, arbitrators should entertain and consider motions whenever that process will contribute to the efficiency and efficacy of the arbitration proceeding.

Statutes, case law, and institutional rules expressly recognize arbitrators' authority to hear and rule upon particular types of motions. For example, AAA Rule 34, JAMS Rule 24(e), CPR Rule 13 and Section 8(b)(1) of the RUAA provide authority to entertain motions for preliminary relief. JAMS Rule 18 provides authority to grant dispositive motions. Courts have acknowledged that the AAA rules implicitly permit the use of summary disposition motions,

Schlessinger v. Rosenfeld, Meyer & Sussman, 40 Cal. App. 4th 1096 (1995), and that the NASD Code of Arbitration Procedure also permits such motions. *Reed v. Mutual Service Corp.*, 106 Cal. App. 4th 1359 (2003). Section 15(b) of the RUAA explicitly authorizes arbitrators "to decide a request for summary disposition of a claim or particular issue." Particular types of motions are discussed in more detail below and in other chapters of this Guide.

III. TYPES OF MOTIONS

During the course of an arbitration, energetic counsel and parties will often attempt to present any kind of motion that could be filed in court, and sometimes more. The most common types of motions generally directed to arbitrators are addressed below.

A. Service of Process

Arbitrators should discourage motion practice regarding the formalities of "service of process" of the demand for arbitration or any other pleading, except when such formalities are prescribed by the arbitration agreement or applicable rules.

In arbitration, jurisdiction does not depend on formal "service of process" in the manner usually prescribed by statutes governing court proceedings (*e.g.,* personal service, service by mail, service by publication, etc.) Moreover, the failure to serve a responsive pleading does not result in any default but is deemed a general denial. AAA Rule 4(c). Therefore, the only pertinent question is usually whether respondent (or claimant with respect to a counterclaim) has received actual notice of the claims asserted. However, when the arbitration agreement or applicable rules prescribe certain procedures for commencing an arbitration, *e.g.,* delivery of the demand for arbitration to a particular arbitral institution or service of the demand in a particular manner, such procedures must be satisfied unless waived, and motions asserting a failure to satisfy them should be seriously considered.   Otherwise, arguing over the formalities of "service of process" in arbitration is an enormous waste of time and money. Arbitrators should simply be sure that, once notice is received, all parties have had adequate time to respond.

B.   Jurisdiction and Arbitrability

Arbitrators often require that any issues relating to arbitrability or jurisdiction be addressed in a formal motion.   For a more detailed discussion of those issues, see Chapter 4, *supra*.

C.   Consolidation and Joinder

On occasion, a party files a motion seeking to consolidate the pending arbitration with one or more other arbitrations, or to join an additional party in the arbitration. Issues relating to consolidation and joinder are addressed in Chapter 6, *supra*.

D.   Preliminary Relief

If inclined to grant preliminary relief, arbitrators should ensure that they have authority and, if so, may grant such relief when they determine it is necessary to ensure the efficacy of the ultimate award.

Preliminary relief is addressed in the rules of various arbitral institutions. Such rules typically provide for arbitrators to take such measures as they deem necessary, including measures that are necessary to ensure the protection, conservation, and/or preservation of goods or property, and the sale or disposition of perishable or disposable goods. AAA Rule 34; JAMS Rule 24(e); CPR Rule 13; NAF Rule 27. The AAA, JAMS and NAF rules provide specifically for issuance of a preliminary injunction. *See also J. Brooks Securities, Inc. v. Vanderbilt Securities, Inc.*, 126 Misc. 2d 875, 484 N.Y.S.2d 472 (Sup. Ct. 1985). The rules typically permit arbitrators to require the posting of security by the party receiving the interim relief.

There is substantial case law that has arisen under the FAA with regard to the enforcement of arbitrators' interim measures through the judicial confirmation process. Additionally, Sections 8 and 18 of the RUAA provide, respectively, for the issuance and enforcement of such interim measures. It is important to note, however, that these sections of the RUAA, taken together, require that, in order for it to be subject to judicial confirmation, the arbitrators' ruling must be incorporated into a document entitled an "award." This nomenclature is probably not required for orders granting interim measures when enforcement would be governed by the FAA. For a further discussion of interim and partial final awards, see Chapter 10, *infra*.

Parties may, in the alternative, apply to courts for provisional relief pending an arbitration, rather than seeking it from the arbitrators. The right to seek such relief is explicit under certain state arbitration statutes. *See* Cal. Code. Civ. Proc. § 1281.8(b). Most courts agree that a party may apply to a court for provisional remedies pending arbitration. *See PMS Distributing Co., Inc. v. Huber & Suhner*, 863 F.2d 639, 642 (9th Cir. 1988) (right to seek provisional relief from court to preserve status quo pending arbitration is available under FAA); *Davenport v. Blue Cross of California*, 52 Cal. App. 4th 435, 451 (1997).

Arbitrators are not limited to granting the kinds of relief a court could provide. *See Sperry Int'l Trade, Inc. v. Government of Israel*, 689 F.2d 301 (2d Cir. 1982); *Cook v. Mishkin*, 95 A.D.2d 760, 464 N.Y.S.2d 761 (1st Dep't 1983). Cases provide examples of relief not referred to in the rules, such as escrow of assets, that may be granted by arbitrators. *See Sperry, supra* (escrow proceeds of letter of credit in names of both parties, applying New York law); *Konkar Maritime Enterprises, S.A. v. Compagnie Belge D'Affretement*, 668 F. Supp. 267 (S.D.N.Y. 1987) (respondent ordered to place amount in dispute in joint interest-bearing escrow account).

On the other hand, some types of interim relief may only be granted by courts. For example, arbitrators are generally held to be unable to appoint receivers. *See, e.g. Wanderlust Pictures, Inc. v. Empire Entertainment Group, L.L.C.*, 2001 WL 826095, No. 01Civ.4465 (JSM) (S.D.N.Y. July 19, 2001). However, the same objective may be accomplished by providing for one party to run the affairs of the business under restraints, including supervision by a representative of the other party, *see Cook v. Mishkin*, 95 A.D.2d 760, 464 N.Y.S.2d 761

(1st Dep't 1983), or crafting a mechanism for appointment of a liquidating entity. *See D'Amato v. Leffler*, 290 A.D.2d 475, 736 N.Y.S.2d 689 (2d Dep't 2002).

E.   Pleadings

Arbitrators must strike a balance between arbitration's informality in pleading requirements and the need of a respondent to obtain enough information about claims to respond effectively.

Commercial arbitration generally reflects a strong proclivity to avoid court-like motion practice to refine pleadings or to dismiss a matter for failure to state a claim properly. However, respondents require enough information about claims to enable them to defend effectively. Respondents may therefore attempt to bring demurrers or motions to strike before arbitrators. Although most institutional rules require minimal information in pleadings, *see* AAA Rule 4(a)(i), CPR Rule 3.3 and JAMS Rule 9(b), they do not provide explicit authority for an arbitrator to dismiss a case for failure to comply with these rules.

Arbitrators should analyze whether a respondent has enough information about a claim and whether more information will be provided through discovery so that additional pleadings may not be necessary. The arbitrators can then (1) order a party to provide a more detailed pleading, (2) order certain discovery to provide further information about the claim, and/or (3) deny any motion for more information about the claims pled.

Since awards can be vacated, remanded, or corrected when arbitrators have either exceeded their authority or failed to issue an award that addresses all of the claims, a reasonably well-pled statement of claim can be very important in light of the traditional standards for vacatur and for correcting an award.

F.   Discovery

Unresolved issues relating to discovery often result in the filing of motions in arbitrations. Given the significant role discovery continues to play in commercial arbitrations in the U.S., issues concerning discovery are addressed in a separate chapter of the Guide. *See* Chapter 8, *infra*.

G.   Bifurcation

Arbitrators should bifurcate proceedings in the exercise of sound discretion if it is clear that bifurcation will reduce costs and streamline the arbitration process.

AAA Rule 30(b) gives arbitrators authority to bifurcate proceedings in order to achieve economy and streamline the arbitration process. JAMS Rule 22, which provides arbitrators with the general authority to vary the order of proof and to organize the arbitration, implicitly grants to arbitrators the discretion to bifurcate proceedings. However, arbitrators should be mindful that bifurcation could have the effect of lengthening, rather than shortening, the proceedings. Arbitrators should, therefore, be cautious when bifurcating proceedings *e.g.*, between liability and damages, because, if there is a finding of liability, the delay in scheduling the second portion of the bifurcated proceeding might mean that the claimant will receive an award much later than if the proceeding had not been bifurcated. However, it is common to bifurcate the issue of attorneys' fees until after a decision and award on the merits. *See, e.g., Rosenquist v. Haralambides,* 192 Cal. App. 3d 62 (1987).

Arbitrators should be mindful of case law indicating that arbitral decisions regarding the initial phases of bifurcated proceedings may be treated by courts as subject to confirmation or vacatur. Thus, parties who do not seek vacatur of such decisions within the applicable time frames may later be barred from doing so when the final award is ultimately rendered. See Chapter 10, *infra*, regarding interim and partial final awards.

H.   Dispositive Motions

To avoid the risk of having an award vacated for refusing to hear evidence, arbitrators should only

> grant dispositive motions when the party opposing the
> motion has had a reasonable opportunity to gather and
> present evidence on the pertinent issues and the
> arbitrator is confident that, on the undisputed facts,
> the movant is clearly entitled to an award in its favor.

Section 15 of the RUAA and JAMS Rule 18 specifically provide for dispositive motions. It has been held that the AAA Rules do so implicitly. *Schlessinger v. Rosenfeld, Meyer & Sussman*, 40 Cal. App. 4th 1096, 1108-9 (1995).

Although FAA Section 10 provides for vacatur of an award when the arbitrators were "guilty of misconduct . . . in refusing to hear evidence pertinent and material to the controversy," it has been held that an arbitrator can grant a dispositive motion without holding a full-blown evidentiary hearing so long as the party opposing the motion receives notice and an opportunity to be heard. *Max Marx Color & Chemical Co. v. Barnes*, 37 F. Supp. 2d 248 (S.D.N.Y. 1999); *Prudential Securities, Inc. v. Dalton*, 929 F. Supp. 1411, 1417 (N.D. Okla. 1996).

In view of the foregoing ground for vacatur, an arbitrator should not grant a dispositive motion except in a clear case. It has been held to be manifest disregard of the law to grant a dispositive motion when issues of fact exist. *Neary v. Prudential Ins. Co.*, 63 F. Supp. 2d 208 (D. Conn. 1999).

Dispositive motions have also been held to be appropriate only in arbitrations in which full discovery has been had and completed; otherwise the party defending the motion may be at a disadvantage due to inability to obtain relevant information that creates a triable issue of fact. *Schlessinger v. Rosenfeld, Meyer & Sussman, supra*, 40 Cal. App. 4th 1096.

I.   Motions in Limine or to Preclude Testimony

> Motions in limine or to preclude testimony are within
> arbitrators' sound discretion; however, granting such
> motions can imperil an award or subject it to an attack.
> Such motions should therefore generally be
> discouraged and the parties reminded that arbitrators

will ultimately decide both the credibility and weight of the evidence offered.

Motions in limine are intended to exclude evidence on the basis that it is irrelevant, inadmissible, or prejudicial. Such determinations are within arbitrators' discretion, and strict conformity to rules of evidence, except with respect to principles of legal privilege, is not required unless the parties so designate. *See* CPR Rule 12.2; AAA Rule 31(a) and (c); JAMS Rule 22(d); NAF Rule 35(C). AAA Rule 31(b) provides that arbitrators shall determine the admissibility, relevance, and materiality of the evidence offered and may exclude evidence deemed by the arbitrators to be cumulative, irrelevant, or privileged. *See also* JAMS Rule 22(d) (permitting arbitrators to exclude immaterial or unduly repetitive evidence).

While arbitrators have discretion to do so, excluding or rejecting evidence, except on the basis of privilege, can imperil an award, or at least subject it to an allegation that a party was not afforded a fair opportunity to be heard. *See* 9 U.S.C. § 10(a)(3), RUAA § 23(a)(3). Accordingly, motions in limine should be discouraged and the parties reminded that the arbitrators will ultimately decide both the credibility and weight of the evidence offered.

Arbitrators' determinations concerning what evidence is pertinent and material will be set aside only if they deprive a party of a fundamentally fair hearing. *See, e.g., DeSilva v. First Union Securities, Inc.,* 249 F. Supp. 2d 286 (S.D.N.Y. 2003); *Matter of Solartechnik, Ges., M.B.H.* 227 A.D.2d 94, 652 N.Y.S.2d 654 (3d Dep't 1997), *rev'd on other grds,* 91 N.Y.2d 482 (1988).

J. Sanctions

Sanctions may be granted in the arbitrators' sound discretion when and as authorized by the clause, applicable arbitral law, or applicable institutional rules.

Any authority to issue sanctions in an arbitration proceeding must be derived from either the rules the parties have agreed to utilize, *see, e.g.,* JAMS Rule 29, the parties' agreement to arbitrate, or applicable statutory or common law. For example, if the parties' agreement provides for discovery pursuant to the California Discovery Act, Cal. Code Civ. Proc. § 1281.05, the arbitrator has the power to enforce those provisions, including the power to impose discovery sanctions as permitted by that act. The RUAA also vests arbitrators with authority to grant broad relief, including an award of fees and expenses, and sanctions for noncompliance with discovery orders. RUAA §§ 17(d), 21(b) and (c).

Many cases also acknowledge the authority of arbitrators to award sanctions. *See, e.g., Polin v. Kellwood Co.,* 132 F. Supp. 2d 126 (S.D.N.Y. 2000) (finding it was proper under AAA rules for arbitrator to award sanction of one-half of cost of arbitration when counsel made false offer of proof, unduly prolonged the hearings, asserted a frivolous claim, and generally acted in contempt of panel). At least one federal case arising under the FAA holds that arbitrators have inherent power to award fees as sanctions arising out of bad faith conduct. *Todd Shipyards Corp. v. Cunard Line, Ltd.,* 943 F.2d 1056 (9th Cir. 1991).

However, caution is advisable, especially in the absence of an enabling clause or rules. For example, there are cases holding that arbitrators have no inherent power to impose particular types of sanctions. *See, e.g., Thompson v. Jesperson,* 222 Cal. App. 3d 964 (1990); *Luster v. Collins,* 15 Cal. App 4th 1338 (1993) (arbitrator did not have the statutory power to compel compliance with arbitral orders by imposing monetary sanctions in the form of a fee for each day of noncompliance); *Certain Underwriters at Lloyd's London v. Argonaut Insurance Co.,* 264 F. Supp. 2d 926, 944 (N.D. Cal. 2003) (order to pay $10,000 per day was "akin to civil contempt," a power not granted to arbitrators under FAA).

Arbitrators may also wish to impose evidentiary sanctions, such as precluding the admission of testimony or documentary evidence, as a sanction for party non-compliance with arbitral orders. While this approach is permissible when the applicable clause or rules so authorize, arbitrators should be cautious in imposing such a sanction. Under the FAA, failure to receive material and relevant evidence can constitute a basis to vacate an award. *See, e.g.,* 9 U.S.C. § 10(a)(3). However, this provision has been narrowly construed so as "not to impinge on the broad discretion afforded arbitrators to decide what evidence should be presented." *Ripa v. Cathy Parker Mgmt., Inc.*, 1998 WL 241621, No. 98 Civ. 0577 (S.D.N.Y., May 13, 1998). *See also Pompano-Windy City Partners v. Bear Stearns & Co.*, 794 F. Supp. 1265, 1277 (S.D.N.Y. 1992) ("the arbitrator is the judge of the admissibility and relevancy of evidence submitted in an arbitration proceeding"). *See also Glen Rauch Securities, Inc. v. Weinraub*, 2 A.D.3d 301, 768 N.Y.S.2d 611 (1st Dep't 2003) (sanction precluding related exhibits and testimony of witness held to be proper in light of failure to comply with order directing production of documents).

K.   Continuances

While motions for continuance are within arbitrators' sound discretion, refusing to grant such a motion can provide potential grounds for vacatur of an award. In addressing such motions, arbitrators should therefore carefully weigh the reasons for the request, the delay in the proceedings, and the risk to the award, and should document the reasons for refusing such a request.

Motions for postponements or continuance are generally within arbitrators' sound discretion. Section 15(c) of the RUAA provides for adjournment by the arbitrator for good cause shown, as do the institutional arbitration rules. *See, e.g.,* AAA Rule 28; NAF Rule 9(E). While arbitrators have discretion to refuse a postponement, FAA Section 10 and many state arbitral laws include an arbitrator's "misconduct in refusing to postpone the hearing, upon sufficient cause shown" as a ground for vacatur.

The cases provide guidance as to when sufficient cause has been shown. *See, e.g., Tube & Steel Corp. v. Chicago Carbon Steel Products*, 319 F. Supp. 1302 (S.D.N.Y. 1970) (award vacated; party out of town and unable to attend); *Allendale Nursing Home, Inc. v. Local 1115 Joint Board*, 377 F. Supp. 1208, 1214 (S.D.N.Y. 1974) (award vacated; key witness seriously ill); *Whale Securities Co. v. Godfrey*, 271 A.D.2d 226, 7005 N.Y.S.2d 358 (1st Dep't 2000) (not improper to reject third request for postponement when lead lawyer was only unavailable for last day of hearing, party was not precluded from submitting affidavits or a written closing statement, and associate lawyer who had attended remainder of hearing was available); *Herskovitz v. L..B. Kaye Associates*, 170 A.D.2d 272, 565 N.Y.S.2d 804 (1st Dep't 1991) (not inappropriate to reject respondent's requests for postponement when petitioner presented all of her evidence in support of her claim in one hour on the first day of hearing and all other days had been used by respondent for counterclaims, respondent had two months' notice of the scheduled hearing date and ten days' notice that the AAA would require a court order to postpone the hearing, and no court order was sought).

Thus, refusal to grant a postponement is a serious decision that requires a weighing of factors including the reasons for the request, the number of prior adjournments sought by both sides, delay, and prejudice. Absent strong evidence of prejudice to the opposing party, it is probably safest to grant a short continuance, even if the showing in support of the request is less than overwhelming.

L.   Disqualification of Arbitrators

In administered arbitrations, disqualification motions should be referred to the arbitral institution. In ad hoc arbitrations, arbitrators should hear and decide the motion on the merits.

A principal advantage in the use of an arbitral institution is that the institution ordinarily will resolve motions to disqualify an arbitrator. For example, AAA Rule 17 allows the AAA to determine whether an arbitrator should be disqualified for failure to remain impartial, perform his or her duties with diligence and in good faith, and for any other ground as provided by law. Therefore, the arbitrator's sole task in connection with such motions is to refer the motion to the institution.

Some institutional rules that are meant to be used in ad hoc arbitrations also provide for a procedure by which the institution provides limited services relating to the resolution of a disqualification motion. For example, CPR Rule 7, which is intended to apply to ad hoc arbitrations governed by the CPR Rules, establishes an efficient process by which any challenges that cannot be resolved by the parties are resolved by the CPR.

There appears to be little authority defining an arbitrator's role in addressing a motion to disqualify in the absence of such a rule or institutional procedure. In such a case, the arbitrator should probably hear the motion as would a judge and decide it on the merits. See Chapter 2, *supra*, for further discussion of disqualification of arbitrators.

M.   Modification of Award

With respect to motions to modify final awards, partial final awards, and interim awards which are final in nature, see Chapter 11, *infra*.

For a discussion of motions to modify interim awards that are preliminary and non-final in nature, *e.g.*, on grounds of new evidence, changes in circumstances, changes in the law, or alleged errors in the arbitrator's analysis, see Chapter 10, *infra*. As is discussed there in more detail, when such a non-final interim award is issued, arbitrators are not *functus officio* with respect to the issues tentatively determined in the award and must reconsider their determination or reopen the record for good cause shown.

CHAPTER 8

DISCOVERY

Arbitrators' goals in managing discovery are (1) to ensure an efficient and fundamentally fair hearing, and (2) to afford each party a reasonable opportunity to obtain material evidence relating to its claims or defenses.

I.   INTRODUCTION

A.   Background

Prior to the adoption of the Federal Civil Discovery Rules, civil litigation was generally conducted without benefit of discovery. Each party to the litigation relied on the documents in its possession and the testimony given by its witnesses at the hearing. Cross-examination then was indeed an art form. However, by the 1930s, many states had begun to enact discovery procedures so that counsel could have a broader base for determining the facts in a given case.

The Federal Rules of Civil Procedure, enacted in 1938, contained discovery rules intended to prevent surprise at trial. While these rules may be said to have achieved their purpose, the rules are often abused in litigation. A plaintiff can file an action without significant factual support and then hope to find the necessary facts through discovery. A wealthier party can force a less affluent opponent to spend himself into submission by engaging in extensive and expensive discovery. Lawyers concerned about malpractice exposure may feel obligated to leave no stone unturned in their use of discovery, protecting themselves at the expense of their clients.

Traditionally, arbitration has involved very little discovery, thus making it more expeditious and less expensive than litigation. In some cases, this has been its main appeal. In other cases, particularly when stakes are high and the facts and law are complex, the parties may want about the same amount of discovery as is available in litigation but may still prefer arbitration for other reasons, for example, the opportunity to have their dispute determined with finality in a non-public forum by a decision-maker of their own choosing. Thus, arbitrators in commercial arbitrations should work with the parties to ensure that the kind and extent of discovery is appropriate in view of the nature of the case, and should honor the parties' intent, when reasonably apparent, that reduced discovery was among the reasons for the parties' agreement to arbitrate.

While there are, of course, some limits on party autonomy (no court, for example, would enforce an "arbitration agreement" that required the parties to resolve their differences through a duel), arbitration is fundamentally a creature of party agreement. When sophisticated parties agree to the extent of discovery to be allowed in a particular arbitration and understand the consequences, in time and costs, of their choice, arbitrators should generally accept that choice and help the parties design appropriate arrangements to implement it. When the parties are in agreement but it is not clear that they have a realistic appreciation of the consequences of their discovery choices, arbitrators should discuss with them the likely impact of their choices on the arbitration process. When parties are not in agreement concerning the extent of discovery, arbitrators should give them the benefit of their experience in this regard, discuss with them the degree of discovery that appears necessary and appropriate for the case, and attempt to forge a consensus regarding the recommended discovery process.

B.   Absence of a Statutory or Common Law Right to Discovery in Arbitration

When appropriate, arbitrators may remind the parties that most state and federal arbitration statutes, and the common law, do not provide parties with a right to conduct discovery in arbitration.

The FAA and most state arbitration statutes do not provide parties with a right to conduct discovery in arbitration. *See e.g.,* Cal. Code

Civ. Proc. §§ 1283.05 and 1283.1. Moreover, in arbitrations governed by the FAA, court-ordered discovery in aid of arbitration is available only "in extraordinary circumstances." *Application of Deiulemar di Navigazione*, 153 F.R.D. 592, 593 (E.D. La. 1994); *Deiulemar Compagnia di Navigazione v. M/V Allegra*, 198 F.3d 473, 479-80 (4th Cir. 1999) (finding extraordinary circumstances for need to perpetuate testimony of witnesses leaving the jurisdiction on a ship and for need to preserve evidence of ship repairs and condition of a vessel departing the jurisdiction). In jurisdictions in which arbitration discovery is not available as of right, it may be useful to remind the parties of this significant difference between arbitration and litigation when taking up the matter of how much discovery arbitrators should allow.

C. Relevance of Applicable Arbitration Rules and Parties' Arbitration Agreement

In determining the scope and nature of discovery, arbitrators must comply with applicable arbitration rules and the parties' arbitration agreement.

Arbitration is sufficiently flexible that it may be tailored to suit the nature of the matter at hand. In their arbitration agreements, parties often agree on practical limitations on discovery or, conversely, may expressly agree to full discovery. Virtually all jurisdictions will respect this exercise of party autonomy. Moreover, the parties' arbitration agreement often provides that any arbitration will be administered by an arbitral institution, or that the arbitration will be conducted ad hoc under the arbitration rules of one of those institutions. In all such cases, arbitrators must honor the parties' contractual agreement and faithfully implement any applicable institutional rules relating to discovery.

D. Soliciting Agreement by Parties Relating to Scope and Nature of Discovery

To the extent the parties wish to conduct discovery beyond that specifically guaranteed by applicable rule

> or the parties' arbitration agreement, arbitrators should encourage the parties to agree on the scope and nature of discovery and, if the parties are able to do so and there are no compelling countervailing considerations relating to reasonableness and efficiency, should accept and enforce such agreement.

Arbitrators will typically find that the parties' arbitration agreement and any applicable rules do not fully resolve the question of what discovery, if any, should be permitted in the proceeding. In that event, and no later than the preliminary conference, arbitrators should seek the cooperation of the parties in developing a discovery plan and schedule. In some instances, the parties might agree that no discovery will be conducted; in such an instance, arbitrators can, when necessary, protect against unfair surprise at the hearing by providing that all documents on which each party intends to rely be produced to the other party well in advance of the hearing and/or that all direct testimony be submitted in affidavit form a sufficient time prior to the hearing to enable each party to prepare its cross-examination before, rather than during, the hearing. (Many arbitrators exempt from the requirement of advance production documents used only to impeach witness credibility, on the theory that prior production destroys the document's utility for that purpose. When such an exemption is made, arbitrators should make clear to the parties that "impeachment" relates only to credibility on collateral issues and may not be used as an excuse to avoid production of documents that relate to the merits of the claims and defenses at issue.) In the more typical situation, the parties should be encouraged to agree on such matters as the number and length of depositions, if any, the scope and number of document requests, and the exchange of expert reports; just as importantly, arbitrators should solicit the parties' agreement relating to the time within which such discovery is to commence and be completed.

Arbitrators' first objective should be to arrive at a discovery plan that the parties will carry out themselves, contacting the arbitrators only with problems they cannot resolve on their own. Arbitrators should have on the agenda of the first preliminary conference the subject of the timing and scope of discovery. Arbitrators should set the tone by informing the parties that they are expected to confer and agree to as much as possible, keeping in mind that discovery in arbitration is intended to be expeditious and cost effective. *See, e.g.,* AAA Rule 21(a); CPR Rule 11.

II. DOCUMENT PRODUCTION

A. Applicable Arbitration Rules

As is reflected in virtually all institutional rules, tailored document production is generally allowed in arbitration and is the heart of most arbitration discovery, and arbitrators thus should normally permit at least a limited document exchange.

Institutional rules generally grant arbitrators wide authority in managing discovery, particularly in the area of production of documents. For example, AAA Rule 21 provides that, on request of a party, arbitrators "may direct . . . the production of documents and other information." Similarly, under Rule 4 of the AAA Large, Complex Case Rules, arbitrators may establish the limits of document production if the parties are unable to agree. CPR Rule 11, which allows arbitrators to require and facilitate such discovery as they determine to be appropriate in the circumstances, is equally general. In contrast, some institutional rules, including the NAF and JAMS rules, are much more detailed. NAF Rules 29(A) and 29(B)(1) thus mandate cooperative discovery and provide that, if the parties cannot resolve their disputes over document discovery, a party may request the arbitrators to order the disclosure of documents when the information is relevant, reliable, and informative, and the information sought is not unduly burdensome and expensive. Interestingly, JAMS Rule 17, which provides for the exchange of all "relevant non-privileged documents," is the only institutional rule that virtually guarantees that document production will occur. In the absence of an applicable rule, arbitrators should consider the realistic needs of the parties in light of considerations related to fairness and the efficient conduct of the proceeding and should order the exchange of only those documents necessary to accomplish those objectives.

B.   Documents on which Party Intends to Rely

Arbitrators should ensure that all documents on which a party intends to rely during the hearing are exchanged prior to the commencement of the hearing.

This category of documents is the most basic, and most institutional rules thus contain separate rules for the exchange of these documents. *See, e.g.,* NAF Rule 31(A)(3) (requiring the delivery of all documents to be introduced at the hearing); JAMS Rule 17. The exchange of such documents is essential in order to maximize the efficiency of the hearing and avoid undue surprise and confusion.

C.   Document Requests

Arbitrators may, when consistent with applicable rules and party agreements, permit the exchange of document requests, which should be limited to seeking only those documents that are relevant. Arbitrators should establish a schedule for document production and require the parties to adhere to it.

In addition to requiring that, shortly before the hearing, the parties are to exchange documents on which they rely, arbitrators will normally, at a minimum, permit a limited number of document requests seeking specific, relevant evidence. Since the parties often do not know at the pre-hearing conference exactly what documents they will want produced, the best procedure usually is to accord to the parties a reasonable period of time within which to exchange document requests and to further specify the date by which the requested documents will be produced or objections to the requests will be asserted.

Documents may be requested by category, provided that the categories are reasonably and narrowly tailored to obtain relevant, non-privileged documents.   Naturally, if a document request is challenged, arbitrators should require the party requesting documents to demonstrate that the request should be allowed. The relevance and the non-privileged status of the documents requested should be shown. It is important to curtail "fishing expeditions" so as to avoid the very sort of protracted discovery that the parties may have sought to escape by choosing arbitration over litigation, while allowing each party to obtain access to the other's relevant, non-privileged documents.

D.   Computer-Based "Document" Discovery

Arbitrators should recognize that electronically stored information can present unique issues relating to document production and   should thus seek creative solutions that best ensure the production of such information.

Arbitrators face challenges when the requested discovery is maintained in computer-based files. Whether the information is located in the hands of the parties, or is in the possession of third parties (such as companies that maintain servers that store instant messages), technical knowledge of the difficulty and expense of retrieval can sometimes be vital. When the parties cannot agree on the accessibility of the relevant data and the necessary steps to preserve and retrieve it, arbitrators may need to hold a hearing on the matter or allow computer experts of the parties to investigate the matter and provide reports to the arbitrator and parties, subject, if necessary, to cross-examination.   Sequentially gathering information concerning (1) the data storage devices, (2) types of software used on the company's computer systems, and (3) the backup of information will aid in defining what information exists and where it can be found. Shifting to the requesting party all or some of the costs associated with retrieval of the information is a solution that has been useful in the electronic discovery arena if the request otherwise would be unduly burdensome. *See, e.g., Zubulake v. UBS Warburg,* LLC, 217 F.R.D. 309, 322 (S.D.N.Y. 2003) (identifying seven factors relating to when cost shifting is justified).

E.   Duty to Supplement

Arbitrators should formally require the parties to supplement any document productions whenever the existence of additional documents becomes known to a party.

It is good practice to establish in the preliminary conference order that the parties have a continuing duty to supplement document production through the last day of the evidentiary hearings. This duty is imposed explicitly by some rules. *See, e.g.,* JAMS Rule 17(d). Since the duty to supplement is now firmly established under federal and most state rules of civil procedure, the application of the same principle in arbitration should come as no surprise to the parties.

F.   Claims of Privilege

In the absence of an applicable legal exception, arbitrators should not require a party to produce privileged documents.

The evidentiary rules of privilege normally obtain in arbitration and, as a result, it occasionally becomes necessary for arbitrators to rule on privilege claims. *See, e.g.,* AAA Rule 31(c). Arbitrators should order the party claiming privilege to produce a privilege log in a specified format; one alternative is to require the log to satisfy the requirements set forth in Fed. R. Civ. P. 26(b)(5). If the pertinent documents must be reviewed to determine whether they are privileged, the chair (or sole arbitrator) typically will conduct the review. In cases in which the allegedly privileged documents are exceptionally voluminous, arbitrators might solicit party agreement to the appointment of a master to conduct an *in camera* review of the documents and render recommended decisions to the arbitrators, reserving to the parties the right to object to particular recommendations.

III. DEPOSITIONS OF PARTY WITNESSES

A. Arbitrators' Authority

In the absence of a contrary rule or contractual provision, arbitrators normally are authorized to permit a discovery deposition of a party witness.

With the exception of the AAA's Commercial Arbitration Rules, most domestic commercial arbitration rules either expressly provide that the parties may take one or more depositions, or that the arbitrator may authorize the taking of depositions. *See, e.g.*, JAMS Rule 17(c) (providing that each party may take one deposition of an opposing party or of an individual under the control of an opposing party); AAA Procedures for Large, Complex Commercial Disputes, Rule 4(d); NAF Rule 29(b)(1). In an ad hoc arbitration in which the arbitration clause is silent on the subject of discovery, statutory and common law principles apply. Despite the fact that the FAA is silent on the issue, courts generally acknowledge that arbitrators may authorize whatever discovery between the parties the arbitrators deem reasonable. In express recognition of this case law, Section 17 of the RUAA, and the comments thereto, now specifically provide that arbitrators are so authorized. *See* RUAA § 17(c) (permitting the arbitrator to allow "such discovery as the arbitrator decides is appropriate in the circumstances") and Comment No. 3 ("The approach to discovery in Section 17(c) . . . follows the majority approach under the case law of the UAA and FAA which provides that, unless the contract specifies to the contrary, discretion rests with the arbitrators whether to allow discovery"). *See, e.g., Stanton v. Paine Webber Jackson & Curtis, Inc.*, 685 F. Supp. 1241, 1242 (S.D. Fla. 1988); *Corcoran v. Shearson/American Express, Inc.*, 596 F. Supp. 1113, 1117 (N.D. Ga. 1984); *Chiarella v. Viscount Industrial Company*, 1993 WL 497967 at *1, *4 (S.D.N.Y. 1993) (arbitrators had authority to order parties "to mutually exchange all documents and witness lists (*i.e.* Full Discovery)").

B.   Limiting Discovery Depositions

The number, scope, and duration of any depositions should be determined in light of considerations relating to efficiency and need.

Discovery is the largest single component of the high cost of litigation, and depositions are, in turn, often the largest part of that component. Arbitrators should manage depositions so that they bear a rational relationship to the size and complexity of the dispute. Otherwise the arbitration will fail to be cost effective. Arbitrators enjoy wide latitude in accomplishing that goal since, in the absence of issues requiring peculiar treatment, such as dispositive motions or claims involving public policy, courts are unlikely to disturb arbitrators' discovery orders.

In managing the deposition process, arbitrators should thus consider limitations on the number of depositions, their scope, and their duration. Additionally, the timing of depositions should be regulated to ensure that subsequent depositions of the same witnesses are not necessary during the discovery process. Finally, arbitrators should specifically incorporate such deposition limitations into the preliminary conference order.

C.   Disputes Relating to Discovery Depositions

When necessary, arbitrators should take an active role in resolving disputes relating to deposition discovery.

Occasionally, counsel will encounter a witness or an opposing counsel who is obstreperous during a deposition. An expeditious means of dealing with this problem is to have an arbitrator available by telephone to hear and rule on objections while the deposition is in progress. The availability of immediate rulings often quickly dampens the offending conduct. In an extreme case, arbitrators may attend and preside over depositions and rule on all objections as they are made.

IV. INTERROGATORIES AND REQUESTS FOR ADMISSIONS

A. General Rule

Arbitrators should not normally allow the parties to conduct discovery through the use of interrogatories and requests for admission.

Absent agreement of the parties, interrogatories and requests for admissions generally are discouraged in arbitration. Interrogatories often are burdensome and inefficient when compared to other available means of discovering the types of information sought. For example, the identification of witnesses--often given as a reason for interrogatories--can more efficiently be obtained by requiring in the preliminary conference order that the parties identify witnesses and the expected subject matter of their testimony at an early date.

Requests for admissions are similarly disfavored because they are not very useful in most cases. Arbitrators should consider any arguments in favor of the use of such discovery devices, but normally such requests should be denied.

When interrogatories and requests for admissions are permitted, arbitrators should normally limit their number and scope.

B. Unique Rules

When applicable rules guarantee the right to use interrogatories and requests for admission, arbitrators should limit their number and scope.

Arbitrators must be aware, of course, of any applicable rules that may create a different result. For example, NAF Rule 29 provides a party with a qualified right to conduct limited discovery through "written questions." When such rules apply, arbitrators should nonetheless seek to limit the scope and number of interrogatories and admission requests to the extent possible. NAF Rule 29(b), for example, limits interrogatories to twenty-five. In keeping with this objective, arbitrators' orders permitting such discovery can specify the general nature of the inquiries to be propounded, or the nature or extent of the responses to be provided.

V.   DISCOVERY OF EXPERT WITNESSES

A.   Discovery of Experts in General

Due to the complexity of expert testimony, arbitrators often can maximize the efficiency of the hearing on the merits by permitting pre-hearing discovery of expert witnesses.

It is the rare commercial arbitration that does not involve some form of expert testimony. In the absence of pre-hearing discovery relating to the opinions of experts and the bases for those opinions, the risk often exists that the cross-examination of an expert during the actual hearing will be prolonged and inefficient. For that reason, and in the interest of avoiding surprise, it is often efficient to allow the parties to conduct at least some discovery of expert witnesses.

B.   Scheduling Discovery of Expert Witnesses

Arbitrators should schedule discovery of expert witnesses in a manner that takes into account any burdens of proof and that allows each party a reasonable opportunity to develop and prepare any appropriate rebuttal or surrebuttal testimony.

The preliminary conference order should provide specific deadlines for the exchange of expert witness résumés, as well as their written reports. Depending on the nature of the issues presented, the burden of proof on such issues, and the relative knowledge of the parties, arbitrators might prefer that such reports be exchanged simultaneously or sequentially. To the extent rebuttal reports are to be introduced at the actual hearing, such reports should be required to be produced in the same fashion. When confronted with a representation by a party that there is, or will be, no written expert report, arbitrators should consider granting the opposing party the right to depose the expert for the purpose of determining the expert's unwritten opinions.

In order to focus the experts' ultimate testimony on those subjects that are actually in dispute, arbitrators should also consider whether it would be efficient to direct the expert witnesses to identify those material matters on which they agree and those on which they disagree. With the agreement of counsel, arbitrators might even require the experts to engage in direct dialogue without counsel being present.

VI. DISCOVERY FROM THIRD PARTIES

A. Extent of Arbitrators' Authority to Issue Third-Party Discovery Subpoenas

Arbitrators must be aware of constraints on their authority to issue subpoenas to third parties for the purpose of pre-hearing discovery.

While Section 7 of the FAA does grant arbitrators authority to issue subpoenas "to attend before [the arbitrators] as a witness," the FAA does not expressly grant to arbitrators the authority to issue subpoenas to third parties for the purpose of discovery. As a result, there is a split of authority on the issue of arbitral power under the FAA to compel non-party witnesses to submit to a discovery deposition. There is case authority in the Sixth and Eighth Circuits holding that arbitrators have that power; case authority in the Third and Fourth Circuits is to the contrary. *See Hay Group, Inc. v. E.B.S. Acquisition Corp.*, 360 F.3d 404, 406 (3d Cir. 2004); *Security Life Insurance Company v. Duncansen & Holt, Inc.*, 228 F.3d 865, 870-71 (8th Cir. 2000); *COMSAT Corp. v. National Science Foundation*, 190 F.3d 269, 275-77 (4th Cir. 1999); *American Federation of Television and Radio Artists v. WJBK-TV*, 164 F.3d 1004, 1009 (6th Cir. 1999). In contrast, Sections 17(d) and (f) of the RUAA specifically authorize arbitrators to issue discovery subpoenas to third parties, although the language of the provision and the accompanying comments make it clear that such authority is to be exercised with due restraint. Given these conflicting provisions, arbitrators must carefully take applicable statutory and decisional law into account when determining the extent of their authority, if any, to issue discovery subpoenas to third parties. Thus, while most arbitration rules expressly or inferentially provide that arbitrators are authorized to issue subpoenas to third parties, arbitrators may not assume that those rules, standing alone, suffice to establish their authority to issue such subpoenas for discovery purposes.

B.   Form and Issuance of Discovery Subpoenas

Arbitrators should require the requesting party to draft any discovery subpoenas and should entertain any objections to the issuance of the subpoenas.

The requesting party usually drafts the subpoena and submits it for an arbitrator's signature. Prior to issuing any subpoena, arbitrators should determine whether the opposing party objects and, if so, should consider the reasons for that objection. Subpoenas should only be issued for discovery purposes when arbitrators determine that such discovery is permitted by the law of the applicable jurisdiction and is appropriate due to considerations relating to fairness or efficiency. If arbitrators deem such a process to be effective, the preliminary conference order can provide that they will hold any proposed discovery subpoena for a specified period of time; in the event that no timely objection is made to the issuance of the subpoena, the subpoena may be signed and returned to the requesting party for service.

C.   Enforcement of Discovery Subpoenas

Because arbitrators lack the authority to compel compliance with third-party subpoenas, their only option may be to seek creative and reasonable ways to accomplish that objective.

Under the FAA and state arbitration statutes, there are both jurisdictional and territorial limitations on the enforcement of arbitral subpoenas. Lacking contempt power, arbitrators are without authority to compel compliance with subpoenas. If the third party objects, enforcement of the subpoena is a matter for the court. In the circumstance in which the third party refuses to comply with the subpoena, it is sometimes useful to confer with counsel for the parties, and even with counsel for the non-party, in order to explain the advantage to the third party of agreeing to pre-hearing discovery.

The heart of that advantage lies in arbitrators' undoubted authority to subpoena the witness to appear at an arbitration hearing, so long as the hearing locale is within the jurisdictional reach of the subpoena. *See, e.g.,* 9 U.S.C. § 7; Cal. Code Civ. Proc. § 1282.6. Thus, arbitrators can explain that, if the witness refuses to participate in a pre-hearing deposition (which would serve as both discovery and *de bene esse* testimony), arbitrators can convene a hearing (in the witness' jurisdiction) at which the witness must appear and give testimony, after which the arbitrator can recess the hearing until the parties have completed their other discovery and are ready to commence the main hearing. The disadvantage of this course is that the witness will be required to appear at the date and time selected by the arbitrator and may spend a long time on the witness stand while counsel review the witness' documents, which can also be subpoenaed to such a hearing, and attempt to learn basic information that could otherwise have been supplied in advance.

In contrast with this scenario, arbitrators may offer the witness the option of producing non-privileged documents to counsel in advance and then having a deposition of limited length taken at a time and location convenient to the witness (for example, the witness' office). In order to aid arbitrators in evaluating the credibility of such a witness, the deposition can easily be videotaped. Often, when these alternative courses are explained and the parties and arbitrators make efforts to respect the witness' concerns and accommodate reasonable time and scheduling constraints, an agreement for a pre-hearing deposition of a non-party witness can be obtained fairly readily.

VII. SITE INSPECTIONS

Site inspections should be carefully controlled by arbitrators to ensure they are efficient and in compliance with arbitrators' directives.

While most institutional arbitration rules do not specifically address "site inspections" (which can include inspections of equipment or other personal property as well as real property) for discovery purposes, such inspections might occasionally be necessary. Given the expense that can be involved in a site inspection, arbitrators should consider requiring that the inspection be videotaped. A videotape of the inspection often helps avoid the need for a second inspection, and further can prove invaluable in ensuring compliance with arbitrators' orders permitting the inspection and in resolving any disputes that arise in connection with the actual inspection.

VIII. CONFIDENTIALITY AND PROTECTION OF PROPRIETARY INFORMATION

Upon good cause shown, arbitrators should enter an order protecting the confidentiality of the arbitration proceeding itself, as well as business information and trade secrets.

A prime reason for using commercial arbitration rather than litigation is to keep the resolution of their dispute out of the public eye. For example, CPR Rule 17 requires parties and arbitrators to treat the arbitration proceeding, including any related discovery, as confidential. In some instances the parties are particularly concerned about the protection of trade secrets or other proprietary information. Arbitrators should assist in maintaining confidentiality by issuing a protective order upon reasonable request. Usually the best practice is to require the moving party to draft a proposed order for the opposing party's consideration and potential approval. In the event the parties cannot agree on the content of the order, arbitrators should consider the arguments relating to any objections and then revise and approve the proposed order as they deem appropriate.

IX. DISCOVERY DISPUTES

A. Encouraging Parties to Resolve Discovery Disputes

Arbitrators should first approach discovery disputes with the objective of encouraging the parties to resolve their own disputes.

In hotly contested arbitrations, discovery disputes will often surface. When they do, arbitrators can and should take the laboring oar in managing those disputes so as to minimize their expense. Occasionally, parties will choose to raise disputes at seemingly every step of the discovery process, and to bring every one of those disputes to arbitrators for resolution. In addition to the standard admonition to cooperate with one another, in cases involving difficult parties or counsel, arbitrators may want to remind the disputants that the arbitrators are the ultimate triers-of-fact in the case and that it is easier to take a balanced view of the evidence when the proceeding is unencumbered by constant side battles over issues of minor consequence.

Arbitrators will also occasionally encounter a party who seems to take lightly the arbitrators' orders to produce information during the discovery process. One effective tool in dealing with such parties is to emphasize that, in deciding the case, arbitrators are entitled to draw negative inferences from a failure to properly participate in discovery.

B. Formal Resolution of Discovery Disputes

Any formal resolution of a discovery dispute should be prompt, efficient, and cost-effective.

When arbitrators are called upon formally to resolve a discovery dispute, they should establish a process designed to accomplish the goals articulated above. One method is to have the parties simply submit and serve electronically, or by fax, short letter briefs setting forth their positions. In the absence of a perceived need for oral argument, arbitrators can then decide the issue based on the written submissions. When oral argument is requested by a party and granted by arbitrators, such argument often can be presented by conference telephone call. An alternative to the foregoing procedure is to handle the matter by telephonic conference call without the prerequisite of letter briefs. There are, of course, situations in which the complexity of the issue or the volume of documents dictates full briefing and an in-person hearing.

Regardless of how the dispute is presented, arbitrators should resolve it fully and quickly, so as not to jeopardize the entire discovery and hearing schedule, and should memorialize all rulings in a concise order that makes clear what discovery needs to be provided and what does not. Given the broad discretion accorded arbitrators in managing the arbitration process, particularly as that discretion relates to discovery, it is not necessary to include in such orders a statement of the reasons for the rulings unless the matter involves especially novel or unique circumstances or discovery of extraordinarily sensitive matters.

X.   DISCOVERY AS A LITMUS TEST FOR A SUCCESSFUL ARBITRATION

As was suggested in the introduction to this chapter, one primary objective of arbitration is to avoid the pitfalls frequently associated with discovery procedures that are available in civil litigation. On the other hand, the premise of discovery is that it can often maximize the efficiency of an adjudicatory process and further ensure a fundamentally fair hearing. In this sense, the nature and scope of the discovery process arbitrators employ can often substantially determine the efficacy of the arbitration proceeding. Arbitrators thus should always give due consideration to all matters relating to discovery and should address discovery issues carefully on a case-by-case basis.

CHAPTER 9

THE HEARING ON THE MERITS

The arbitrators' goals with respect to the hearing on the
merits are (1) to provide each party with a fair opportunity
to present its evidence and argument, (2) to make the hearing
as smooth, efficient, and expeditious as possible, and (3)
to provide arbitrators with all the information they need to
properly resolve the issues presented.

I. DESIGNING THE APPROPRIATE HEARING PROCESS

Arbitrators should utilize their broad discretion
concerning management of the hearing to establish
and carry out arrangements and procedures that are
fair, appropriate to the particular case, and, to the
extent reasonably possible, acceptable to all parties.

Consistent with the common law, the rules of most arbitral
institutions accord arbitrators broad discretion in managing
arbitration hearings. *See, e.g.,* CPR Rule 9.1 ("Subject to these
Rules, the Tribunal may conduct the arbitration in such manner as
it shall deem appropriate."); JAMS Rule 22(a) ("The Arbitrator
will ordinarily conduct the Arbitration Hearing in the manner set
forth in these Rules. The Arbitrator may vary these procedures if
it is determined reasonable and appropriate to do so."); AAA Rule
30(b) ("The arbitrator, exercising his or her discretion, shall
conduct the proceedings with a view to expediting the resolution
of the dispute and may direct the order of proof, bifurcate
proceedings and direct the parties to focus their presentations on
issues the decision of which could dispose of all or part of the
case."). Courts seldom disturb arbitration awards for reasons

relating to the hearing procedures utilized by arbitrators. As a practical matter, arbitrators have nearly unlimited authority to conduct hearings as they think best.

However, such broad discretion does not suggest that arbitrators should feel unconstrained in how they conduct hearings. To the contrary, the manner in which arbitrators exercise this discretion can have profound consequences for the case at hand and for the future growth of commercial arbitration in general. To the extent that arbitrators are perceived by counsel and the parties as fair, conscientious, creative, and efficient in conducting hearings, those parties and counsel will be much more likely to cooperate with arbitrators in carrying out the procedures established for the hearing and more inclined to use arbitration in the future.

Accordingly, arbitrators should devote major attention to working with counsel to develop in each case hearing procedures that are just, efficient, and well suited to the particular case. Such procedures should afford all parties a fair opportunity to present their evidence and arguments and also aid the arbitrators in obtaining the information they need to properly decide the case. All hearing procedures should be determined at the preliminary conference, or as soon thereafter as practicable, and memorialized in one or more orders. Since counsel generally select arbitrators at least partly because of their expertise in managing the arbitration process, arbitrators should lead the effort in arriving at appropriate procedures by sharing with counsel their experience and wisdom concerning the efficacy of various techniques. However, building a collaborative relationship with counsel requires that arbitrators seriously consider counsel's suggestions as well. To increase the parties' commitment to the integrity of the arbitration process, and to further diminish any remote prospect of vacatur due to particular procedures used during the hearing, arbitrators should strive to secure party agreement to all the procedures established for the hearing and should recite that agreement in the order setting forth those procedures.

II.   DOCUMENT HEARINGS

Occasionally, parties will agree to waive the live presentation of evidence and argument and submit the case to the arbitrators entirely on documents (usually, affidavits, pertinent exhibits, and briefs). NAF Rule 28 sets forth basic procedures for the conduct of such a "Document Hearing," and AAA Expedited Procedures, Rule E-6 provides for "Proceedings on Documents." Because such hearings are relatively rare in commercial cases of any complexity, the balance of this chapter will address procedures for "participatory hearings" in which some or all of the evidence and argument are presented to the arbitrators in person.

III.   SETTING THE BASIC CONSTRUCT OF THE HEARING

Arbitration hearings proceed more smoothly and efficiently if arbitrators, working with counsel, determine well in advance the basic construct for the particular hearing so that all participants know what to expect and can plan accordingly.

A.   Standards for Admission of Evidence

Arbitrators should advise counsel of what standards will govern the admission of evidence at the hearing and should encourage counsel, in planning their presentations, to focus their attention on evidence that is likely to be accorded greater weight by the arbitrators.

It has long been settled that arbitrators may consider evidence that would normally be inadmissible in court trials, and the rules of most arbitral institutions reflect this more liberal approach to admissibility. *See, e.g.,* CPR Rule 12.2 ("The Tribunal is not required to apply the rules of evidence used in judicial proceedings, provided, however, that the Tribunal shall apply the lawyer-client privilege and the work product immunity."); JAMS Rule 22(d) ("Strict conformity to the rules of evidence is not required, except that the Arbitrator shall apply applicable law relating to privileges and work product."); AAA Rule 31 ("Conformity to legal rules of evidence shall not be necessary. . . . The arbitrator shall take into account applicable principles of legal privilege, such as those involving the confidentiality of communications between a lawyer and client."). However, the fact that arbitrators are not required to apply the rules of evidence does not necessarily mean that they will not do so. Counsel will be greatly aided in planning their presentations if arbitrators will disclose at an early stage in the arbitration the standards they intend to apply in the admission of evidence.

Most arbitrators are generally very liberal in the admission of evidence and will receive any non-privileged evidence unless it is plainly irrelevant or unduly repetitious. Thus, for example, hearsay evidence is freely received in most arbitrations, and arbitrators usually dispense with the necessity of laying formal foundations for business records, past recollection recorded, and similar evidence. Documents are generally presumed authentic unless a genuine and specific objection is raised regarding a particular document. Lay witnesses are ordinarily allowed to express non-expert opinions. Evidence is usually received for any purpose for which it may be relevant, and admission for limited purposes is rare.

Arbitrators frequently observe that "the evidence will be received for what it is worth." Counsel may not appreciate how significant that observation can be. While arbitrators are unlikely to require the party offering a business record to prove all the normal prerequisites of the state or federal "shopbook rule," they may well accord little weight to such a record if it concerns a critical finding in the case and there has been no evidence regarding the person or persons who create such records for the business, the extent of their training and knowledge, how quickly after the event they make their records, the source of their information concerning what they record, and similar factors affecting the accuracy and reliability of such records. Similarly, while hearsay evidence of a statement by an absent observer concerning a crucial happening may well be received, the arbitrators may be reluctant to give it much weight if the absent observer could have been presented for cross-examination.

In short, if arbitrators intend to apply a very liberal standard in the admission of evidence, they should so advise the parties but should also urge counsel to consider presenting the most direct and persuasive evidence available on important points, even if weaker evidence would be received.

In rare cases, the parties' agreement may provide that admission of evidence will be governed by the Federal Rules of Evidence or some other evidence code. In other cases, arbitrators may conclude that the sensitivity, public importance, or very high stakes of the dispute mandate a strict application of evidentiary rules as to some or all of the issues. In these situations, arbitrators should identify for the parties the rules of evidence that will be strictly applied and the issues for which such application will obtain.

B.   Order of Proof

Arbitrators should determine a fair and efficient order of proof for each hearing.

Most arbitration rules provide that arbitrators shall determine the order of proof. NAF Rule 34(C); CPR Rule 9.3(a). Some rules indicate that the order of proof should generally be similar to a court trial but that arbitrators have discretion to vary this order. AAA Rule 30(a); JAMS Rule 22(b).

Often, the "court trial" model (plaintiff's direct case, defendant's direct case, plaintiff's rebuttal case, and possibly defendant's surrebuttal case) works fine in commercial arbitrations as well. Sometimes, however, there may be advantages gained, for example, avoiding the introduction of unnecessary evidence or increasing the clarity of focus on genuine disputes, by varying this order of proof. Arbitrators and counsel should think creatively about such possible variations when establishing procedures for the hearing.

One traditional variation sometimes utilized in court as well as arbitration is to bifurcate the hearing in order to sequentially consider issues relating to liability and damages. This procedure can substantially reduce the length and cost of the hearing if evidence concerning damages is voluminous, complex, and easily separable from evidence of liability and the arbitrators are able to determine after the liability phase that liability was not established. Such bifurcation is probably inadvisable when damages evidence is intertwined with liability evidence or is distinct but relatively brief.

Other "sequencing" of the hearing may be appropriate in particular cases. For example, when a statute of limitations defense involves fairly limited evidence and, if successful, would end the case or greatly reduce the balance of the hearing by eliminating several claims, it may make sense to receive evidence and argument on that defense in Phase I of the hearing and proceed to any subsequent phases based on the rulings made at the end of Phase I. Similarly, if proper interpretation of a key contract provision requires some parol evidence but will greatly influence what evidence is relevant in the balance of the hearing, Phase I could be restricted to that contract interpretation issue, with subsequent phases dependent upon the Phase I rulings. In setting up the schedule for hearings that will proceed in sequential phases, arbitrators should be sure to allow sufficient time after each phase for them to determine the pertinent rulings and for the parties to prepare any subsequent presentations accordingly.

Arbitrators should also be mindful of the considerations discussed in Chapter 10, *infra*, concerning awards that determine some, but not all, of the issues in the case.

Even in cases in which there are no critical threshold issues, it may be useful to consider whether some or all issues can most effectively be presented on an issue-by-issue basis (by having the pertinent witnesses for each side testify sequentially, or even concurrently, as discussed below), with the arbitrators possibly ruling on each issue after all evidence and argument on that issue have been presented. In considering such an arrangement, arbitrators should attempt to weigh the advantages of more clearly focused and logically sequenced presentations against the possible burdens of recalling some witnesses to testify repeatedly at successive stages of the hearing.

In cases in which the arbitration hearing is likely to be long and expensive, arbitrators may wish to advise the parties, perhaps in the order setting out the agenda for the preliminary conference, that they will be willing to consider any joint proposals of the parties for structuring the hearing in a fashion that facilitates settlement discussions between the parties. For example, the arbitrators could initially hear and decide certain crucial issues and then recess the hearing for a short time to allow the parties to discuss settlement. Similarly, in cases with multiple claimants or multiple respondents, arbitrators could allow each side to pick two or three representative claims, out of the much larger number pending, and hear those; the rulings on those "sample" claims might point counsel to a settlement of the remainder. Such creative structuring, with the agreement of all parties and the assistance of counsel, can considerably reduce the time and cost of resolving the dispute. However, since the parties may have dramatically different strategies and interests with respect to whether the dispute should be promptly settled or the arbitration truncated, arbitrators should not design the order of proof so as to facilitate settlement unless all parties jointly request such a design.

IV. MANAGEMENT OF EXHIBITS

In many commercial arbitrations, a considerable volume of exhibits is introduced, and in some cases the exhibits run to tens of thousands of pages. Frequently, many of these exhibits turn out to be unnecessary. Sometimes arbitrators have some success in strongly encouraging the parties to pare down their exhibits to what is truly essential, but many counsel are reluctant to do so for fear of leaving out some document that becomes important as the hearing unfolds. Thus, in most commercial arbitrations, there will be a large volume of exhibits that must be managed. Arbitrators can ease the burden of dealing with those materials by establishing some simple ground rules for the management of exhibits.

A.   Core Exhibits

Arbitrators should require the parties to jointly assemble and submit, as soon after the preliminary

> conference as is feasible, a tabbed and indexed notebook containing paginated copies of the key documents in the case (sometimes referred to as the "core exhibits" or "the common bundle").

In many cases all parties recognize that there is a core set of documents (perhaps ten to twenty-five in number) that are critical to the various claims and defenses in the case. These may include such items as the governing contract and amendments, notices of termination or default, important correspondence, photographs of construction sites or other locales, diagrams of pertinent equipment, and the like. Often, counsel will be able to readily agree on the identity of such documents and submit to each arbitrator a tabbed, indexed notebook containing them. The exhibits can be labeled **JX** (for Joint Exhibit) **1**, **JX 2**, etc. Sometimes it is also helpful to ask counsel to highlight the important portions of each document. All highlighting can be done in the same color or different parties can use different colors. Having such a notebook at an early stage in the arbitration can assist arbitrators in becoming familiar with the background of the dispute and dealing more readily with any motions or discovery disputes that arise before the hearing. The notebook will also be a key resource for arbitrators to use during the hearing.

In cases in which there will be substantial document discovery, it may be appropriate to ask counsel to provide, relatively early in the arbitration, a notebook containing the key exhibits known to them at that time and then to supplement that submission by providing, close to the time of the hearing, such additional documents as the parties have subsequently determined to be of particular importance.

B.   Evidentiary Exhibits

> Arbitrators should require each party to submit, in advance of the hearing, tabbed, indexed notebooks containing paginated copies of all evidentiary exhibits (beyond the core exhibits) which that party intends to use at the hearing for any purpose other than impeachment of credibility.

Rules of most major arbitral institutions require that parties exchange their hearing exhibits, usually five to fourteen days before the hearing. *See, e.g.,* AAA Rule 21(b) (5 business days); NAF Rule 31(B) (10 days); JAMS Rule 20(a) (14 days). While such an arrangement may be satisfactory in relatively simple cases with few documents, it is, for three reasons, often unsuitable in cases with many documents. First, receipt of thousands of pages of documents a week or two before a hearing does not afford a party sufficient time to review and analyze them, consult with witnesses, and develop plans for dealing with the documents at the hearing. (While many of the documents may be known to the receiving party as a result of the underlying events or through discovery in the arbitration, others may be unfamiliar, particularly documents relied on by expert witnesses.) Second, when parties exchange exhibits simultaneously, many of the same documents are typically offered by multiple parties, thus greatly increasing the volume of exhibit binders. Third, if written testimony is to be submitted (*see* Section V.A, *infra*), it is preferable to have exhibits submitted beforehand so that witnesses can discuss and identify by exhibit number the pertinent documents offered by all parties.

Thus, assuming a hearing date of "X" for a case with voluminous exhibits and written testimony, a more efficient arrangement may be to proceed as follows: 60 days before X ("X – 60"), claimant submits all exhibits it relies on to support its position. On X - 50 days, respondent submits all exhibits (beyond those submitted by claimant) it relies on to support its position. On X - 40 days, claimant submits any rebuttal exhibits (beyond those already submitted). Each exhibit is paginated (by Bates stamp or otherwise) for easy reference during the hearing. Claimant's exhibits are labeled **CX 1, CX 2**, etc. Respondent's exhibits are labeled **RX 1, RX 2**, etc. (Alternatively, the hearing exhibits may be labeled in a single sequence by having the numbering of each successive submission of exhibits begin where the numbering of the preceding submission left off.) If written testimony is to be submitted, then claimant's direct testimony is submitted on X - 30 days, respondent's direct testimony on X - 20 days, and claimant's rebuttal testimony on X - 10 days.

The foregoing schedule can be adjusted to fit the circumstances of particular cases. For example, if respondent has asserted counterclaims that involve substantially different issues than those that form the basis for claimant's claims, X - 60 days could be designated as the date for both claimant and respondent to submit exhibits in support of their respective claims, X - 50 days as the date for each to submit exhibits in response to the claims of the other, and X - 40 days as the date for each to submit rebuttal exhibits. The schedule for submission of written testimony could be similarly adjusted.

If written testimony will not be used, the three-step document submission dates might be changed to X – 30 days, X – 20 days, and X – 10 days. The intervals set forth above can, of course, be increased or decreased to reflect the nature and volume of exhibits and written testimony likely to be submitted. When multiple claimants or respondents are independently pursuing separate claims or defenses, it is best to dispense with the **CX** and **RX** designations and instead require that their exhibits be labeled in a manner that reflects the name of the party, *e.g.,* **Jones Ex. 1, Smith Ex. 2.**

Arbitrations in which there are many exhibits can get bogged down if each exhibit must be expressly offered in evidence by a party and expressly admitted or denied by the arbitrators. Accordingly, most experienced arbitrators discuss with counsel, and memorialize in an order, streamlined procedures governing the admission of exhibits. One technique frequently used is to provide that all exhibits furnished in accordance with the arbitrators' order for pre-hearing exchange of exhibits will be deemed admitted at the outset of the hearing, without necessity of any formal offer, save only for documents whose authenticity is genuinely disputed in an objection submitted by a specified date. (Such documents will not be admitted until the offering party presents evidence of authenticity at the hearing.) Any party may, at the close of the hearing, withdraw any of its exhibits that were not used during the hearing, although an opposing party may then offer such exhibits as its own.

An alternative approach is to provide that only those exhibits specifically mentioned by a witness during the hearing, or expressly moved into evidence by counsel, will be received in evidence. Of course, the parties may always agree, during or at the end of the hearing, to limit the admission of exhibits in some way, *e.g.,* by stipulating that only exhibits cited by expert witnesses will be deemed to be in evidence.

Absent a showing of good cause, documents not exchanged as required by pre-hearing orders should not be received at the hearing, except for documents used solely to impeach witnesses on collateral matters. Documents that provide substantive support for a party's position, and incidentally impeach an opposing witness, must still be included in the pre-hearing exchange.

On the date of delivering any exhibits or testimony to opposing parties, copies of the same should also be delivered to each arbitrator unless an arbitrator requests that the exhibits be delivered at a later time. (Some arbitrators prefer to have all exhibits delivered to them in the hearing room at the commencement of the hearing.) In addition, when the hearing begins, each party should place at the "witness stand" one set of that party's exhibits, and the core exhibits, to be utilized successively by witnesses during their testimony.

C.   Demonstrative Exhibits

Arbitrators should make clear what, if any, documents or other objects are excluded from the foregoing exchange requirement on grounds they are "demonstrative exhibits" and should fix appropriate deadlines for their production to the other side.

A wide variety of things can be shown to arbitrators during hearings but not offered in evidence. These include charts, graphs, summaries of data, enlargements of photographs or other exhibits, diagrams, maps, models, power point presentations used by counsel or expert witnesses, samples of materials or products, and similar items. Frequently, counsel assert that these are simply "demonstrative" or "illustrative" exhibits and thus are not subject to the advance exchange requirement applicable to evidentiary exhibits.

The use of such materials can be very helpful to the arbitrators' understanding of the case and should be welcomed, even encouraged.

However, there is a potential for unfair surprise and prejudice if one party suddenly displays, in the midst of the hearing, a demonstrative exhibit that the other side has never previously seen. Usually, some reasonable amount of time is required to verify that a summary of data is accurate, a diagram is correct, a model properly depicts the operation of the particular turbine involved in the case, and so on. Thus, it is important to establish some ground rules for the use of "demonstrative exhibits" during the hearing. The two most important concerns relate to (1) what is embraced by the term "demonstrative exhibits," and (2) how far in advance of their use at the hearing must such exhibits be shown to the opposing party.

Because of their great diversity, it is difficult to develop a comprehensive definition of what a demonstrative exhibit is. The better course is probably to define demonstrative exhibits by what they are not. Thus, a fairly workable definition for a demonstrative exhibit is anything that is shown to arbitrators during the hearing but is not part of the evidence in the case and thus cannot provide substantive support for any factual findings. This definition discourages a party from "sandbagging" an opponent by withholding from the exchange of evidentiary exhibits certain data, diagrams, or other items that it relies upon to prove any facts essential to its case. If the purported "demonstrative" actually furnishes evidence of facts in the case or an analysis of such facts, then it is really an evidentiary exhibit and not a demonstrative at all.

Frequently, all parties intend to utilize demonstrative exhibits during the hearing and may well be able to agree on the deadline for advance production, which agreement arbitrators should ordinarily accept. If the parties cannot agree on the deadline, the arbitrators must fix it based on the complexity and number of demonstratives likely to be used during the trial. A possible guideline might be that demonstratives that consist solely of visual material (such as photographs, sketches, and illustrations) need only be produced to the other side twenty-four hours before their use at the hearing, whereas demonstratives that contain data (such as graphs, charts showing measurements, calculations based on exhibits in evidence) must be produced one week before their use in the hearing, so there will be adequate time to investigate their accuracy. Whatever definition and production requirements arbitrators adopt should be memorialized in the preliminary conference order or a subsequent order.

D.   Exhibits Created During the Hearing

Arbitrators should make appropriate provisions for identifying and preserving exhibits created during the hearing.

In some arbitrations, exhibits are created during the course of the hearing. One witness may be asked to walk over to a flip chart and draw a diagram of a construction site or accident scene, or list the names of the persons who attended a particular meeting, or write out the language he recalls proposing for a certain provision during contract negotiations. Another may be asked to place marks on a map to depict the locations at which various events took place. An expert may be ask to perform certain calculations on the flip chart or show how she arrived at a critical number contained in her report. The list of ways in which such exhibits may be so created is virtually endless. When this happens, two important questions arise.

First, will the exhibit be treated as an evidentiary or demonstrative exhibit? As suggested in the preceding section, the exhibit should be regarded as evidentiary if it supplies information that could support a factual finding by the arbitrators (*e.g.,* the expert's calculations) and demonstrative if it merely illustrates facts already in evidence (*e.g.,* the witness' rough diagram of the accident scene he already described in his testimony.) Once the arbitrators determine this question, they can assign to the exhibit the appropriate evidentiary or demonstrative exhibit number.

Second, how will the exhibit be preserved? In some cases, the parties are content to let the arbitrators maintain sole custody of the original exhibit. In others, they may wish to have the exhibit copied, usually at reduced size, so that copies can be provided to each arbitrator and each party.

V.   MANAGEMENT OF TESTIMONY

In the United States and other common law countries, the testimony and credibility of witnesses remain critical components of most adjudicative processes. Thus, it is important that arbitrators and counsel work out fair and efficient arrangements for the presentation of witness testimony at the hearing.

A.   Possible Use of Written Testimony

Arbitrators should discuss with counsel the possible submission of some or all direct testimony in writing.

In international arbitrations, and in many state and federal administrative law proceedings, it is customary for each party to submit, in advance of the hearing, written sworn statements of the direct testimony of witnesses, with reference to relevant exhibits, leaving oral testimony confined to cross-examination, perhaps with brief introductory questions on direct. This practice is now being adopted by some domestic arbitrators as well. The practice has definite pros and cons that merit careful consideration by arbitrators and counsel in each case.

On the one hand, presentation of written direct testimony saves the time of the many people involved in the hearing (lawyers, parties, party representatives, reporters, and arbitrators), thus resulting in substantial cost savings. Additionally, the use of such testimony may obviate the need for depositions of the witnesses, thus effecting further cost savings. Finally, having the direct testimony of some or all of the witnesses in advance permits counsel to prepare more effective cross-examination and permits arbitrators to focus their attention on the key issues in dispute.

On the other hand, in cases with high stakes, written testimony of witnesses is likely to be drafted by counsel and to go through innumerable reviews and redrafts, thus generating legal fees that may equal or exceed the costs saved by reducing hearing time by a few hours. The fact that such testimony is often written by attorneys rather than the witness effectively means that the witness' entire direct testimony is presented in the form of an affirmation to one long, leading question ("Now, Mr. Witness, isn't what happened here the following: _____?"). Finally, the fact that the witness will have little or no opportunity to tell his story in his own words but will immediately find himself on the defensive from cross-examination is viewed by some arbitrators as a serious impediment to their ability to evaluate the credibility of various witnesses. (This concern can be ameliorated by giving the witness a reasonable amount of time to summarize, in his own words, the key points of his testimony and to relax and settle in at the hearing before cross-examination begins.)

Accordingly, arbitrators should review these and other pertinent considerations with counsel in order to determine the extent to which written direct testimony should be used in any particular case. It may be, for example, that the advantages of the technique outweigh the potential adverse consequences with respect to expert witnesses, who traditionally write (albeit in consultation with counsel) their own reports and submit them to the other side before the hearing. The technique may also be worth employing with secondary witnesses whose testimony is not significantly disputed, although it is possible that a stipulation as to such undisputed facts might be even more efficient. With respect to critical lay witnesses, the use of written testimony should probably be approached with caution and only ordered if all parties consent.

To the extent written testimony is to be used, arbitrators should include in the preliminary conference order the deadline for its submission and the applicable procedures relating to the examination of the witnesses at the hearing.

B.   Expert Witness Testimony

Arbitrators should consider adopting procedures to focus the principal disputes between expert witnesses and to gauge more effectively their respective abilities to defend their opinions.

One of the most frustrating aspects of court trials today is that the so-called "battle of the experts" is often not really a battle at all but rather a case of "ships passing in the night." Plaintiff's expert appears on Monday, gives her analysis, and leaves. Defendant's expert appears on Thursday, gives a somewhat different analysis, and leaves. Judge and jury are often left to wonder what the key differences between these experts' opinions really are and how effectively the witnesses would be able to support their opinions in a true dialogue between the two.

In cases increasingly dominated by experts, some commercial arbitrators are becoming frustrated by the same unsatisfactory quality of traditional expert presentations and are utilizing their hearing-management discretion to implement steps to address the problem. One technique is to require that experts meet before the hearing, outside the presence of counsel, to draw up a list of the points on which they agree and those on which they disagree. If this is done, their expert reports or written testimony can briefly address the agreed points and provide a more focused exposition of their opinions concerning the points in dispute.

Another technique that can be employed is to ensure that a genuine dialogue or conversation between experts occurs at the hearing. This can be accomplished in various ways. One alternative is to have opposing experts on the same subject "take the stand" at the same time and answer seriatim the same questions put by counsel and the arbitrators. A variation on this approach is to have all experts on the same topic present in the hearing room at the same time and to let each testify in the presence of the others and comment on the testimony of others, with counsel and the arbitrators recalling witnesses successively to respond to the arguments of one another until the arbitrators are satisfied that the respective arguments and counter-arguments have been fully articulated. Either variation of the "concurrent testimony" approach puts the experts in the position of having to answer directly each other's arguments.

The two foregoing techniques (the pre-hearing expert meeting and the hearing dialogue) can be used separately or together. Other techniques are possible as well. The techniques to be used should be thoroughly discussed with counsel and memorialized in an order.

Regardless of whether any of these techniques are used, it is usually advisable to defer the examination of experts until after both parties have presented the lay witnesses who will testify to the factual material upon which the expert testimony is based.

C.   Lay Witness Testimony

Arbitrators should discuss with counsel whether any procedures should be adopted to expedite and focus the testimony of lay witnesses.

To a lesser extent, presenting lay testimony in the traditional sequence can occasion some of the same frustrations that occur in connection with expert witnesses. Arbitrators should discuss with counsel the possibility of varying that sequence to make the presentation of lay testimony more efficient and effective.

For example, when there are discrete factual issues on which opposing parties' witnesses are in dispute, there may be advantages to having such witnesses take the stand at the same time and be present during each other's testimony. When this is done, claimant's witness would present direct testimony and be cross-examined, respondent's witness would testify next and be cross-examined, and then both witnesses would be questioned by the arbitrators. As with expert witnesses, this process has the potential of sharpening the focus of disagreements and giving arbitrators a better opportunity to evaluate the credibility and reliability of competing witnesses. One disadvantage of the process is that, if a witness on one side opposes the testimony of various witnesses on the other side, the hearing could devolve into a succession of separate match-ups in which the same witnesses are recalled again and again to debate points with different witnesses from the other side without ever having a chance to tell their story in a coherent and comprehensive way.

In some cases, one or more parties will present multiple witnesses whose testimonies overlap or are repetitive. Instead of having these witnesses testify sequentially, arbitrators may wish to discuss with counsel the possibility of presenting at the same time "panels" of witnesses, either from one party or from both sides, so that they can be examined and cross-examined as a group. *See* Robert J. McPherson, Richard F. Smith, and Roy S. Mitchell, *Innovations in Arbitration: Improving the Presentation of Evidence in Construction Arbitration*, 58 Disp. Resol. J. 30, 33 (Oct. 2003). Presenting lay testimony in this way can save significant hearing time but also increases the opportunity for witnesses from the same side to conform their testimony to that of one another.

D.   Testimony from Witnesses at Other Locations

Arbitrators should determine from counsel whether special arrangements need to be made to obtain live testimony from a witness at a location other than the hearing site.

Occasionally, counsel will wish to present the testimony of a witness beyond the applicable subpoena range who could not be deposed and is unwilling to travel to the hearing site. While the hearing could be adjourned and reconvened at the witness' location, the expense of transporting the hearing participants to the witness' locale may be quite excessive if the move is only needed to obtain some relatively brief testimony from a single witness. In such a situation, arbitrators should consider arranging for the witness to testify by speakerphone or, better yet, by videoconferencing equipment. If the witness is to be examined concerning documents, these can be placed in a sealed envelope and sent to a court reporter, notary, or other independent person who, at the direction of the examining counsel, will open the envelope and show the exhibit to the witness.

Of course, as discussed in Chapter 6, *supra*, when there are substantial numbers of witnesses located in cities A and B, it may be most efficient and economical to first convene the hearing in city A to take testimony from witnesses there and then reconvene in city B to take testimony of the witnesses who are there.

E.   Previously Recorded Testimony

Arbitrators should make appropriate arrangements regarding previously recorded testimony.

Some institutional rules expressly permit arbitrators to receive affidavits and previously recorded testimony and to give that evidence such weight as they deem appropriate. *See, e.g.*, JAMS Rule 22(e); AAA Rule 32(a). Rules of other institutions are plainly broad enough to permit this procedure. While the evaluation of credibility is best done when witnesses appear in person before arbitrators, there are situations in which this is impossible or infeasible; in those cases, counsel may wish to present the testimony of such witnesses in pre-recorded form, most commonly via a transcribed and/or videotaped deposition.

In such circumstances, arbitrators should explore with counsel how best to handle the presentation of such testimony. One possibility is to have the parties designate and counter-designate portions of the deposition and then present the arbitrators with a redacted transcript or video clip containing only the designated portions. Sometimes these materials are presented to arbitrators for review before or after the hearing. Sometimes counsel prefer to present them at what they consider the most effective stage in the hearing.

Affidavits or declarations may also be received by arbitrators and almost invariably are, absent truly extraordinary circumstances. What weight to give such evidence will depend on the facts of each case. On less critical points, arbitrators may be willing to rest their findings on such evidence. On the key facts, it would normally be the rare case in which arbitrators would accept the affidavit account of an absent witness over the credible testimony of a witness who appeared and stood cross-examination.

F.   Sequestration of Witnesses

Arbitrators should generally sequester lay witnesses if any party so requests unless the arbitrators determine, in their discretion, that there are compelling reasons to do otherwise.

While each party has a right to be present throughout the hearing, in person or through a designated corporate representative, witnesses do not; thus, whether to sequester witnesses is generally a matter to be determined in the arbitrators' discretion. AAA Rule 23 ("Any person having a direct interest in the arbitration is entitled to attend hearings. The arbitrator shall otherwise have the power to require the exclusion of any witness, other than a party or other essential person, during the testimony of any other witness. It shall be discretionary with the arbitrator to determine the propriety of the attendance of any other person other than a party and its representative."); JAMS Rule 26(c) ("Subject to the discretion of the Arbitrator or agreement of the Parties, any person having a direct interest in the Arbitration may attend the Arbitration Hearing. The Arbitrator may exclude any non-Party from any part of a Hearing.").

Sometimes counsel are concerned that witnesses who are allowed to attend the hearing may adjust their testimony to conform to the testimony of others or perhaps to arbitrator rulings. Absent exceptional circumstances, the usual practice is to sequester witnesses when all parties so request and not to sequester them when no party so requests. If some parties request sequestration and other parties oppose it, arbitrators must weigh the competing arguments and determine the matter in a sound exercise of discretion. Since there is seldom a compelling reason why witnesses need to attend the hearing, and there is usually some risk of testimony being "adjusted" when witnesses do attend, most arbitrators tend to err on the side of caution and order sequestration if any party requests it.

A traditional exception to this "rule on witnesses" is expert witnesses who are ordinarily permitted to hear the testimony not only of other experts (so they can better present their points of agreement and disagreement) but also of lay witnesses (so they can better understand the facts on which their expert opinions are supposedly based.).

G.   Restrictions on Counsel's Communications with Witnesses During Testimony

Arbitrators should discuss with counsel whether any restrictions should be placed on counsel's communications with witnesses during their testimony.

In some cases, particularly when witnesses may be on the stand for extended periods, some counsel may be concerned about the possibility that the witness' testimony may be influenced by communications, during breaks and overnight recesses, with the counsel who called the witness. Thus, arbitrators may be asked to impose some restrictions on the right of offering counsel to talk with a witness while the witness is "on the stand." If counsel can reach agreement on this matter, either that particular restrictions should be observed by all counsel or that no restrictions should be imposed, arbitrators should generally accept such agreements. If counsel cannot agree on the matter, one formulation that is generally fair and reasonable is to provide that offering counsel may freely confer with a witness during direct- and re-direct examination but may not discuss the case with the witness from the time cross-examination commences until it is concluded. Any restrictions to be imposed should be clearly recited in an order.

VI.   MANAGEMENT OF HEARING TIME

A.   Introduction

Arbitrators should institute fair, realistic, and reasonable measures to ensure that the hearing is conducted efficiently and that it is likely to be completed in the time allotted.

One of the most precious resources available to arbitrators and parties in a commercial arbitration is the time allotted for the hearing. If the hearing is not completed on the days reserved for it, it may be many weeks or months before busy arbitrators and counsel can find another block of time when all are available to resume the hearing. Sometimes medical emergencies or other unexpected circumstances make it impossible to complete the hearing in the time reserved. However, in most instances, if arbitrators and counsel were realistic at the preliminary conference in setting the dates for the hearing, then the hearing can usually be completed in the time reserved, provided that arbitrators institute and enforce fair and reasonable measures for making use of that time.

B.   Setting and Maintaining a Realistic Daily Schedule

Arbitrators should devise with counsel an agreeable and realistic schedule for hearing days and then ensure that the schedule is maintained throughout the hearing.

Assuming that the arbitrators and counsel derived at the preliminary conference a reasonable estimate of the total number of hearing hours required for the case, that estimate should serve as the basis for establishing the daily hearing schedule.

For example, if claimant and respondent report at the preliminary conference that they will each need a total of forty hours at the hearing, and the arbitrators satisfy themselves that these estimates are realistic, they might proceed as follows: Assigning each side a ten percent increase in their estimate for unexpected developments would result in forty-four hours per side or eighty-eight total hearing hours. Thirteen hearing days, which provide for seven hours of hearing time per day, would yield ninety-one hours, and thus afford a little margin of safety. To yield seven hours of hearing time per day, the arbitrators might schedule the hearing to run from 9:00 am to 5:30 pm each day with lunch from 12:00 to 1:00 pm and ten-minute recesses at 10:30 am, 2:30 pm, and 4:00 pm. Other scheduling variations are, of course, possible.

It is important to be realistic in determining the amount of real hearing time that can be obtained in a normal business day. Lunch breaks and periodic recesses will typically consume one and one-half to two hours per day. Thus, an estimate that assumes that each day will yield eight hours of hearing time is not realistic unless all participants are prepared to be at the hearing site approximately ten hours per day.

Once the daily hearing schedule is set, it is important that it be consistently maintained so that the expected number of hearing hours can be achieved and counsel can schedule witness meetings, conference calls, and other matters with confidence. The best way to assure conformity to the schedule is for arbitrators to be sitting in their chairs, ready to go, when each scheduled break is due to end and for them to make clear that they expect counsel and parties to do the same.

C.   Monitoring Compliance with the Hearing Schedule

Arbitrators should establish with counsel some system for ensuring that the parties actually complete their cases within the time available.

While all parties may start the hearing with the good intention of completing it in a timely fashion, those intentions may be insufficient to assure that that goal is achieved. Arbitrators, working with counsel, should establish a system for daily monitoring of where each side stands in relation to the pre-hearing projections. If it becomes clear early on that the time reserved for the hearing will be insufficient, additional time can often be obtained by starting earlier and/or going later on some or all days or by scheduling additional hearing days on the weekend. If arbitrators do not discover until late in the hearing that one or more parties needs substantial further time to complete the presentation of evidence, there is usually little that can be done at that point to secure such additional time aside from a continuance to a later (often, much later) date.

For these and other reasons, many arbitrators find it very helpful to have an administrative session at the end of each hearing day (*i.e.*, at 5:30 pm in the example given above) in order to take stock of where each party stands in relation to its hearing time, to review the witness schedule for the following day, and to take up any other administrative matters that any party wishes to raise. Some arbitrators also insist that objections to evidence or the use of demonstrative exhibits, arguments on motions, or other disputes between the parties be addressed in these "after hours" sessions so as to avoid consuming time set aside for testimony.

Various methods are available to monitor whether the parties are on track to complete the presentation of their evidence within the hearing time reserved. One method favored by some arbitrators is the "chess clock" system, under which each party is allocated a specified amount of time, typically a pro-rata share of the total hearing time reserved, to present its case. All time used by a party-- for example, in examining or cross-examining witnesses, making or responding to objections, presenting arguments or statements, setting up audio-visual equipment, or even in locating witnesses who are wandering the halls--is charged against that party's allotted time. Throughout the day, arbitrators maintain a running tally of the time used by each party and those totals are reported to all parties at the end-of-the-day administrative session. Such a system leaves it up to each party to decide how best to use its time and can serve as a self-regulating device to discourage repetitive evidence or other wastes of time.

Other arbitrators prefer to sit down with counsel in advance of the hearing and prepare a schedule showing the date and time when each witness will testify. If subsequent developments require changes in the schedule, it is promptly modified so as to take account of those developments and still complete the hearing on time. In virtually all arbitrations, witnesses are taken "out of turn" when scheduling constraints or other good cause require it.

Still other arbitrators prefer to simply establish target dates by which each side is expected to complete the presentation of certain evidence and to remind counsel that those targets must be met if the hearing is to conclude on time.

D.   What To Do If a Party Runs Out of Time or Requests a Continuance

Arbitrators should respond with care and discretion when a party runs out of hearing time and seeks more time or requests an adjournment to gather additional evidence.

Sometimes a party operating under the chess clock system will use all of its allotted time and then tell the arbitrator that it still has important evidence to present and thus requires additional time. Frequently, an opposing party who has managed to present its evidence within its allotted time will oppose the other party's request. This situation calls for the exercise of great care and discretion by the arbitrator.

If the parties have agreed to the time allocations, arbitrators presumably have the authority to enforce the agreement and deny any additional time to the requesting party. Indeed, the rules of some arbitral institutions suggest that arbitrators have this authority even in the absence of party agreement to the allocation. *See, e.g.,* CPR Rule 9.2 ("The Tribunal is empowered to impose time limits it considers reasonable on each phase of the proceeding, including without limitation the time allotted to each party for presentation of its case and for rebuttal. In setting time limits, the Tribunal should bear in mind its obligation to manage the proceeding firmly in order to complete proceedings as economically and expeditiously as possible.")

On the other hand, Section 10 of the FAA, which applies to most commercial arbitrations, lists, as one ground for vacating an arbitration award, "the arbitrators were guilty of misconduct in refusing to postpone the hearing, upon sufficient cause shown, or in refusing to hear evidence pertinent and material to the controversy." 9 U.S.C. § 10(a)(3). Section 23 of the RUAA contains substantially the same provision. Neither statute, nor the AAA or JAMS rules, specifically authorizes the imposition of binding time limits on the parties. Indeed, the JAMS rules suggest that arbitrators may not terminate hearings so long as one or more parties still has relevant and material evidence to present. JAMS Rule 22(h) ("When the Arbitrator determines that all relevant and material evidence and arguments have been presented, the Arbitrator shall declare the hearing closed.")

Thus, while arbitrators can and should strongly encourage parties to complete their presentations within the time allotted, it is generally unwise to deny additional time to a party who can identify relevant and material evidence that it still wishes to present. The better course is usually to allow that party a reasonable enlargement of time and to try to schedule the completion of the hearing as promptly as possible.

A somewhat analogous problem arises when one party asserts that, because of unexpected developments during the hearing, it requires an adjournment to secure additional relevant and material evidence. If the evidence is truly relevant and material and could not have been reasonably anticipated before the hearing began, the party may have made a showing of good cause for such relief. However, any adjournment should be as short as reasonably possible, and the additional testimony could be taken via a videotaped deposition, telephone testimony from a remote location, or possibly a supplemental evidentiary hearing.

In some instances, the party requesting additional time should have reasonably anticipated the need for the evidence and was negligent in not doing so. Arguably, this circumstance defeats the showing of good cause and justifies a denial of the adjournment request. However, the denial of the request still involves some risk of vacatur since a reviewing court may assess the arguably negligent conduct differently. If there are strong reasons for denying the request for adjournment, for example, great prejudice to the opposing party or an imminent deadline in the arbitration agreement for issuing the award, arbitrators may certainly do so but should carefully recite those reasons in the order denying the request. Absent such factors, a wiser course may be to grant the adjournment on condition that the requesting party reimburse the other party the reasonable costs occasioned thereby, *e.g.*, the round trip fare of counsel and other participants who may be required to return a second time to the site of the hearing.

VII. MANAGEMENT OF LOGISTICS

> **Arbitrators should ensure that appropriate arrangements have been made for all necessary logistical support for the hearing, including use of technology, appropriate hearing room space, transcripts, interpreters and/or signers, access for handicapped participants, and other special needs.**

Quite often, arbitrators and counsel become preoccupied with the substantive issues involved in arbitration hearings and tend to overlook the various logistical matters that are required to support the proceedings. Arbitrators should give early attention to these matters in order to assure a smooth, efficient, and comfortable hearing process.

A.   Use of Technology

Arbitrators should encourage appropriate utilization of technology and ensure that necessary arrangements are made for its efficient use at the hearing.

Many technological devices are now available that can facilitate the presentation of evidence and the arbitrators' comprehension of it. These include "Elmos" and other overhead projectors, power point, computer animation and projection, CDs, videotape and DVD players, big screen projectors, and video-conferencing equipment. In appropriate cases, arbitrators should encourage the use of such technology by all parties. Arbitrators should determine at an early stage what, if any, technological equipment will be used at the hearing and should make sure that the hearing room can reasonably accommodate that equipment. Arbitrators should also inquire whether counsel can cooperate in the use of a common system, or whether one party can provide the other party with access to such technology at the other party's cost. Arbitrators should also require that paper copies of any slides or other items projected on screens be given at the time of projection to each arbitrator and opposing counsel, since it is somewhat difficult to read the fine print on the screen and arbitrators often like to make marginal notations on a copy of the document as it is being discussed.

Finally, it is advisable for arbitrators to caution counsel not to let technology take over. In some cases counsel become so obsessed with putting on an impressive "show" that they devote more attention and energy to the medium than to the message. At bottom, arbitration is about winning the minds of arbitrators. Counsel should focus first on making sure they have a persuasive case to present and then consider what technological devices may assist them in its presentation.

B.   Transcripts

Arbitrators should discuss with counsel whether having a transcript will be advisable and, if so, should make appropriate provisions therefore in an order.

In cases that involve lengthy hearings, technical or otherwise complex facts, or highly subtle and nuanced determinations, a transcript can greatly aid counsel in post-hearing briefing and greatly benefit arbitrators in arriving at sound results and preparing reasoned awards. In cases with fairly high stakes, arbitrators can usually convince counsel that these advantages significantly outweigh the marginal cost increase occasioned by having a court reporter record and transcribe the hearing, or critical portions thereof. Ordinarily it will be sufficient to secure such a transcript at the court reporter's standard rates, and production at "expedited" rates will not be necessary.   Production of "overnight" transcripts should be discouraged in all but the most exceptional cases, as they significantly increase the costs of arbitration and protract the hearing through lengthy cross-examination based on such transcripts.   Arbitrators should also determine whether a "real-time" transcript of testimony will be available electronically during the hearing and, if so, assure that each party has equal access to that technology at its own cost.

C.   Hearing Room Logistics

Arbitrators should take an active role in ensuring that hearing room logistics maximize the efficiency of the hearing.

Arbitrators should take personal responsibility to confirm well in advance of the hearing that the hearing room is of adequate size and properly configured for a hearing; that there are clear views of the witnesses; that the acoustics are satisfactory; that there is adequate and appropriate space for exhibit binders, briefs, demonstrative exhibits, projection screens, VCR's, computers, overhead projectors, models, blueprints, or any other items needed for the hearing; and that there are comfortable chairs and adequate space for arbitrators, parties, counsel, witnesses, and court reporter, if applicable.

D. Special Needs

Arbitrators should determine if any hearing participants have special needs and should make appropriate arrangements therefor.

If any witnesses, parties, or counsel require sign language or interpreter services, the arbitrators should ensure that counsel have made appropriate arrangements for such services and should ask counsel to agree on the competency of any such interpreters or signers. If any hearing participant is wheelchair bound or otherwise handicapped, arbitrators should assure that appropriate arrangements have been made for such person's full participation in the hearing. Any other special needs should be identified and provided for as far in advance of the hearing as possible.

VIII. SITE VISITS

Arbitrators should consider whether an inspection of particular sites, pieces of equipment, or other physical objects that cannot be brought to the hearing room would significantly aid them in resolving the case, and if so, should make appropriate arrangements for such inspections.

When detailed knowledge about a physical location, structure, or large item of equipment is critical to the resolution of issues in the case, much hearing time can sometimes be saved, and more reliable information can be presented to the arbitrators, by not relying simply on photographs or drawings, but instead by having the arbitrators actually view the location or object. Michael J. Altschuler, *Seeing is Believing: The Importance of Site Visits in Arbitrating Construction Contracts*, 58 Disp. Resol. J. 36 (October 2003). The timing of the visit will depend on the circumstances of the case. In a large, complex dispute that will involve multiple hearing days, a site visit early in the hearing process might help clarify the issues in dispute. A site visit just before the last hearing days could be useful to allow arbitrators to view items of importance that could not have been anticipated prior to hearing the testimony of key witnesses.

Care should be taken by the arbitrators, in consultation with counsel, to plan the site visitation process in such a way as to ensure fairness. They will want to consider such matters as sharing transportation to the site, how explanations and questions and answers will be handled, avoidance of side conversations, the provision of such amenities as meals, and making a record (by videotape or otherwise) of what occurred during the visit. Indeed, a site visit can sometimes be obviated if parties, jointly or separately, can make a high-quality videotape of the location or object in question and present that to the arbitrators who can review it as necessary during the hearing and deliberations.

While some rules, for example, AAA Rule 33, permit arbitrators to make site visits without counsel, provided that the arbitrators make an oral or written report of their visit to the parties and afford them an opportunity to comment, this procedure should probably only be utilized in exceptional circumstances and with counsel's consent.

IX.   ARBITRATOR CONDUCT DURING HEARINGS

Arbitrators should conduct themselves during the hearing in a manner designed to expedite and facilitate the receipt of the parties' evidence and arguments and to assure the parties of their impartiality and neutrality.

The conduct of arbitrators during hearings is extremely important. By the actions they take and the example they set, arbitrators can greatly enhance the fairness, efficiency, and professionalism of the proceedings and can demonstrate to the parties and counsel that they are approaching the case in a conscientious, thoughtful, and impartial way. To achieve this goal, arbitrators are encouraged to adhere to the following guidelines:

A. Controlling the Hearing

Arbitrators should make clear that they, not counsel, are in control of the hearing. They should keep proceedings moving along at an appropriate pace, guide the presentation of evidence so as to avoid wasteful repetition and useless proof of uncontested matters, and firmly curb any apparent filibuster.

Arbitrators should control hearings in a firm but not overbearing manner. They should insure that each hearing day begins as scheduled, that breaks do not exceed the time allotted for them, and that the hearing proceeds at a pace that is efficient but not rushed.

Except in "panel witness" situations, examination of witnesses should generally proceed in the normal fashion (direct, cross, redirect, recross, etc.), and arbitrators should allow the parties to continue to examine a witness until it is clear that meaningful inquiry has been exhausted. In order to avoid wasting time, arbitrators should encourage counsel to stipulate to uncontested matters and to refrain from offering unduly cumulative evidence. Counsel and witnesses should not be permitted to make long speeches that appear calculated to use up hearing time to the prejudice of other parties. If the chess clock system is used, this should serve as an automatic restraint on counsel using time unprofitably.

B. Setting the Tone

Arbitrators should set a tone of easy informality, but the needs of counsel and witnesses for flexibility should be accommodated, and arbitrators should not deny any party the right to present material evidence.

While arbitration hearings are generally more relaxed and informal than court trials, it is important for arbitrators to be attentive to the legitimate needs of counsel and witnesses and to ensure that all parties receive a full, fair opportunity to present their case.

C.   Maintaining an Open Mind

Each arbitrator should at all times keep an open mind (and the clear appearance of an open mind).

Arbitrators should avoid giving any indications of how they may be inclined to decide the case, since such conduct can later be cited by the losing party as evidence of partiality or pre-disposition. However, arbitrators can, without any hint of partiality, tell counsel that a point has been understood and they may safely move on, or, conversely, that a point has not been understood and counsel may wish to clarify it. Most counsel appreciate this sort of guidance from arbitrators, since it helps counsel make most effective use of their time.

D.   Questioning Witnesses

Arbitrators should carefully consider when, and to what extent, they become involved in the questioning of witnesses.

Arbitrators have varying views relating to the questioning of witnesses by arbitrators. Some arbitrators prefer to ask questions of witnesses or counsel whenever they arise in the hearing, taking care, of course, not to become too intrusive or adversarial, or to take over the role of counsel. Usually the better practice is for arbitrators to allow counsel to fully develop the evidence, and confine themselves simply to clarifying questions, until examination and cross-examination have been concluded (except in cases where arbitrators may be taking the lead in questioning expert witnesses or other witnesses who are appearing as a panel).

If an arbitrator perceives that questioning by counsel leaves a significant gap in the evidence, there is a question as to whether the arbitrator should seek to close that gap. There may be different reasons for the gap, ranging from incompetence of counsel to strategic decisions not to address certain matters; and there may be different perceptions among arbitrators as to what is truly significant. One recommended practice in tripartite arbitrations is for the arbitrator, before pursuing such an inquiry, to consult with the other arbitrators as to whether they agree that the issue is significant; if they do, then the chair can raise the issue with counsel in terms such as "We notice that Party X has not addressed Issue Y; do you wish to do so? Does the opposite party have any view on the subject?" If, based on the responses, the arbitrators determine that the matter should be pursued, then they should feel free to ask the necessary questions. In cases with only one arbitrator, the same practice, save for consultation with other arbitrators, generally can be followed.

E.   Discussing the Case with other Arbitrators

In tripartite arbitrations, arbitrators should consider how to handle conversation within the tribunal concerning the merits before the case is submitted for decision.

Some arbitrators prefer to discuss the case with their fellow panelists while the case unfolds, believing that such discussion is the best way to ensure that all the arbitrators are cognizant of all the issues that have arisen during the hearing. Other arbitrators believe that discussing the merits of the case may unduly influence the views of other arbitrators and should be avoided until all evidence and arguments have been presented. There are respectable arguments for both positions. Arbitrators should not worry about determining which position is "right" but should select the approach with which they feel most comfortable under all the circumstances of the particular case.

F.   Dealing with Non-Appearance of Witnesses

If an expected witness fails to appear, arbitrators should invite the views of counsel as to the appropriate action.

If the witness is under subpoena, a recess of the hearing pending judicial enforcement may be necessary, but arbitrators should look for a fair way to obviate what might be an extended delay. If the missing witness is employed or controlled by a party, it may be appropriate to preclude proof of an issue by the offending party or, less drastically, to draw an inference adverse to the offending party. Whether a sanction is warranted and, if so, the propriety of the sanction selected should be established on the record.

G.   Making Further Disclosures

If an arbitrator needs to make a new disclosure during the hearing, proceedings should be temporarily suspended so that any potential objections can be resolved.

If an arbitrator discovers during the hearing that a new disclosure is necessary, the disclosure should immediately be brought to the attention of counsel. Sometimes the nature of the disclosure is so minimal that all counsel will immediately waive any objection to the arbitrator's continued service. When this occurs, the arbitrator should promptly memorialize in an order or letter to counsel that the disclosure was made and objection was waived by all parties. However, if there is any question as to the possible effect of the disclosure, there should be an immediate suspension of the proceedings for a period reasonably necessary to determine if there is an objection and, if so, to resolve it. Under the rules of some arbitral institutions, such as the AAA, the disclosure process should be administered by the arbitral institution.

H.   Addressing Arbitrator Performance Problems

Arbitrator performance problems should be addressed with care and discretion.

Very rarely an arbitrator performance problem may occur during the hearing, *e.g.*, the appearance of bias on the part of a neutral arbitrator, inattention, absence, tardiness, unduly intrusive questioning, or serious irregularity on the part of the chair. A member of a tripartite tribunal perceiving such a problem should ask for a private conference. A respectful but firm remonstrance will usually resolve the problem. In cases with a single arbitrator, it may be necessary for counsel to raise the matter with the arbitral institution or, if there is none, directly with the arbitrator.

I.   Calling for Additional Evidence

Arbitrators should exercise with care their right to call for additional witnesses or exhibits.

The rules of most arbitral institutions make clear that arbitrators are not limited to deciding the case on the basis of evidence the parties have chosen to present but may call upon the parties to present additional evidence. *See, e.g.*, AAA Rule 31(a) ("The parties may offer such evidence as is relevant and material to the dispute and shall produce such evidence as the arbitrator may deem necessary to an understanding and determination of the dispute."); CPR Rule 12.3 ("The Tribunal, in its discretion, may require the parties to produce evidence in addition to that initially offered.").

Arbitrators should carefully exercise this discretion to call for the production of additional evidence. Arbitrators should normally be reluctant to call for additional witnesses or exhibits simply because one party has not supplied any proof, or sufficient proof, to establish a required element of its claim or defense. In that instance, the additional evidence, if produced, could shift the outcome of the case, and the losing party (who would have won had the arbitrators not solicited such evidence) may question the arbitrators' neutrality. On the other hand, if arbitrators believe that the evidence offered by both sides on a particular issue is confusing or incomplete, it may be appropriate for the arbitrators to state that they believe the evidence presented to date may not be sufficient for them to understand and determine that issue and to then invite both sides to submit additional evidence to clarify the matter.

J.   Confirming that All Evidence has been Presented

At the conclusion of the parties' presentations, arbitrators should ask the parties whether they have any further evidence to present and, in the event of a negative answer, should indicate in the record that they do not.

For two reasons, it is important to memorialize in a transcript or order that the parties advised the arbitrators on a certain date that they had no further evidence to present. First, properly recording this declaration of the parties will significantly reduce the possibility of vacatur, under the FAA or RUAA, for refusing to receive relevant and material evidence. Second, under some institutional rules, when the arbitrators determine that all relevant evidence and arguments have been presented, they must declare the hearing closed. *See, e.g.,* JAMS Rule 22(h). Thus, in a case in which post-hearing briefing and argument have been waived, the completion of evidence requires the closing of the hearing record, thus commencing the running of the arbitrators' time within which to issue an award. However, arbitrators may defer the closing of the record to an agreed date for the submission of post-hearing briefs and arguments, upon receipt of which the hearing is deemed closed. *Id.*

X.   DETERMINING REQUESTS FOR FEES, COSTS, AND INTEREST

Arbitrators should determine whether evidence concerning interest, fees, and costs will be received during the main hearing or through supplemental proceedings and should establish the procedures for any such proceedings.

In some cases, a prevailing party may be entitled to pre-award and/or post-award interest on its damages and possibly attorneys' fees and costs as allowed by a statute, rule, or contract provision. In almost all cases, the arbitration agreement and/or the arbitration rules require arbitrators to determine how arbitrator fees and costs shall be allocated between the parties. The awarding of such ancillary relief cannot be finally determined until the arbitrators have decided which party prevailed on all the claims before them. There are two basic ways to handle the matter.

In fairly straightforward cases, the parties may be willing to stipulate at the end of the hearing to the reasonable amount of any fees and costs, and the calculation of any interest, to which each party would be entitled if it prevailed. In such cases, the evidentiary record can be declared closed at the completion of the hearing (upon receipt of the stipulation) and the arbitrators will simply insert in their final award the stipulated numbers for fees, costs, and interest depending on which party prevailed.

In other cases, the above procedure may be unworkable for a number of reasons. First, in cases in which there will be substantial post-hearing briefing and argument, it may be difficult to reasonably estimate at the end of the hearing the amount of legal fees and costs that will be occasioned by such post-hearing activities. Second, there may be disputes concerning the reasonableness of certain fees and costs, and the parties may wish to present expert witness testimony, by affidavit or possibly live, concerning such disputes. Third, there may be a need to brief which costs are properly recoverable under the applicable law, rule, or contract provision, or whether interest should be allowed and, if so, at what rate. In a case in which a claimant may receive some but not all of the damages it is seeking, interest cannot be calculated until the arbitrators determine the precise amount of damages to be recovered.

In these kinds of situations, arbitrators typically review the parties' evidence concerning liability and damages and issue an interim award determining those matters. That award includes a schedule setting the date by which any party seeking fees, costs, or interest shall file a brief and relevant documents in support of such request; a date by which the opposing party will file a brief and documents in opposition to such request; and a date on which the arbitrators will hold an evidentiary hearing or oral argument if needed. After these proceedings are concluded, the arbitrators then issue a final award that includes their interim award and, potentially, the arbitrators' reasoning relating to the supplemental requests for interest, fees, and costs. See Chapter 10, *infra*, for certain cautions relating to interim awards.

XI.   BRIEFING

A.   Pre-Hearing Briefs

Arbitrators should determine at the preliminary conference what will be included in pre-hearing briefs and when they will be exchanged and should include those determinations in their preliminary conference order.

Arbitrators vary considerably in their preferences concerning pre-hearing or post-hearing briefs. Some arbitrators like to receive very complete briefs in advance of the hearing so that they can be thoroughly prepared when the hearing begins and also be able to begin writing their award as soon as the hearing ends, while the evidence is fresh in their minds. Other arbitrators prefer to receive a summary statement of each party's position before the hearing and then a comprehensive post-hearing brief, with citations to the record, after the hearing is completed. In addition to their own preferences, arbitrators need to be mindful of the preferences of counsel, specific provisions in any applicable rules (for example, CPR Rule 12.1, requiring fairly detailed pre-hearing memoranda), and the costs that excessive briefing requirements may impose on the parties.

Nearly all arbitrators will want to receive from each party, at a date reasonably in advance of the hearing, a pre-hearing brief containing, or accompanied by, the following items:

1.   A concise statement of that party's claims and/or defenses.
2.   A list of the party's witnesses, including experts, in the order in which they will be called, with a short description of the

anticipated testimony of each witness and an estimate of the length of their direct testimony.

3.   Copies of the curriculum vitae or biography of each expert.

4.   A statement of any relief requested, including the amount of any damages.

5.   A concise statement of the applicable law and authorities upon which the party relies, with citations to the pertinent pages of each authority.

6.   A tabbed, indexed, notebook containing the principal cases or other legal authorities on which that party relies.

In fairly simple cases, it may be reasonable to ask that counsel include in their pre-hearing briefs a statement of all the facts they intend to prove at the hearing. In very complex cases, such statements could run to hundreds of pages and requiring them would be unduly burdensome.

How far in advance of the hearing such briefs should be filed will vary with the complexity of the case. In uncomplicated cases, receipt of the briefs a week or so before the hearing may be adequate. In more complex cases, it may be desirable for the arbitrators and opposing counsel to receive the briefs fifteen to thirty days or more before the hearing.

B.   Post-Hearing Briefs

In protracted and complex cases, many arbitrators find it very useful to receive thorough post-hearing briefs in which parties set forth their factual and legal positions in detail with citation to the hearing transcript and exhibits. Some arbitrators (and some counsel) like these briefs to be in the form of proposed findings of fact and conclusions of law. Some arbitrators require that, in addition to whatever else the parties wish to say, they address in their briefs certain questions specified by the arbitrators in the order setting the briefing schedule. While such an order can sometimes be issued before the hearing begins, it is usually best to issue, or at least supplement, it after the hearing has closed so that the arbitrators can request briefing on the particular matters that concern them or on issues that arose unexpectedly during the hearing.

The schedule for such post-hearing briefing usually follows one of two models. In the first model, all parties file an opening brief on date X and a responsive brief on date Y. In the second model, the briefing is staggered as follows: On date A, claimant files a brief in support of its claims; on date B, respondent files a brief in opposition to claimant's claims and in support of its counterclaims; on date C, claimant files a brief that includes its reply concerning its claims and its opposition to respondent's counterclaims; and on date D, respondent files a reply brief concerning its counterclaims. In cases in which respondent has no counterclaims, the briefing ends on date C.

Which model to use, the intervals of time between briefs, and even the question of whether there will be any post-hearing briefing are matters to be discussed with counsel and resolved, if possible, by consensus.

C.   Other Materials That May Assist Arbitrators

In addition to formal briefs, arbitrators should not be shy about asking that counsel provide to them, either before or after the hearing as appropriate, any other sorts of materials that might help them better understand and decide the case. Such materials might include the following:

1.   A chronology or time-line of pertinent events.
2.   (In a long hearing with many witnesses) Photographs of each witness.
3.   A tabbed and indexed notebook containing the party's most important exhibits, with pertinent passages highlighted.
4.   A tabbed and indexed notebook containing the portions of testimony that the party considers most important.
5.   For each major witness, a one page, bullet point list of the most important points made by that witness (with transcript citations).
6.   Precise formulations of the relief sought to be ordered.

Naturally, copies of all such materials (including the highlighting) should be served on opposing counsel as well as the arbitrators, and those counsel should have a reasonable opportunity to point out to the arbitrators any alleged inaccuracies in the submissions.

XII. STATEMENTS AND ARGUMENTS OF COUNSEL

A. Opening Statements

Arbitrators should generally allow a reasonable amount of time for counsel to make opening statements at the beginning of the hearing and to respond to any questions the arbitrators might have.

Unless all counsel waive the opportunity and the arbitrators are sure that they thoroughly understand the case as a result of reviewing pre-hearing briefs, arbitrators should usually afford counsel a reasonable amount of time to make opening statements at the beginning of the hearing. Often counsel will make a power point presentation, in which event each arbitrator should be provided with a copy of all slides included in the presentation. Opening statement is also a good opportunity for arbitrators to seek clarification of any points they found to be unclear in the pre-hearing briefs. Arbitrators need not be too concerned with enforcing the rigid rule, often applied in jury trials, that counsel's opening must be a "statement" of the evidence expected during the hearing but not an "argument." Experienced arbitrators can readily distinguish evidence from argument and treat each appropriately.

B. Mini-Summaries

Arbitrators should consider allowing counsel to provide "road map" commentaries or "mini-summaries" at various points during the hearing.

In some multi-issue, protracted hearings, counsel present their witnesses and exhibits in such a sequence or manner that arbitrators are uncertain what issue is being addressed or what connection this evidence has with other issues in the case. In such cases, the arbitrators' understanding of the evidence may be enhanced if counsel are permitted, at appropriate points during the hearing, to give brief introductory statements explaining what issues a witness is being called to address or how this testimony will relate to other testimony to come. It can also be useful to permit counsel, if they wish, to periodically summarize for the arbitrators what they contend they have established thus far in the hearing and where they will be going next in their presentations. Though such statements will inevitably contain a degree of argument, there is no more harm to that than that which arises from mid-trial arguments made to judges concerning relevance or admissibility of evidence, motions in limine, motions for directed verdict, and similar matters. Of course, time utilized for such mini-summaries is charged to the party making them.

C. Final Arguments

Arbitrators should allow counsel to present their final arguments at a time and in a manner that is helpful to the arbitrators but also affords counsel a reasonable opportunity for advocacy.

Final argument is the last, and, say some, the most important, opportunity for advocacy by counsel who are contending for different outcomes in a matter that may have very great consequences, financial or otherwise, for their clients. Fairness and integrity of the arbitration process demands that counsel be given a reasonable chance to collect their thoughts and present their best arguments to the arbitrators before the case is submitted for decision.

Arbitrators who like to begin work on their awards immediately following the conclusion of the hearing will typically request that counsel be prepared to deliver their final arguments immediately upon close of the evidentiary hearing or within a few days thereafter. If the argument will be presented a few days after the hearing ends and arbitrators and counsel are then located in different cities, the argument can be held by conference phone or video conferencing. If counsel wish to make the argument in person, all participants can reassemble at the hearing site or other convenient location.

Arbitrators who prefer to receive thorough post-hearing briefs will generally want to schedule argument in one of two ways. Some arbitrators wish to have argument at the close of the hearing and to receive briefs thereafter. Other arbitrators prefer to hold argument at a time that will permit them to carefully review the briefs and related materials prior to the argument. Some arbitrators, having conducted that review, like to send counsel a list of questions to address in argument. Some like to send counsel an itemization of all the issues the arbitrators understand they must address in any reasoned award so that counsel can advise them at argument if they have inadvertently overlooked or misstated any issues. Some arbitrators prepare and send to counsel, for comment at the argument, a proposed analytical structure or "decision tree" for considering the issues in the case. Some even prepare and send to counsel a tentative award that sets forth their preliminary conclusions about the case, inviting counsel to point out at the final argument any errors or omissions in their analysis.

How much time to allow for final argument will obviously depend on the complexity of the case, the number of issues, and the size of the record. In simple cases, one hour per side may be sufficient. In complex cases, several hours or even one day per side may be required.

Occasionally, issues will arise in the final argument that warrant further briefing. When this occurs, arbitrators should set an expedited schedule for submissions or supplemental briefs on particular, specified issues.

If the case is one in which the parties stipulated to the amounts of fees, costs, and interest to which each party would be entitled if it prevailed, then the record is usually declared closed, and the arbitrator's time to issue a final award commences to run, on the date final argument ends or any post-argument submissions are completed. If submissions on interest, fees, or costs were to be handled through supplemental proceedings following issuance of an interim award, then the record is generally declared closed at such time as the interim award is issued and all such supplemental proceedings are completed.

If arbitrators have any concern that, due to the size of the record or other unusual circumstances, it may be difficult or impossible for them to issue a final award within the time allowed by the arbitration agreement or applicable rules (typically, thirty days), they should ask counsel, at or before the time of final argument, to consent to a reasonable extension of that deadline and should promptly memorialize that consent in a written order. Some arbitrators believe it is best to have counsel countersign such an order.

CHAPTER 10

AWARDS

**In issuing awards, arbitrators' goals are to craft awards that
are (1) clear, (2) supported by the evidence and substantive
law, (3) appropriate to the circumstances of the particular case,
and (4) consistent with applicable law and rules relating to
timeliness, finality, and the scope of their authority.**

I.   INTRODUCTION

In many respects, due in part to varying state and federal legislative
enactments and judicial decisions, there is no uniform agreement on
the meaning and preferred usage of many arbitration terms and
phrases. Thus, even though the ultimate objective in arbitration is the
issuance of a final "award," the word "award" is actually used by
arbitrators for a broad variety of purposes. Generally, three distinct
types of awards are issued by arbitrators in domestic arbitrations: (1)
"final awards" that conclusively resolve all issues; (2) "partial final
awards" that finally determine some, but not all, issues involved in a
proceeding; and (3) "interim awards" that tentatively or preliminarily
determine some, but not all, issues involved in a proceeding.

The distinctions between these types of awards can be critical since,
depending on the content of the award and the intent of the arbitrators
and/or parties, the issuance of the award might trigger the application
of the doctrine of *functus officio* or related institutional rules or
statutory provisions that provide that the arbitrators' jurisdiction has
been terminated with respect to issues determined in the award. (For a
more detailed discussion of the doctrine of *functus officio* and the
related rules and statutes, see Chapter 11, *infra*.) Just as significantly,
when "finality" does attach to the award, the issuance of the award
may trigger a party's right to seek confirmation or vacatur of the

award. Moreover, at least when the FAA applies to the procedural aspects of the confirmation or vacatur proceeding, the issuance of such an award may actually commence the running of the statutory time limitations within which such relief must be sought.

Given these considerations, it is important for any discussion of awards to address, at least briefly, not only final awards, but also the other forms of awards mentioned above. Therefore, while this chapter will chiefly focus on the final award to be issued in the arbitration proceeding, it will also include a discussion of both interim awards and partial final awards.

II.   FINAL AWARDS

A.   Making a Definite and Final Award Upon the Matter Submitted

> Arbitrators must ensure that the final award (1) clearly determines every issue submitted to the arbitrators, and only such issues, (2) is issued on a timely basis, and (3) grants only that relief authorized by the parties' agreement and applicable rules and law.

The FAA provides that a court may vacate an arbitration award when "the arbitrators exceeded their powers, or so imperfectly executed them that a mutual, final, and definite award upon the subject matter submitted was not made." 9 U.S.C. § 10(a)(4). Nearly all state arbitration acts contain comparable provisions. Awards can and have run afoul of these provisions when the award indicates that the arbitrators failed to decide all of the submitted issues (for example, when arbitrators improperly delegated to counsel or others the authority to determine the quantum of damages), decided issues that were not submitted to the arbitrators, ordered relief not within the authority of the arbitrators, ordered relief inconsistent with stipulations entered into by the parties, ordered relief in favor of or against a party not obligated to arbitrate, decided issues reserved for the courts, or failed to issue an award within time limits prescribed by statute or applicable arbitral rules.

Experienced arbitrators have fashioned practical steps that can help to identify and avoid such problems. One primary means of accomplishing this purpose is to obtain from the parties, at the earliest reasonable time, a statement of each of the claims or issues the arbitrators are being asked to decide, accompanied by a statement of the specific relief each party seeks. Some arbitrators seek such submissions early in the case, in initial pleadings or at the first preliminary conference. Others do so in the pre-hearing briefs or in written submissions to be made at the hearing. Arbitrators in complex cases involving multiple claims, such as large construction cases, will sometimes ask the parties to format such submissions in the form of spreadsheets; arbitrators can use such spreadsheets to keep track of the specific issues and the parties' positions on them, and also to note references to, and comments about, the evidence. With the aid of these and similar materials, the arbitrators' final review can ensure that the award addresses all of the issues to be decided and relief sought. Any doubts regarding the arbitrators' authority to grant the specific relief requested, or the arbitrability of any given claim with respect to any person or entity in favor of whom or against whom relief is to be ordered, should trigger a request for briefing or argument on those questions. Finally, most experienced arbitrators include a "sweeper" provision in their awards providing that all claims not specifically addressed elsewhere in the award are denied.

B. Form of Award

Arbitrators should examine the parties' agreement and any applicable rules, and should consult with the parties, regarding whether the award is to contain reasons or findings of fact and conclusions of law. Arbitrators should either issue an award that conforms with those requirements and the parties' expectations or, in the absence of clear guidance, should exercise their discretion in determining the nature of the award.

Arbitrators should determine whether the arbitration agreement or applicable rules specify the form of award. If arbitrators have not resolved this question prior to the commencement of the hearing, they should consult with counsel and make the determination as soon as reasonably possible. When the applicable rules or an agreement between the parties provide for an award without a statement of reasons, arbitrators should issue such an award. In international arbitrations, reasoned awards are the norm. In domestic arbitrations, arbitrators traditionally have chosen between three alternatives: (1) a short-form or "bare" award that simply identifies the parties, recites the source of their duty to arbitrate, and announces the prevailing party and relief awarded; (2) a narrative or "reasoned" award that includes all of the elements of the short-form award, but also explains the principal reasons for the arbitrators' decision; or (3) an award that includes not only the elements of a short-form award, but also formal findings of fact and conclusions of law.

A lively debate exists among arbitrators as to whether reasoned awards are appropriate or desirable in domestic cases in which the parties have not agreed on a particular form of award. One school of thought is that bare awards best protect the finality of the award, avoid much of the expense of award preparation, are potentially desirable for reasons not always apparent to the arbitrator (e.g., insurance considerations), and best preserve the confidentiality of the dispute, particularly because awards must be filed of record in a court in vacatur or confirmation proceedings. Other arbitrators take the view that fairness, to both the prevailing and losing parties and to a reviewing court, requires an explanation of the principal reasons for the decision, and also that preparation of a written statement of the arbitrators' analysis in a complex case is usually essential to arrive at an analytically sound decision. In some instances, for example, when the arbitrators' decision affects the parties' future performance in an ongoing contractual relationship, the declaratory nature of the arbitrators' decision might make it essential that the award contain sufficient reasoning to allow the parties to understand, and comply with, their continuing obligations under a contract.

When a question exists regarding the nature of the award to be issued in the arbitration, there are several practical approaches arbitrators can take to help confine and focus the debate. Arbitrators should always raise the question relating to the form of the award early in the case, perhaps at the initial preliminary conference. Arbitrators should explain the alternatives and ask the parties whether they have agreed on the form the award should take. If no agreement exits, arbitrators should either require the parties to discuss the issue and then advise them of any agreement, or should proceed to discuss and resolve the issue immediately. If the issue cannot be resolved in the course of the preliminary conference, arbitrators should direct that any subsequent agreement reached by the parties be communicated to them no later than the beginning of the hearing. Arbitrators' analysis of the issue should always include a review of any applicable arbitral rules, most of which include provisions relating to the form of the award.

Whenever the parties reach an agreement on the form of the award and timely communicate that agreement to the arbitrators, arbitrators must prepare the award in the agreed format. If the arbitrators believe that the parties' agreement is unwise or unworkable, they may explain the reasons for that opinion and ask the parties to reconsider. Like other aspects of the process, however, a final agreement by the parties on the form of the award is binding on the arbitrators. When the parties do not agree on the form of the award, arbitrators should solicit argument on the issue, since there might be obscure considerations that are important to only one of the parties, or that are unique to the particular case. After arbitrators have heard the parties' competing viewpoints and resolved the issue, their decision regarding the form of the award should be communicated to the parties, preferably in writing, before the hearing commences.

C. Content of Award

1. Architectural Framework of Award

> Arbitral awards should generally be structured in a logical sequence that portrays the chronological

> history of the proceeding, commencing with the
> initiation of the arbitration and culminating in the
> granting or denial of relief.

All forms of arbitral awards normally begin by identifying the parties and counsel, the parties' agreement to arbitrate, the arbitrators, and the arbitral rules, if any, under which the arbitration has been conducted. Most experienced arbitrators then provide a summary of the procedural aspects of the case beginning with the demand or submission agreement, an identification of the filing dates of the claims and counterclaims and any amendments thereto, references to any significant pre-hearing orders, a description of the hearing, a statement of the date when the hearing was closed, and a summary of any interim awards or orders issued previously. In cases involving a large evidentiary record, the number of witnesses who testified and some indication of the number of exhibits admitted into the record may also be included. If the hearing was transcribed, and the parties agreed or the arbitrators determined that the transcript would be the "official record" of the hearing (*see* AAA Rule 26), the award should recite that fact. At this point, a bare award normally will proceed directly to announce the relief awarded. In contrast, a narrative, reasoned award will provide further information, potentially including a brief statement of the facts, the issues to be decided, an identification of the applicable law, and the analysis and reasons that support the arbitrators' decision. When the award includes findings of fact and conclusions of law, the award generally will cover the same ground as is provided in a reasoned award, only in more detail and in a format that separates and numbers the individual findings and conclusions. The award will then conclude with a statement of the precise relief awarded, the date of the award, and the signatures of the arbitrators who join in the award. Legal requirements vary from state to state as to whether awards must be notarized and how they must be delivered.

If an interim award has been issued, the final award should reference the issuance and scope of the interim award. When an interim award has been issued in which the arbitrators finally resolved factual and legal issues that are also pertinent to the final award, the relevant portions of the interim award should be included *verbatim* in the final award. If, due to additional evidence or briefing, changes in the law, changed circumstances, or reconsideration by the arbitrators, the final award reaches different factual or legal conclusions from those preliminarily announced in an interim award, the final award should make clear how it differs from the interim award and why.

2. Detailed Sections of Award

a. Identifying Arbitral Process and Issues to be Determined

All awards should contain an identification of the issues determined by the arbitrators, together with a brief description of the proceeding and its procedural history.

There is no single "right" approach to award preparation, which must be sensitive to the realities of the particular case. Arbitrators' first and foremost objective, of course, is to ensure that they determine all of the submitted issues. Toward that end, when arbitrators have required the parties to provide a statement identifying the issues to be determined and the requested relief, they should rely on that statement in an effort to ensure that they fashion an award that addresses all issues and requests for relief. It is often useful to include in the section relating to the procedural record a statement that, at the end of the hearing, counsel for all parties were asked whether they had any further proofs to offer or witnesses to be heard and replied to this inquiry in the negative.

b. Analyzing the Law and Evidence

Reasoned awards should contain a concise analysis of the critical evidence and applicable law, and a discussion of how the arbitrators' view of the evidence and law relates to the arbitrators' decision.

When the format of the award permits, it is generally desirable to summarize the salient evidence and avoid overly detailed descriptions of particular exhibits or testimony. Any greater degree of specificity usually is not warranted, both because the parties are already familiar with the evidence and because an arbitration award generally will not serve as a type of "case law precedent" in which a detailed recitation of the facts might determine the decision's applicability to another case. Arbitrators might nevertheless desire to explain important credibility decisions or choose to indicate generally that the factual summary or findings incorporate their assessments of the credibility of the various witnesses, without going into detail as to why certain testimony was deemed more or less credible.

The award should explain the facts and identify the applicable law that supports the arbitrators' conclusions with respect to each issue determined in the award. When there is little or no dispute regarding what law applies to a particular issue, the discussion of the law may be quite minimal; in such instances, the evidence should be sufficiently discussed to explain the basis for the arbitrators' decision. In the circumstance in which the resolution of a disputed issue turns on the applicable law, it may be appropriate to explain the arbitrators' reasons for following and applying a particular interpretation of the law.

c. Awarding Section

Arbitrators must ensure that the awarding section of the award accurately describes the nature and extent of any relief that is granted or denied, and that it is clear from the award which parties are entitled to such relief and which have been determined to be liable.

When multiple parties are involved in the proceeding, the statement of relief awarded must be specific in identifying the parties against whom any and all relief is awarded, and the parties in favor of whom such relief is awarded. Awards of damages also should address whether pre- or post-award interest is awarded and, if so, in what amounts and at what rates, and should be accompanied by a reference to the legal authority supporting such an award. Any award of injunctive relief should specify the acts to be performed or enjoined and the dates and time period covered by any such relief. Any award of attorneys' fees and litigation expenses should reference the source of the arbitrators' authority to make such an award.

D. Preparation and Issuance of Award

The award must be issued in a timely manner, and should be carefully prepared in recognition of the fact that strict limitations on arbitrators' post-award authority, and the general absence of merits-based judicial review, make it unlikely that the award can or will be altered subsequent to its issuance.

Issues relating to the preparation of the award implicate subjects addressed in other chapters of the Guide, such as management of the arbitrators' deliberative process during the hearing, relations between neutral and non-neutral arbitrators, and post-award limitations on modifications and corrections of awards; those matters, therefore, will not be discussed here. It is nevertheless important to emphasize that award preparation is itself a project that must be managed. As is true in all arbitrations, the preparation and drafting of the award must be done in light of finality requirements that obligate responsible arbitrators to "get it right" before the final award issues.

One concern relating to the issuance of the final award often relates to the question of when to "close" the hearing. Some arbitral rules and contractual provisions provide that the arbitrators will lose jurisdiction if the award is not issued within a specified number of days—often thirty—after the "closing" of the hearing. Arbitrators should take care to set a schedule for award preparation that will result in issuance of the final award within that allowed time. In tripartite arbitrations, arbitrators should also ensure that their personal schedules permit adequate time for panel deliberations, which deliberations preferably should be scheduled to take place as soon as possible after the evidentiary hearing and any post-hearing briefing and arguments have been concluded.

Arbitrators should prepare the award with the realization that, once the final award is issued, they will effectively lose meaningful authority to correct any mistaken decisions on the merits. As a result, and because judicial review of awards normally does not extend to merits-based "appellate" review of the correctness of awards, the award is not only final in terms of the arbitrators' authority, but also is final in the sense that it serves to finally resolve the parties' dispute. If arbitrators have a concern that an issue is not clear, the last best opportunity for help—which typically comes from counsel—is to ask for it, perhaps by requesting additional briefing or supplemental argument, *before* the award is issued. While many arbitral rules expressly grant arbitrators the discretion to reopen the hearing in appropriate circumstances, arbitrators nonetheless should be aware that the request for additional briefing or argument can implicate the closing of the hearing and that, when necessary, they will need to either reopen the hearing or request that the parties extend any deadlines relating to the date by which the award must be issued.

III.   INTERIM AWARDS

In appropriate circumstances, arbitrators may issue "interim awards" that are preliminary and non-final in nature, but which advise the parties of the arbitrators' intended resolution of some, but not all, of the submitted issues.

As was generally mentioned in the introduction to this chapter, arbitrators sometimes have reason to issue awards that are not final in nature but which serve to advise the parties of their intended ruling on certain issues in the arbitration. These awards, which are most commonly referred to as "interim awards," typically are issued in bifurcated proceedings (in which case they normally adjudicate issues relating to liability) or when arbitrators have adjudicated all of the parties' claims but still need to address ancillary issues such as attorneys' fees or costs. The purpose of issuing such an interim award, as opposed to a "partial final award," is to avoid the implication that the arbitrators have lost at least some of their authority due to the application of *functus officio* principles, and to preserve the opportunity to ultimately incorporate all of the arbitrators' determinations into a single final award. Such objectives are perfectly logical, and most arbitral rules therefore expressly authorize arbitrators to issue "interim" or interlocutory awards. *See, e.g.,* AAA Rule 43(b) (authorizing the issuance of "interim, interlocutory, or partial rulings, orders, and awards"); CPR Rule 14.1 (authorizing the issuance of "final, interim, interlocutory and partial awards"); JAMS Rule 24(d) (authorizing "interim or partial rulings, orders and Awards").

In issuing interim awards for this purpose, however, arbitrators must be aware that some courts will not accept that the label "interim award," in and of itself, establishes that the award is not final with respect to the issues it addresses. *See, e.g., National Mutual Insurance Company v. First State Insurance Company,* 213 F. Supp. 2d 10, 16-17 (D. Mass. 2002) (holding that an "interim award" adjudicating liability issues in a bifurcated proceeding was final for purposes of FAA confirmation and vacatur proceedings); *The Home Insurance Company v. RHA/Pennsylvania Nursing Homes, Inc.,* 127 F. Supp. 2d 482 (S.D.N.Y. 2001) (finding that an "interim award" adjudicating certain issues was final and subject to FAA confirmation proceedings). Rather, such courts tend to analyze the content of the award, and the underlying arbitration proceedings, for the purpose of determining whether the arbitrators and/or the parties expected the interim award to contain a final determination of the issues addressed in the award.

These observations are particularly important with respect to arbitrations in which any subsequent confirmation or vacatur proceedings will be governed by the FAA. Some courts have ruled that, when an arbitrator issues an interim award that is final in nature, the time limitations, respectively under Sections 9 and 12 of the FAA, within which to commence a proceeding to confirm or vacate the interim award, begin to run upon the issuance of the award. *See National Mutual Insurance Company, supra.* As a consequence, under this line of cases, the issuance of an interim award that is even arguably final in nature might compel parties to commence such proceedings.

Given these factors, when arbitrators issue interim awards that are not intended to be final in nature, they should express that fact in the interim award. *See* CPR Rule 14.1 (authorizing arbitrators to issue interim awards and stating that the "Tribunal may state in its award whether or not it views the award as final for the purposes of any judicial proceedings in connection therewith"). Moreover, to the extent such a non-final interim award is issued, arbitrators must faithfully recognize that they are not *functus officio* with respect to the issues tentatively determined in the award and that they must reconsider their determination, or reopen the record, for good cause shown. Since all of these considerations can be accommodated by the careful drafting of the interim award, they should not serve to deter arbitrators from utilizing interim awards.

Indeed, most experienced arbitrators would argue that the use of non-final interim awards is a critical tool. Many arbitrators use the interim award as an effective device when there remains a need to address a prevailing party's claims for attorneys' fees and costs. Although a final award can be issued more expeditiously if the evidence relating to fees and costs is simply introduced along with the merits evidence at the hearing, many parties prefer to delay submission of such evidence until after arbitrators have resolved the merits of the parties' claims and defenses. This desire can be accommodated by adopting a two-step approach discussed in Chapter 9 § X, *supra*, that involves the initial issuance of an interim award determining all issues except those relating to fees and costs, followed by the subsequent filing of written applications and any objections concerning the fees and costs issues, and culminating in the issuance of a final award that incorporates not only the rulings contained in the interim award, but also the arbitrators' adjudication of the fees and costs issues.

When arbitrators choose to employ this two-step approach, they should take into account certain related matters. For example, arbitrators should not "close" the hearing after the conclusion of the first phase, thus triggering the due date for the final award. Moreover, to the extent arbitrators are inclined to offer the parties the option of utilizing either the one-step, or two-step, approach, they should raise that question early in the case, preferably no later than the preliminary conference, so that the scheduling of the bifurcated process can be taken into account at the time the remainder of the proceedings are scheduled.

When arbitrators do issue one or more interim awards, they should ensure that the final award fully incorporates all interim awards, whether by reference, by attaching the interim award to the final award, or by incorporating the language of the interim award *verbatim* into the final award. This last practice will provide a service to the parties in any subsequent confirmation or vacatur proceedings, since the parties will find it convenient to have a single document—in the form of a final award—reflecting the entirety of the arbitrators' rulings.

Since the best practice often is to incorporate interim awards into the arbitrators' final award *verbatim*, arbitrators normally should ensure that the form of an interim award conforms to the form the arbitrators anticipate the final award will take. In other words, if the final award is to contain reasons or, alternatively, findings of fact and conclusions of law, then the interim award also should take that form and should reflect the same level of specificity that the final award will contain.

IV.   PARTIAL FINAL AWARDS

Arbitrators may issue "partial final awards" in which the arbitrators finally determine some, but not all, of the submitted issues, with the caveat that the issuance of such an award will normally prohibit the arbitrators from reconsidering the merits of the issues decided in the partial award.

As was briefly mentioned in the introduction to this chapter, a "partial final award" is an award that does not dispose of the entirety of the case but does contain a final determination on some issues and therefore is subject to immediate confirmation and vacatur proceedings under Sections 9 and 12 of the FAA, respectively, and perhaps also under other state statutes. As was true with respect to non-final interim awards, most institutional rules expressly provide that arbitrators may issue partial final awards. *See, e.g.,* AAA Rule 43(b); CPR Rule 14.1; JAMS Rule 24(d). The FAA also generally acknowledges that partial final awards may be issued by arbitrators, and further acknowledges that such awards can be confirmed or vacated prior to the time the final award is issued. *See* 9 U.S.C. § 16(a)(1)(D). Indeed, in light of recent decisions such as those mentioned in the preceding section, it would appear that parties sometimes have compelling reasons to consider seeking the immediate confirmation or vacatur of partial final awards. While the RUAA and some, if not all, state statutes, do not expressly grant courts authority to confirm or vacate a partial final award prior to the issuance of the final award, some courts recently have recognized the finality of a "partial final award" and have determined that state courts have the jurisdiction to confirm or vacate those awards despite the fact that the final award has not yet been issued. *See, e.g., Hightower v. Superior Court,* 86 Cal. App. 4th 1415, 1419 (2001).

Partial final awards should be issued only when the parties' arbitration agreement or applicable rules compel their use or when arbitrators have determined that the issuance of one or more such awards is reasonably necessary to the efficient resolution of the closed portions of the proceeding and the dispute as a whole. When issuing a partial final award, arbitrators should explicitly reserve jurisdiction to issue a later final award on the remaining issues, and should expressly state that the partial final award does not include a determination of all the issues submitted to them.

Because a partial final award, by its very nature, cannot normally be altered by the arbitrators, it is important that arbitrators ensure that the form of a partial final award is consistent with the form the final award will take. Thus, when the final award will contain reasons or findings of fact and conclusions of law, the partial final award should also take that form. Just as importantly, all of the remaining details that should be included in a final award—*e.g.,* a complete description of the parties and the proceedings, and an awarding section that accurately describes the relief granted and denied—must be set forth with the same degree of specificity that would obtain had the partial final award been the final award in the proceeding.

V.   REMEDIES

A.   Authority to Craft Remedies

Subject to any limitations imposed by statute, the parties' agreement, or any applicable rules, arbitrators generally have wide latitude in determining the appropriate remedies in an arbitration proceeding.

Arbitrators generally have broad authority to craft remedies. *See, e.g.,* JAMS Rule 24(c) ("any remedy or relief that is just and equitable and within the scope of the Parties' agreement"); AAA Rule 43. Moreover, arbitrators generally are not restricted to granting only those remedies that would be available in a court of law. *See, e.g., Advanced Micro Devices, Inc. v. Intel Corp.,* 9 Cal. 4th 362, 385-87 (1994) (arbitrators' authority is broader than the remedies available in court so long as the remedy bears a "rational relationship" to the contract and its breach). *See also* RUAA § 21(c) ("the fact that such a remedy could not or would not be granted by the court is not a ground for refusing to confirm . . . or for vacating an award"). However, arbitrators' remedial powers can be limited by constraints set forth in the arbitration agreement. Remedies outside those limits can be vacated as acts in excess of arbitral power. *O'Flaherty v. Belgum,* 115 Cal. App. 4th 1044, 1055-56 (2004); *Jordan v. Department of Motor Vehicles,* 100 Cal. App. 4th 431, 450-453 (2002).

Arbitrators normally have the power to issue permanent injunctions, grant declaratory relief, order an accounting, and provide for other equitable remedies. *See, e.g.,* JAMS Rule 24(c). Some cases hold, however, that arbitrators are without power to appoint a receiver. There is also case law limiting arbitrators' power to issue injunctions in certain circumstances involving statutes providing for injunctive relief on behalf of the general public. *Broughton v. Cigna Healthplans of California,* 21 Cal. 4th 1066, 1079-80 (1999); *Cruz v. PacifiCare Health Systems, Inc.,* 30 Cal. 4th 303, 307 (2003).

B.   Punitive Damages

In the absence of a contractual provision to the contrary, arbitrators usually have the authority to issue an award of punitive damages in an appropriate case.

Cases applying either state arbitration law or the FAA and interpreting broadly worded arbitration clauses and institutional rules generally hold that punitive damages are within the arbitrators' powers to grant. *See* RUAA § 21(a) and Comment No. 1 (collecting cases). Thus, while there are some older cases to the contrary, the weight of authority now holds that arbitrators do not need a specific grant of power to authorize an award of punitive damages. Nonetheless, particularly in cases that do not involve interstate commerce or maritime transactions and in which the FAA therefore does not apply, arbitrators must consider whether other applicable laws prohibit an award of punitive damages. Conversely, contractual clauses that prohibit punitive damages awards are generally enforceable, rendering an award of such damages "in excess of powers." *See, e.g., Investment Partners, L.P. v. Glamour Shots Licensing, Inc.* 298 F.3d 314, 318, n. 1 (5th Cir. 2002); *Mastrobuono v. Shearson Lehman Hutton, Inc.,* 514 U.S. 52 (1995).

C.   Attorneys' Fees, Arbitrators' and Arbitral Institution Fees, and Costs

In the absence of a specific statute, contractual provision, or rule, arbitrators normally do not have authority to award attorneys' fees, arbitrator or arbitral institution fees, or costs to a prevailing party.

1. Attorneys' Fees

In arbitration, just as in litigation, the "American Rule" applies, with the result that an award of attorneys' fees requires a contractual or statutory basis. Generally, arbitrators are empowered to grant attorneys' fees whenever such relief would be allowed by law in a civil action. *See, e.g.,* RUAA § 21(b). Some institutional rules (*e.g.,* CPR 16.2(d)) provide that attorneys' fees may be awarded in the arbitration. AAA Rule 43(d)(ii) is unique in providing that attorneys' fees may be awarded not only when authorized by law or the parties' arbitration agreement, but also "if all parties have requested such an award." In instances in which the parties have agreed to utilize such rules, and the parties have not otherwise agreed that attorneys' fees and costs may not be awarded, such rules serve to provide a contractual basis for an award of fees and costs. Moreover, the parties certainly can contractually provide that the arbitrators must award attorneys' fees to the prevailing party, and arbitrators therefore must faithfully comply with any such provision. *See, e.g., DiMarco v. Chaney,* 31 Cal. App. 4th 1809 (1995) (arbitrator exceeded his power by denying attorneys' fees when the arbitration agreement provided that the prevailing party "shall" be entitled to such fees). Obviously, the parties also can contractually provide that arbitrators do not have authority to award attorneys' fees, and arbitrators must also comply with that provision.

2. *Arbitrators' and Arbitral Institution Fees and Expenses*

Most institutional rules acknowledge the parties' right to contractually define and/or limit arbitrators' authority to allocate arbitrators' and arbitral institution fees and expenses in the final award. *See, e.g.,* AAA Rule 50; JAMS Rule 24(f); CPR Rule 16.3. The rules differ, however, with respect to the situation in which the parties have not reached an agreement on the issue. For example, JAMS Rules 24(f) and 31 provide (1) that in the absence of an agreement by the parties or applicable law, the parties generally can only be held to be obligated to pay their pro-rata share of such fees, but (2) that in the circumstance in which an opposing party has failed to deposit its proportional share of fees, or has deposited a lesser sum, arbitrators may enter an award permitting a party to recover any excess deposits it made with JAMS. In contrast, the AAA and CPR rules provide that in the absence of an agreement by the parties, arbitrators may exercise their discretion in assessing such fees and expenses in the final award. *See* AAA Rule 50; CPR Rules 16.2 and 16.3.

3. *Other Costs and Expenses*

The institutional rules are even more divergent with respect to arbitrators' authority to award other types of costs and expenses. The CPR rules are particularly specific in this regard and clearly delineate a broad variety of costs that may be assessed in the final award in the absence of a contrary agreement by the parties. *See* CPR Rules 16.2 and 16.3 (generally permitting arbitrators to assess the "costs of expert advice and other assistance engaged by the Tribunal," travel and other expenses incurred by witnesses, costs for legal representation and expert advice and testimony, and the costs of transcripts and hearing facilities). Conversely, while the AAA rules also permit arbitrators to award costs relating to witnesses or proof "produced at the direct request" of arbitrators, the AAA rules specifically state that "[t]he expenses for either side shall be paid by the party producing such witnesses." AAA Rule 50. The JAMS rules provide no further guidance on the topic of costs and expenses and arbitrators, thus, must seek guidance from applicable law when determining whether they have authority to assess such costs and expenses in their award.

The above-mentioned distinctions in the AAA, CPR, and JAMS rules illustrate that arbitrators must be familiar with the provisions of any applicable institutional rules when determining whether to award fees, expenses, and/or costs. Arbitrators also must be cognizant of any applicable law that might determine whether fees and costs may be awarded. When arbitrators are unsure of the intent of a particular rule or applicable law, the best practice is to request the parties to present either written and/or oral argument on the issue. Finally, it should be noted that while arbitrators necessarily have the authority to interpret institutional rules, some institutional rules provide for an internal mechanism by which, in the absence of a majority consensus on a tripartite panel, the institution itself will provide guidance with respect to the meaning and intent of the rule. *See, e.g.,* AAA Rule 53.

4. *The Issuance of Interim or Partial Awards Pending Determinations Relating to Fees and Expenses*

When it is necessary to conduct further proceedings for the purpose of allowing the prevailing party to submit affidavits and other material in support of a request for attorneys' fees, arbitrators must ensure that they do not prematurely issue a "final award" reflecting their decision on the merits of the parties' claims. Rather, in order to ensure that they retain jurisdiction to adjudicate the attorneys' fee issue, arbitrators' determinations on the merits should be contained in an interim award, or a partial final award, or in such other form of award that achieves that purpose. If arbitrators elect to utilize an interim award, the ultimate final award should not only reflect their ruling on the attorneys' fee issue, but should incorporate their prior determinations by adopting one of the alternatives discussed in the above sections pertaining to interim and final awards.

D.   Sanctions

When arbitrators formally issue "sanctions" against a party or counsel, such sanctions should be reflected in an award that is final in nature.

As was discussed in Chapter 7 § III(J), *supra*, arbitrators often have the authority to issue a broad variety of sanctions. Because sanctions essentially provide a form of relief that is inherently "final" in nature, the issuance of sanctions usually should be memorialized in a written award that is, itself, final and thus subject to confirmation and enforcement. Of course, it is not always necessary to issue formal sanctions in order to ensure compliant conduct by parties and counsel. A warning that sanctions may be included in a final award can serve as an effective deterrent against improper conduct by a party or counsel; when the offending party or lawyer becomes aware that such conduct might actually influence a determination on the merits or be memorialized in writing, that party or individual is more likely to reconsider its actions and to become more compliant with the arbitrators' expectations or orders.

In instances in which arbitrators have determined that a party or counsel must be sanctioned in a final award for recalcitrant or abusive conduct, arbitrators should consider whether such sanctions are more likely to be enforced by a reviewing court when the sanctions relate to a form of relief or determination that is clearly within the scope of the arbitrators' discretionary authority. For example, arbitrators might prefer to sanction the offending party by providing in a final award that the offending party shall pay all or a portion of the aggrieved party's fees and/or costs. Similarly, the arbitrators might conclude that it is within their authority to sanction a recalcitrant party by stating in a reasoned award that certain evidence lacked credibility due to the offending party's obstructive conduct. In all such cases, arbitrators must ensure that their reasoning, and the ensuing award, are not infected by any bias that might have arisen due to the nature of the objectionable conduct.

Finally, in instances in which arbitrators conclude that sanctions are not only permissible but are warranted, they might further conclude that it is necessary to keep the hearing "open" in order to permit the parties to submit additional materials relevant to the arbitrators' consideration of the sanctions issue. In such an instance, just as pertains in the circumstance in which arbitrators conduct supplementary proceedings on the issue of attorneys' fees, they must take due precautions—for example, by issuing an interim award or by obtaining the parties' agreement regarding when the record is closed and the award is due—to ensure that they do not lose jurisdiction and become *functus officio* prior to the time the sanctions issue is resolved.

CHAPTER 11

POST-AWARD MATTERS

In addressing post-award matters, arbitrators' goals are to act
promptly and appropriately, while avoiding (1) alteration of
the award, except on the limited grounds permitted by
applicable law and rules, and (2) conduct that might
give rise to allegations of partiality or bias.

I. LIMITED GROUNDS FOR POST-AWARD RELIEF

A. Doctrine of *Functus Officio*

An arbitration has a finite life. The common law doctrine of
functus officio thus holds that once arbitrators render a final decision,
they cease to have jurisdiction over the dispute and have no authority
to alter the final award. This doctrine is based on an "unwillingness to
permit one who is not a judicial officer and who acts informally and
sporadically, to re-examine a final decision which he has already
rendered, because of the potential evil of outside communication and
unilateral influence which might affect a new conclusion." *La Vale
Plaza, Inc. v. R.S. Noonan, Inc.,* 378 F.2d 569, 572 (3d Cir. 1967).

Some courts are reluctant to apply the *functus officio* doctrine.
Indeed, courts occasionally ignore the doctrine altogether and remand
cases to an arbitration panel without even mentioning the rule. This
tendency is due perhaps to the fact that some courts view the doctrine,
which "originated in the bad old days when judges were hostile to
arbitration and ingenious in hamstringing it," as antiquated. *See, e.g.,
Glass Workers International Union, Local 182B v. Excelsior Foundry Co.,*
56 F.3d 844, 846 (7th Cir. 1995) (*quoting Courier-Citizen Co. v. Boston
Electrotypers Union No. 11,* 702 F.2d 273, 278 (1ˢᵗ Cir. 1983)).

Nevertheless, the doctrine remains alive and well, albeit somewhat misunderstood.

1. Arbitrators' Lack of Authority to Alter Determination on the Merits After Issuance of a Final Award

In the absence of a contractual provision to the contrary, arbitrators are prohibited from modifying a final award for the purpose of correcting legal or factual substantive errors that affect the arbitrators' determination on the merits.

As is true of many aspects of arbitration, the relevance of the *functus officio* doctrine depends, in the first instance, on whether the parties' arbitration agreement has provided for arbitration procedures that render the doctrine moot. Since there is no legal prohibition against parties agreeing that arbitrators may reconsider the merits of their awards, parties are free to provide that *functus officio* principles do not apply or apply only after the passage of a stated amount of time. *See UHC Management Co., Inc. v. Computer Sciences Corp.*, 148 F.3d 992, 997 (8th Cir. 1998) ("Parties may chose to be governed by whatever rules they wish regarding how arbitration itself will be conducted"); Ian R. Macneil, Richard E. Speidel & Thomas J. Stipanowich, 3 FEDERAL ARBITRATION LAW § 37.6.4.2 (1994). In the absence of such an agreement, however, and unless the applicable rules provide otherwise, the principles underlying the doctrine of *functus officio* strictly prohibit arbitrators from reconsidering the merits of a case once they have issued a final award.

This principle is illustrated by *Landis v. Pinkertons, Inc.*, 122 Cal. App. 4th 985, 991 (2004), in which the arbitrator erred in applying the law pertaining to damages for emotional distress. In granting a post-award motion filed by the respondent, the arbitrator "corrected" the award by striking that portion of the award granting damages for emotional distress. On review, the court, while not expressly referring to *functus officio*, observed that the arbitrator's alteration of the award was not based on the limited statutory grounds upon which an arbitrator may correct or clarify an award and, as a consequence, held that the corrected award could not be confirmed but the erroneous award could.

For the same reasons relating to the perceived need for "finality" in arbitral decisions, arbitrators are prohibited from correcting substantive errors relating to the application of evidence or factual matters in a final award. Thus, in *WMA Securities, Inc. v. Wynn*, 105 F. Supp. 2d 833, 840 (S.D. Ohio 2000), *aff'd*, 32 Fed. Appx., 2002 WL 504965, No. 00-4232 (6th Cir. Apr. 1, 2002), the court applied the *functus officio* doctrine in an instance in which the arbitrators had purported to correct an award, entered in a rescission case, that had ordered the respondent to return the purchase price of securities to the claimant without requiring the claimant to return the securities.

As was discussed in Chapter 5 § VIII and Chapter 10 § III-IV, *supra*, interim and partial awards themselves can be considered to be "final" when such awards are intended to conclusively determine the merits of separate issues or claims. Because the doctrine of *functus officio* is inextricably related to the finality of arbitral awards, arbitrators must be aware that they can be held to be *functus officio* with respect to the issues or claims determined in such interim or partial awards. *See Trade & Transport, Inc. v. Natural Petroleum Charterers, Inc.*, 931 F.2d 191, 195 (2d Cir. 1991).

2. *Exceptions to* Functus Officio

There are three generally recognized exceptions to the doctrine of *functus officio*. These exceptions are designed to ensure that an award may be corrected or clarified to render effective the "intent" of the arbitrators. For similar reasons, Section 11 of the FAA permits a court to correct or modify a final award "so as to effect the intent thereof." 9 U.S.C. § 11.

a. *Clerical, Computational, and Similar Errors*

Arbitrators generally retain authority to correct clerical, computational, or other similar errors in a final award.

The first recognized exception to *functus officio* is that arbitrators retain the authority to correct a clerical, typographical, computational, or similar mistake that is evident on the face of the award. *See La Vale, supra,* at 573. Errors of this nature tend to involve mistranscriptions of data or misdescriptions of persons, places, or things. The very nature of such errors usually demonstrates that their correction will not be inconsistent with the arbitrators' intent as reflected in the final award.

b. Submitted but Unadjudicated Issues

Arbitrators generally retain the authority to correct or supplement an award to determine an issue that had been submitted for determination but that, for whatever reason, the arbitrators had failed to resolve.

The second generally recognized exception to *functus officio* permits arbitrators to decide an issue after they have rendered an award when the award fails to adjudicate an issue that had been submitted for determination. *Id.* Again, the exception does not jeopardize the finality of the original award, since the award in such a circumstance actually is silent with respect to the relevant issue.

c. Clarifications Regarding Intent of Award

Arbitrators generally retain the authority to issue a clarification of the intent of the original award.

The third generally recognized exception to *functus officio* provides that arbitrators may clarify an award when there is demonstrable ambiguity regarding the intention of the award or relating to the question whether the parties' claims and defenses have been fully determined. *Id.* In so clarifying an award, arbitrators must exercise every caution to ensure that the clarification does not in any way alter the intention of the original award. Occasionally, the exercise of attempting to clarify an award reveals that the reasoning that gave rise to the original award was erroneous. In such a circumstance, arbitrators must avoid the impulse to correct the substantive error in the original award and must recognize that their original determination is final and that they are without power to correct it.

B. Interrelationship Between the *Functus Officio* Doctrine, Institutional Rules, and Arbitration Statutes

In determining the scope of their post-award authority, arbitrators should consider the interrelationship between any applicable institutional rules, the relevant arbitration law, and the doctrine of *functus officio*.

Most of the major domestic institutional arbitration rules have expressly adopted the *functus officio* doctrine together with the recognized exceptions thereto. Thus, when parties agree to conduct their arbitration under these rules, they contractually accept the application of the doctrine to their arbitration and further agree that, in order to obtain the type of corrections, modifications, and clarifications provided for under these rules, they must seek such relief within the time periods stated in the rules. *See, e.g.,* JAMS Rule 24(i); AAA Rule 46; CPR Rule 14.5; NAF Rules 42 and 43(A)(4). *But see* NAF Rule 43(A)(2) (permitting reconsideration of a final award not only on the grounds that it is ambiguous, but also because the award "contains evident material mistakes"). Most court decisions that interpret institutional rules relating to an arbitrator's limited post-award authority recognize that those rules are patterned after the common law exceptions to *functus officio;* such court decisions, therefore, typically apply a traditional common law *functus officio* analysis in determining whether the arbitrators exceeded their authority under the institutional rules when granting, or refusing to grant, post-award relief.

Some institutional rules contemplate that the governing arbitration law might serve to supplement those rules insofar as concerns arbitrators' authority to grant post-award relief. Thus, the AAA's Guide for Commercial Arbitrators (available at www.adr.org/Guides), which is intended to assist arbitrators in applying the AAA Rules, suggests (1) that arbitrators may respond to a joint request for clarification, even though the AAA Rules do not provide that arbitrators may clarify an award, and (2) that the law of the jurisdiction might be relevant in defining the scope of the arbitrators' authority to modify or correct an award.

While the FAA does not expressly codify the *functus officio* doctrine, it is nonetheless clear that the doctrine applies to arbitrations governed by FAA procedures. In applying the FAA, courts routinely acknowledge the tenets of the doctrine and hold that, in the absence of an applicable rule or contractual provision to the contrary, arbitrators have only the limited authority to grant the forms of post-award relief contemplated by the exceptions to *functus officio*.

The doctrine is even more firmly established in the Uniform Arbitration Act ("UAA") and the RUAA, since both uniform acts expressly recognize arbitrators' authority to grant only those forms of post-award relief permitted by the traditional exceptions to *functus officio*. *See* UAA § 9; RUAA § 20 and Comments 2 and 3 (acknowledging the application of the *functus officio* doctrine to arbitrations conducted under the uniform acts). As a result of the general incorporation of the common law doctrine of *functus officio* into domestic institutional arbitration rules, the UAA, the RUAA, and the FAA, the principles underlying *functus officio* apply to virtually all commercial domestic arbitrations unless the parties contractually agree otherwise.

C.   *Sua Sponte* Corrections of Clerical and Similar Errors and Clarifications to Awards

Depending on the applicable law and institutional rules, arbitrators sometimes are authorized to act independently to correct clerical or similar errors in an award, or to clarify the intent of an award.

In some instances, arbitrators can act on their own initiative to alter a final award. For example, in *Cadillac Uniform & Linen Supply, Inc. v. Union de Tronquistas Local 901*, 920 F. Supp. 19, 22-23 (D.P.R. 1996), the reasoning in the original award expressed the view that the claimant, whose employment had been terminated on the ground that he had been fighting with a fellow employee, should receive the same punishment as his antagonist—*i.e.,* a two-week suspension. Despite this determination, the arbitrator ordered that the claimant be reinstated without pay; this remedy, in effect, imposed a one-year suspension. Subsequent to the issuance of the final award, the arbitrator changed the award *sua sponte* such that the altered award provided that the claimant would be reinstated with pay save for the two-week suspension period. Even though the amended award greatly increased the amount of money that the claimant was to receive, the court ruled that "the arbitrator was not reconsidering his award but just clarifying his intention" and the corrected award was therefore confirmed.

Some institutional rules expressly allow arbitrators to act on their own initiative for the purpose of correcting clerical or mathematical errors, or clarifying ambiguities, in an award. *See, e.g.,* CPR Rule 14.5; JAMS Rule 24(i). In order to ensure early finality, however, those rules provide short periods of time within which such corrections may be made. In instances in which the arbitrator realizes, subsequent to the issuance of a final award, that the award contains a significant error not relating to the determination on the merits, arbitrators should examine the applicable rules and arbitration statute and determine whether they are empowered to correct the error. Such *sua sponte* corrections, when permissible, should be made before the parties are forced to request a clarification.

II. ISSUES ARISING ON REMAND OF FINAL AWARD

Arbitrators, and most institutional rules, tend to assume that final awards will never be remanded to the arbitrator by a reviewing court. As a consequence, institutional rules fail to provide meaningful guidance in such circumstances. Due to this lack of guidance, or for other reasons, arbitrators occasionally are confronted with difficult and potentially awkward problems when a court remands an arbitration award to the arbitrators for correction or clarification.

A.   Following the Court's Remand Instructions

On remand, arbitrators are required to comply faithfully with the instructions of the reviewing court.

Arbitrators must take every precaution to ensure that any corrections or alterations to an award on remand are limited to conform to the court's instructions. Unless ordered to do so by the court, arbitrators may not rehear or redetermine issues that were resolved in the original award. *Paperhandlers Union No. 1 v. U.S. Trucking Corp.*, 441 F. Supp. 469, 474 (S.D.N.Y. 1977). Thus, in *Domino Group, Inc. v. Charlie Parker Memorial Foundation*, 985 F.2d 417, 420 (8th Cir. 1993), the Court of Appeals for the Eighth Circuit held that when the arbitrator not only satisfied the court's directive to clarify the award ordering specific performance but also added for the first time a provision for monetary damages as an alternative to compliance with the specific performance award, the arbitrator exceeded his authority and the award on remand violated the principles of *functus officio*.

This principle can present complicated issues. For example, some arbitration agreements provide that the final award will not be supported by a statement of reasons. Despite the existence of such a contractual provision, the court's directions on remand might require the arbitrators to explain the reasoning underlying the award. In such an instance, arbitrators must decide whether to follow the court's directive or, alternatively, to respond to the remand order by observing they believe they lack the authority to issue such a statement of reasons. While there is no definitive answer to questions such as these, the case law strongly suggests that better practice is to comply with the court's directive. Considerations relating to the objective of achieving finality, the proper respect and deference arbitrators must accord to courts that oversee compliance with arbitration laws, and the possibility that arbitrators will be viewed as acting in "manifest disregard of the law" if they intentionally disregard the court's order, all support the proposition that arbitrators cannot disregard formal judicial directives simply because the arbitrators do not agree that those orders are well-founded. If any parties believe that the court's remand instructions are improper, they may, of course, move the court to reconsider those instructions.

B.   Remands and Insufficient Arbitration Records

If the court's order on remand permits the arbitrators to review the arbitration record in order to satisfy the court's directive, the arbitrators may take any reasonable measures to ensure that such record is available to them.

Due to the formal and public nature of state and federal court proceedings, all rules of civil procedure provide for the creation of a "record" of such proceedings. *See, e.g.,* Fed. R. App. P. 10(a) (describing the contents of "the record" on appeal, including the original exhibits and papers filed in the district court, any transcripts, and the docket relating to the trial court proceedings); Fed. R. Civ. P. 79(a) (requiring the court clerk to keep a "civil docket" that identifies all pleadings, orders, or other materials filed by the parties or the court). Institutional arbitration rules, in contrast, not only do not explicitly require that an official "record" be kept but, in some instances, implicitly acknowledge that an official "record" of the arbitration will not necessarily be maintained. *See, e.g.,* AAA Rule 26 (granting the parties or the arbitrator the *discretion* to designate a transcript as "the official record" of the proceeding); CPR Arbitration Appeal Procedure, Rule 1.3(b) (providing that no appeal may be presented by agreement to an arbitral appeal panel *unless* there is a "record" that includes "all hearings and all evidence (including exhibits, deposition transcripts, [and] affidavits admitted into evidence)").

Given the informal manner in which arbitral institutions, arbitrators, and parties often administer the arbitration "record," it should come as no surprise that a complete record may not be available when an award is remanded by a court, sometimes years after it was issued. The mere passage of time might cause it to be difficult to locate or identify the materials that comprise the record; the document destruction policy of an arbitral institution or arbitrator might have resulted in the disposal of the record; the parties might no longer employ the same counsel, or counsel might not longer be with the same firm. Thus, arbitrators are occasionally faced with the difficult problem of identifying, or reassembling, a record of the original arbitration proceeding for the purpose of refreshing their recollection of the issues and evidence.

Under these circumstances, arbitrators must attempt to satisfy the court's directives and, therefore, may solicit assistance from the parties. It is possible that the parties have duplicate copies of some materials, or that the arbitrators' memory may be refreshed by other means. Obviously, in seeking such assistance, arbitrators must take every precaution to ensure that their review is limited to conformance with the court's instructions. They may not supplement the record unless permitted by the court's directive.

When the arbitration is being administered by an institution that maintains a document destruction policy, arbitrators should consider advising the parties of that policy and the related fact that their personal records and files relating to the arbitration will no longer be available after the time stated in the policy. Similarly, in an ad hoc arbitration involving arbitrators who enforce their own document destruction policy, arbitrators should not only consider advising the parties at the preliminary conference of the existence of that policy, but also should feel free, upon the reasonable request of one or both of the parties, to alter that policy with respect to that arbitration.

C.   Fees and Costs Incurred in Addressing Awards on Remand

Prior to the issuance of a corrected or clarified award on remand, arbitrators should take such reasonable actions as are necessary to best assure the payment of any additional fees or costs occasioned by the remand order.

Arbitrators are entitled to be compensated when they are required to provide additional services, or incur additional costs, as the result of a court-ordered remand of an award. Moreover, a very real possibility exists that the parties will incur additional attorneys' fees and/or costs as a result of the remand order. Since most institutional rules do not address how arbitrators are to handle remands, those rules also fail to address cost and fee issues under such circumstances. Arbitrators generally may take such reasonable measures as might have been taken at the commencement of the arbitration to ensure the payment of all such fees and costs. For instance, arbitrators can require the parties to make an advance payment of the fees and costs that they estimate will be incurred, and can order one party to advance all of such fees and costs when the opposing party refuses to make advance payment of its share. In the situation in which it appears that a party might refuse to pay its share of any arbitrator costs and fees, arbitrators should consider providing for the payment of such costs or fees in the corrected or clarified award. Similarly, arbitrators might be authorized to award additional attorneys' fees if such fees were awardable in the first instance.

III. POST-AWARD ETHICAL ISSUES

No single ethical standard defines what conduct by arbitrators is appropriate subsequent to the issuance of a final award. Depending on the rules of a particular arbitral institution and applicable law, arbitrators might not be governed exclusively by the AAA/ABA Code. Nevertheless, the various codes and guidelines that do exist, including the International Bar Association Guidelines on Conflicts of Interest in International Arbitration and certain state statutes pertaining to arbitrators' ethics, all reflect the policy objectives of protecting the integrity of the arbitration process and ensuring that arbitrators maintain the appearance of impartiality and independence subsequent to the issuance of a final award.

A. Maintaining Confidentiality of the Arbitration Proceeding

Subsequent to the issuance of a final award, arbitrators must ensure the ongoing confidentiality of the arbitration proceeding.

Arbitrators must maintain the confidentiality of all matters relating to any arbitration proceeding. *See, e.g.,* AAA/ABA Code, Canon VI(B). Under Canon X of the AAA/ABA Code, this obligation applies both to neutral and to non-neutral arbitrators, but is subject to exceptions created by applicable law or by agreement of parties.

The obligation of confidentiality with respect to any arbitration is permanent; that is, it does not cease to exist when an award is rendered. Reference in a speech, writing or résumé to an arbitration in which an arbitrator has served should be generic, and comments by an arbitrator in response to inquiries about counsel, a witness, or other arbitrators who were involved in an arbitration should not disclose confidential information.

Consistent with these standards, arbitrators, of course, are expected not to use any information learned in an arbitration for their own personal advantage. AAA/ABA Code, Canon VI(A).

B. Assisting the Parties in Understanding the Award

In the absence of a valid, timely, and formal request for clarification of an award, arbitrators should refrain from responding to requests that they assist the parties in understanding the intent of the award.

Except as provided by law or by agreement of the parties, including applicable arbitration rules, it is unethical for arbitrators to assist a party by clarifying or interpreting an award after it has been rendered, or by aiding a party in its effort to enforce or challenge the award. *See* AAA/ABA Code, Canon VI(C). Statutes such as Section 703.5 of the California Evidence Code thus make an arbitrator "incompetent" to give testimony in a post-award proceeding, except in limited circumstances such as those involving disciplinary proceedings relating to the arbitrator. Even the submission by an arbitrator in a post-award proceeding of a written declaration supporting the award has been criticized as "overexuberant" and "unseemly." *Cobler v. Stanley, Barber, Southard, Brown & Associates*, 217 Cal. App. 3rd 518, 529, n.7 (1990).

C. Post-Award Relationships with Parties and Counsel

For a reasonable or specified period of time subsequent to the issuance of the award, arbitrators should refrain from entering into relationships with the parties or counsel that could be interpreted as evidencing partiality.

The creation of a formal or personal relationship between an arbitrator and one of the parties or counsel immediately subsequent to the issuance of a final award might be interpreted as demonstrating that the arbitrator had some expectation of a relationship that influenced the arbitrator's decision on the merits of the arbitration proceeding. For that reason, the various codes of ethics and some state statutes address whether and when such relationships may come into existence. For example, under the AAA/ABA Code, a "reasonable period" should pass before arbitrators enter into any business, professional, or personal relationship, or acquire any financial interest in a former party, that might reasonably create the impression that they had been influenced in their decision by anticipation or expectation of such a relationship or interest. *See* AAA/ABA Code, Canon I(C).

Similarly, in California a neutral arbitrator is prohibited for two years after the conclusion of any arbitration from accepting any gift, bequest, favor, or honorarium from any party to the arbitration or any other person whose interests were involved. *See* Ethics Standards for Neutral Arbitrators in Contractual Arbitrations (Division VI to Appendix to California Rules of Court), Standard 11(b). Obviously, the variety of "relationships" that might arise subsequent to the issuance of an award is infinite, and not all such "relationships" would be prohibited. For example, a "relationship" of sorts arises when an individual agrees to serve as a neutral arbitrator in an arbitration proceeding. Logically, such a relationship would not be violative of the principles discussed above. Nevertheless, the compelling need to ensure the integrity of arbitration awards dictates that arbitrators should be particularly sensitive to the issue of what relationships are permissible and should fully analyze the propriety of entering into any such relationship in the first instance.

CHAPTER 12

INTERNATIONAL ARBITRATION

Arbitrators who serve in international arbitrations should understand the many characteristics that distinguish such arbitrations from domestic commercial arbitrations as well as the features that they have in common.

I. INTRODUCTION

International arbitration, while probably centuries old, arrived in full force in the United States only during the past thirty-five years. Prior to that time, lawyers generally were wary of submitting disputes to international arbitration due to their uncertainty about, and unfamiliarity with, the applicable laws and procedures, as well as the foreign languages, long delays, and expensive costs that were associated with such arbitration. In addition, most agreements to submit future disputes to arbitration were unenforceable; only agreements to arbitrate existing disputes were capable of specific enforcement.

The first major defining event for international arbitration was the advent of the 1958 Convention on the Recognition and Enforcement of Foreign Arbitral Awards (the "New York Convention"). The United States ratified the New York Convention in 1970, and Congress implemented the Convention through the enactment of Chapter 2 of the FAA. The New York Convention, now with over 135 signatory countries, has two major aims: (1) the enforcement of international arbitration agreements, and (2) the recognition and enforcement of foreign arbitral awards. The New York Convention generally provides that, when the court of a contracting state "is seized of an action" involving an international commercial dispute with respect to which the parties have made a written agreement to arbitrate, the court shall, upon the request of one of the parties, "refer the parties to arbitration" unless it finds that the agreement is "null and void, inoperative or incapable of being performed." In view of the fact that there currently are no treaties that mandate the enforcement of contractual agreements to resolve international disputes by other ADR procedures, such as mediation and conciliation, it may be said that the pro-enforcement nature of the New York Convention accords to international arbitration a special and significant status.

The second major defining event relating to the maturation of international arbitration was the promulgation in 1976 of the United Nations Commission on International Trade Law Arbitration Rules (the "UNCITRAL Rules"). These standard procedural rules for ad hoc international arbitrations, which serve as an alternative to the rules of arbitral institutions, have proved to be very useful in promoting arbitration. Utilization of the rules is increasing and the rules thus have had an influence on the development of the third important defining event relating to international arbitration—the UNCITRAL Model Law.

The most important aspect of the Model Law is that it establishes uniform processes by which national courts can confirm, modify, and/or vacate international awards that are made in their territory. The Model Law, in essence, complements the New York Convention, because the Convention does not specify the grounds on which an international award may be vacated or confirmed by a national court of the award's origin. Rather, the Convention only specifies the grounds on which a "foreign award"—*i.e.,* an international award made in a country other than that of the reviewing court—may be "recognized and enforced" by that court. While many countries have adopted the UNCITRAL Model Law, the United States has not. Instead, when a U.S. court considers an application to confirm or vacate an international award made in the United States, the FAA applies. Awards that are international in nature, but which are made on the soil of the reviewing court, are generally referred to as "nondomestic awards," a term that emanates from Article I of the New York Convention.

Finally, as a prefatory matter it should be emphasized that, while there are many important distinctions between international and domestic arbitrations, some of the management practices discussed in previous chapters of the Guide may be usefully employed in international arbitrations as well. Arbitrators serving in international arbitrations thus may wish to consider, and to discuss with the parties, the possible use of such domestic practices in appropriate instances.

II.   APPOINTMENT PROCESS

A.   Initial Communication Regarding Possible Appointment

Arbitrators should neither solicit appointments to serve in a specific international arbitration, nor disseminate information that inaccurately portrays their qualifications to serve in international arbitrations.

The appointment process for international arbitrators consists of three phases: (1) communication from the parties or arbitral institution to the arbitrator candidate concerning the possible appointment; (2) determination by the arbitrator regarding willingness, fitness, and availability to serve; and (3) disclosure of any information necessary to allow the parties and/or arbitral institution to make an informed decision regarding the appointment. Prior to the formal commencement of this process, consideration of the arbitrator's *curriculum vitae* may be important. Arbitrators should therefore ensure that the information provided in a CV or published in an international arbitration directory is accurate and current. Implicit in the first phase of the appointment process is the recognition that it would be inappropriate for prospective arbitrators to solicit a specific appointment. Communication from a party or parties or arbitral institution about a possible appointment is, of course, necessary and appropriate, but is subject to certain restrictions.

B.   Arbitrators' Determination of Willingness, Fitness, and Availability to Serve

In order to determine their fitness and availability to serve in an international arbitration, arbitrators must first gain a meaningful understanding of the nature of the dispute, the underlying arbitration agreement, the applicable procedural rules, the identity of the parties and counsel, and a variety of other potential considerations.

While the ultimate decision concerning an appointment is made by the parties or arbitral institution, or sometimes a court, arbitrators must take responsibility in the second phase of the appointment process for assuring that it is appropriate for them to take on the matter based on considerations relating to the general nature of the dispute, the arbitrators' qualifications and experience, and availability. Most importantly, arbitrators must be confident of being able to fairly and efficiently determine the dispute, which implies, among other things, impartiality and independence.

Regardless of whether arbitrators will serve as the sole arbitrator, co-arbitrator, or chairperson, they should immediately review certain basic documents, including the arbitration agreement and the arbitration rules. The arbitration clause in the underlying contract is particularly significant, because it provides the general framework of arbitrators' responsibilities. Just as importantly, arbitrators should determine (1) whether there are any time limitations relating to the selection of the chair; (2) whether any specific qualifications are required of them; (3) what law applies in determining the parties' dispute; and (4) whether institutional rules or ad hoc procedures apply. When an institution is named as the administrator of the arbitration, arbitrators should confirm familiarity with the current version of that institution's rules.

The five most commonly employed sets of international rules are similar but nonetheless have major differences in procedures. *See,* International Chamber of Commerce Rules of Arbitration (the "ICC

Rules"); International Centre for Dispute Resolution (American Arbitration Association) Rules (the "AAA International Rules"); London Court of International Arbitration Rules (the "LCIA Rules"); Stockholm Chamber of Commerce Rules (the "SCC Rules"); and the UNCITRAL Rules. For example, under the ICC Rules, the parties nominate arbitrators and the ICC Court makes the appointment after reviewing the arbitrator's statement of independence. In contrast, under other institutional rules the established practice is to confirm the parties' arbitrator appointments unless the arbitration provision or an arbitrator disclosure mandates otherwise. Since the UNCITRAL Rules are designed for ad hoc proceedings, there is no one institution that oversees the arbitrator appointment process under those rules. Instead, Article 7 provides a mechanism whereby either party may request the Secretary-General of the Permanent Court of Arbitration at The Hague to designate an appointing authority. Most parties generally prefer to name their own appointing authority under the UNCITRAL Rules. The ICC, AAA, LCIA, and SCC thus all occasionally act as appointing authorities in arbitrations conducted under the UNCITRAL Rules.

C.   Arbitrator Disclosures

Arbitrators must disclose all matters that might give rise to justifiable doubts concerning their impartiality or independence.

Having learned the general nature of the dispute, the identity of parties and counsel, and other factors affecting availability and fitness to serve—including such matters as the place of arbitration, the language of the arbitration, the anticipated scheduling of the hearing on the merits, any deadline for the issuance of the award, any requirements set out in the arbitration agreement, and the applicable law or arbitral rules, and having decided to accept the appointment, arbitrators must make any necessary disclosures bearing on their impartiality and independence.

All international arbitrators are expected to be impartial and independent of the parties. A shorthand definition of an "impartial" arbitrator is one who is not biased in favor of, or prejudiced against, a particular party or its case. In contrast, an "independent" arbitrator is one who has no close relationship—financial, personal or professional—with a party or its counsel. *See generally*, International Bar Association Rules of Ethics for International Arbitrators, Art. 3(1) (1987). Regardless of whether arbitrators will serve as the sole arbitrator, co-arbitrator, or chairperson, they should immediately review certain basic documents, including the arbitration agreement and the arbitration rules, in order to assist them in making determinations regarding impartiality and independence. All arbitration rules require that, before accepting an appointment, arbitrators must disclose any potentially disqualifying relationships connected to the arbitration. *See, e.g.,* AAA International Rules, Article 7(1); ICC Rules, Article 7(2); UNCITRAL Rules, Article 9; LCIA Rules, Article 5.3; SCC Rules, Article 17(2).

1. *International Bar Association Disclosure Guidelines*

In determining what disclosures, if any, to make, arbitrators should consider the Guidelines published by the International Bar Association.

The new International Bar Association ("IBA") Guidelines on Conflicts of Interest in International Arbitration were published in May 2004 in an effort to achieve greater consistency and fewer unnecessary challenges or arbitrator withdrawals and removals. The Guidelines specify situations that do, or do not, warrant disclosure or disqualification of arbitrators. The Guidelines divide these circumstances into the Red List, the Orange List, and the Green List.

The Red List identifies two different types of mandatory disclosures: (1) disclosures relating to matters that automatically disqualify arbitrators from serving (*i.e.,* non-waivable disclosures), and (2) disclosures that must be made but which can then be waived by the parties. Non-waivable Red List disclosures include situations in which there is a relationship between a party and an arbitrator, when arbitrators are members of a supervisory board or director of a party, or when arbitrators have a financial interest in the outcome of the arbitration. Waivable Red List disclosures include circumstances in which arbitrators have previously given a party legal advice concerning the dispute, own shares in a party, a close family member has a financial interest in the outcome of the arbitration, or there are previous contacts between the arbitrator's law firm and a party. Significantly, the waivable Red List disclosures can only be waived when the parties "expressly waive" any objections. In other words, a waiver of a Red List disclosure cannot occur as a result of a party's failure to object.

In contrast, while the matters identified on the Orange List also must be disclosed, any objections to those disclosures are deemed waived if not made on a timely basis. The Orange List includes matters that may give rise to the appearance of partiality or at least raise questions about impartiality. They may include repeat appointments by one of the parties, serving as counsel for or against one of the parties in an unrelated matter, or serving in a separate arbitration with one of the parties where the issue is related.

The Green List identifies circumstances which the IBA believes create "no appearance of, and no actual conflict of interest," and include such matters as instances in which "the arbitrator previously has expressed an opinion on an issue, an associated firm has rendered service to a party, or the arbitrator has a relationship with another arbitrator or with the counsel of one of the parties through membership in the same professional association or social organization." Matters identified on the Green List need not be disclosed.

While the IBA Guidelines are considered by many international arbitrators to provide the best guidance regarding what disclosures to make in an international arbitration, arbitrators must be mindful of the fact that ethical considerations relating to arbitrator conduct might be governed by a complex interplay of rules and authorities. For example, depending on the situs of the arbitration and/or the agreement of the parties, ethical standards and law established under the FAA and/or the AAA/ABA Code of Ethics might be applicable. In order to ensure that everyone concerned is operating under the same set of controlling principles, the best practice in this regard is for the parties and arbitrators to expressly agree on the governing law and ethical standards relating to arbitrator disclosures and conduct.

2. *"Due Diligence" in Determining Disclosures*

Arbitrators must exercise "due diligence" in determining what disclosures, if any, to make in connection with the appointment process.

If the arbitrator is a member of a law firm, the arbitrator must conduct all reasonable inquiries regarding the firm's prior representation of, or adversity to, the parties and counsel, and whether the firm has had any involvement with any potential witnesses in the new arbitration. If the arbitrator is not a member of a law firm, review of the arbitrator's own records, and dependence on the arbitrator's recollection regarding prior or ongoing relationships with parties, counsel, and witnesses is necessary. Arbitrators should also determine whether they have taken a public position on an issue material to the dispute. As an ongoing precaution, and in the event an arbitrator is appointed to serve in the arbitration, an arbitrator who is a member of a law firm should insert the names of parties and counsel in the firm conflicts system in an effort to prevent the firm from representing or become adverse to those parties or counsel without first consulting the arbitrator.

3. *Challenges to Appointment*

Arbitrators should respond to any challenges dispassionately and with the best interests of the parties in mind.

As in domestic arbitrations, *see* Chapter 2 *supra*, when the appointment of an arbitrator is challenged by a party, the arbitrator should put self-interest aside and should base the decision whether to step down on the need to safeguard the integrity of the arbitration process. Arbitrators should thus consider whether a decision not to step down could impair the award. It is not unheard of for a challenge to be made for purposes of delay or with the objective of eliminating arbitrators whose preliminary decisions have offended the party making the challenge. When a prior or ongoing relationship not previously disclosed by the arbitrator forms the basis of the challenge, the arbitrator should make full disclosure regarding that relationship. In an administered arbitration or ad hoc arbitration in which an appointing authority has been designated by the parties, the arbitral institution or appointing authority will decide the challenge when the arbitrator declines to withdraw. Courts normally refuse to address a pre-award dispute between a party and an arbitrator or arbitral institution, leaving such matters for post-award hearings relating to the confirmation or vacatur of the award.

4. *Arbitrators' Terms of Engagement*

The parties should be advised of the arbitrators' terms of engagement prior to the time arbitrators accept appointment, and such terms should comply with any applicable institutional rules.

Prior to accepting appointment, arbitrators should disclose all material terms of engagement, including rate of compensation, whether they are to be compensated for travel time or in the event of cancellation of the hearing, special requirements (for example, business class airline travel), and other fees and expenses (such as VAT). Some arbitral institutions keep arbitrators' rates of compensation on file; arbitrators should take care to update that information whenever a change occurs. Arbitrator compensation under some sets of rules is based on the amount in dispute. Pursuant to Appendix III to the Arbitration Rules of the ICC International Court of Arbitration, the arbitrators' fees and expenses are fixed exclusively by the Court, and separate fee arrangements between the parties and arbitrators are not permitted. Arbitrators should understand applicable arbitral rules and national law bearing on compensation and other terms of engagement prior to accepting appointment.

5. *Changes in Status During Course of Proceeding*

Arbitrators should be alert to changes in relationships with parties, counsel, and witnesses during the course of the proceeding, and should disclose any changes that could give rise to justifiable doubts about independence or impartiality.

Arbitrators must remain diligent in ensuring that the arbitrator maintains the appearance of impartiality and independence throughout the pendency of the arbitration proceedings. Thus, arbitrators should be alert to the possibility that, for a variety of reasons, it might be necessary for them to make additional disclosures as the proceeding unfolds. For example, the arbitrator, or the arbitrator's law firm, might develop a relationship with one of the parties, counsel, or a witness without realizing their connection to the arbitration. Similarly, additional parties or counsel, or newly identified witnesses, might become involved in the proceeding. The obligation to disclose is an ongoing obligation that requires arbitrators to remain vigilant of potential new conflicts that require such disclosure.

III.   DETERMINING JURISDICTION AND ARBITRABILITY

A.   Challenges to Arbitrators' Jurisdiction

International arbitrators must be prepared to rule on challenges to their jurisdiction to determine the parties' dispute, and should resolve any such challenges in a manner that maximizes the efficiency of the proceeding.

As in domestic cases, the jurisdiction of an international tribunal is fundamental to the decision-making power of the arbitrator. It is thus essential for arbitrators to confirm that they have jurisdiction to determine the parties' claims and defenses. Modern arbitration laws generally hold that participation in the hearings on the merits without raising objection to jurisdiction amounts to a submission to arbitration and a waiver of any such objections. For example, Article 16(2) of the UNCITRAL Model Law provides that any jurisdictional objection must be raised no later than the Statement of Defense.

In contrast to the normal practice in domestic arbitrations, in international arbitrations the question of jurisdiction might not necessarily be determined by the national law of the arbitration forum. There might be an interplay between the contract clause establishing the applicable law and differing laws applicable to the parties and the subject matter of the dispute. Jurisdictional issues should be decided even when one party does not participate in the arbitration.

Parties often raise jurisdictional issues for purposes of delay or for other strategic reasons. The international arbitration doctrine of "competence-competence," which, in effect, is a recognition of the tribunal's authority to determine its own jurisdiction, serves to minimize such delays by ensuring a prompt resolution of such issues. Article 16(1) of the UNCITRAL Model Law thus provides as follows:

> The arbitral tribunal may rule on its own jurisdiction, including any objections with respect to the existence or validity of the arbitration agreement. For that purpose, an arbitration clause which forms part of a contract shall be treated as an agreement independent of the other terms of the contract. A decision by the arbitral tribunal that the contract is null and void shall not entail *ipso jure* the invalidity of the arbitration clause.

The concept established in Article 16 is consistent with the United States doctrine of separability. *See* Chapter 4, *supra.* More importantly, all of the major international institutional rules are consistent with Article 16 of the Model Law in providing both that an arbitration clause contained in a contract shall be treated as an agreement independent and separate from the other terms of the contract, and that arbitrators shall have the power to rule on any challenges to their jurisdiction and any objections with respect to the existence, scope, or validity of the arbitration agreement or the contract of which the arbitration agreement forms a part.. *See, e.g.,*

AAA International Rules, Article 15; LCIA Rules, Article 23.1; UNCITRAL Rules, Article 21(2); ICC Rules, Article 6(4). The ICC Rules also provide that the ICC Court of Arbitration will make a preliminary determination that the arbitration may proceed if it is *prima facie* satisfied that an arbitration agreement exists. ICC Rules, Article 6.

B.   Challenges to Arbitrability of a Party's Claims

International arbitrators must also be prepared to rule on challenges to the arbitrability of a party's claim.

A party may challenge the arbitrators' jurisdiction on the ground that the dispute is not arbitrable, for example, when the subject matter of the dispute is not capable of settlement by arbitration because of some mandatory law requirement or public policy consideration. In the United States, almost all commercial disputes, including disputes relating to mandatory laws, are now generally arbitrable; some foreign countries, however, might still prohibit such an issue from being decided anywhere other than in that nation's courts. Issues concerning arbitrability also might simply relate to the question whether the parties' arbitration agreement contemplates that the asserted claims are arbitrable under that provision. Other common arbitrability issues include such matters as non-signed agreements, assignment, agency, alter ego, bribery, res judicata and estoppel.

C.   Formalizing Arbitrators' Decisions on Jurisdictional and Arbitrability Issues

Arbitrators' determinations of jurisdictional and arbitrability issues can take various forms and can be made at various times, except that a final award should promptly be issued when the arbitrators determine that they do not have jurisdiction to determine the case, or that none of the asserted claims are arbitrable.

There are three well-known ways that international arbitrators have dealt with challenges to their jurisdiction or to the arbitrability of a claim: (1) consider the jurisdictional or arbitrability challenge initially and, if valid, promptly issue a final award determining that the arbitrators have no jurisdiction or that the claim is not arbitrable, (2) consider the issue of jurisdiction or arbitrability and issue an interim award on the jurisdictional or arbitrability point alone, or (3) defer considering the issue until such time as the arbitrators issue the award on the merits. Which procedure to follow in a particular case depends on the totality of circumstances in that case.

Any decision by arbitrators denying jurisdiction or arbitrability of a claim should be in the form of an award, so it can be recognized under the New York Convention. In contrast, a preliminary decision or ruling is sufficient for a finding that jurisdiction exists or that a claim is arbitrable.

IV. PRELIMINARY MEETING

International arbitrators should, to the extent feasible, arrange a preliminary meeting between the arbitrators and counsel for the purpose of organizing and scheduling the arbitration proceeding.

In international arbitrations, a preliminary meeting or conference between the arbitrators and counsel for the parties is particularly desirable in order to identify and resolve the often very divergent procedural expectations of parties from different cultures and legal systems. It may facilitate agreement, or at least understanding, of key procedural steps, such as possible bifurcation, document production, the use of experts, and other matters with which the parties may not be familiar. Such a meeting can also be important to allow the parties and arbitrators to establish personal contact, to identify key issues, to agree on other procedural steps and a timetable (to be incorporated in a procedural order), and conceivably to consider settlement. Because of the long distances and costs involved, however, such a meeting may not be practical. In such cases, a preliminary telephone conference, with a carefully prepared advance agenda, coupled with exchanges of correspondence, may have to do.

V.   TERMS OF REFERENCE

When required or appropriate, arbitrators should actively expedite the finalization of Terms of Reference or other initial framework documents.

In the case of ICC arbitrations, Terms of Reference must be prepared and must be signed by the arbitrators and, hopefully, all parties. ICC Rules, Article 18. While large portions of the Terms of Reference can be prepared and agreed via correspondence, an actual meeting can be helpful to discuss practical matters, including the issues to be decided, the format and scheduling of written submissions, witnesses and witness statements, experts, the language and translation, and timing. Many experienced arbitrators now ask each party to prepare its own short summary of the facts to be inserted in the prospective Terms of Reference; such unilateral submissions, however, are not binding on the other party or on the arbitrators.

Under the ICC Rules, as recently revised, the Terms of Reference can, but need not, include a summary of the issues to be decided. When there are experienced counsel on both sides, it may be preferable that any such summary be very general, referring only to the issues as raised in the pleadings and submissions. On the other hand, when inexperienced counsel are involved, it might be helpful to attempt to focus the issues in advance, even though such an effort might involve considerable time and argument.

Once signed, the Terms of Reference are almost always supplemented by a first procedural order, providing more detail, and by a mandatory time schedule (otherwise known as a "provisional timetable"). ICC Rules, Article 18 (4). The Terms of Reference will usually give arbitrators the power to change the timetable and grant extensions. Any such changes should be memorialized by written order. Extensions relating to the time for the issuance of the award must be granted by the ICC Court. Due to the difficulties of international travel and scheduling, experienced arbitrators try to set and reserve dates for future hearings long in advance of the time they are to occur.

Similar documents—sometimes called Heads of Appointment—can also be used in other non-ICC arbitrations, particularly in ad hoc proceedings (under UNCITRAL or other rules) to set out the agreement between the parties and the arbitrators, as well as the general framework of the arbitration. In ad hoc proceedings, such an agreement also may be necessary to establish the compensation of the arbitrators. A useful guide or checklist, to be used in preparing a preliminary meeting or initial procedural orders, can be found in the UNCITRAL Notes on Organizing Arbitral Proceedings (1996). One important preliminary consideration may be whether to bifurcate the proceedings so that issues relating to liability will be heard in an initial proceeding, with issues relating to damages considered in a second proceeding. The potential economies of avoiding the substantial costs involved in presenting evidence on the issue of damages must be balanced against potential burdens, such as additional travel and duplication of effort. Occasionally, in instances in which the arbitration agreement is silent on the topic, sharp disputes will arise relating to the language of the arbitration proceeding; the resolution of that issue sometimes requires a hearing, and perhaps even the issuance of an interim award. In order to avoid any unnecessary proceedings relating to the language of the arbitration, the arbitrators should attempt to confirm or establish the language of the arbitration at the preliminary meeting.

VI. MOTIONS AND APPLICATIONS

Arbitrators should require that any motions or applications seeking relief are supported with reasons, and should grant a party opposing such a motion or application an opportunity to respond.

Formal motions are used less frequently and less aggressively in international arbitrations than in domestic U.S. practice. Nonetheless, they are commonly used to obtain interim or other relief, and often are presented in the form of "applications" or letters (as distinguished from oral procedural applications in the course of hearings).

Arbitrators should insist that such applications be in writing and be supported with reasons. To the extent the application is substantive, the opposing party should be granted a reasonable opportunity to respond. Moreover, the arbitrators should consider whether the decision on such an application can be contained in a procedural order or, in the event the application seeks a final determination on a substantive matter, whether the decision must be contained in an interim or partial award. Such an award normally is enforceable, but an as award—as opposed to a mere order—may entail further formalities and a possible institutional review (for example, by the ICC Court) with consequent delay. Motions or applications for summary judgment or dismissal for failure to state a claim are relatively rare. Most arbitration rules require a hearing on these, and potentially other, dispositive motions if either party so requests.

Other common subjects of motions/applications include: (1) interim relief, including injunctions, restraining orders, protective orders, and conservatory measures; (2) expert examination; (3) discovery and document production; (4) the deposit or guarantee of eventual costs; and (5) consolidation or joinder of third parties. Each of these categories of potential motions presents its own unique considerations. A request for interim relief can raise issues regarding conflicting jurisdiction with local courts, and the enforceability of an order granting such relief might depend on applicable substantive law or on the *lex loci*. Whereas a request for a so-called "conservatory" expert examination might be a common practice under French law, it might be viewed in other jurisdictions as encroaching on arbitrators' duty to decide the merits of the dispute. Orders requiring the deposit or guaranty of eventual costs are increasingly common, but requests for such relief can present difficult issues, for example, when one party is economically weak. A request for consolidation or joinder of parties might require the consent of parties not presently involved in the arbitration. These, and other, issues illustrate that arbitrators must respond to motions and applications with caution, and must be prepared to address such requests for relief in light of the many unique considerations that can be presented in an international arbitration.

VII. DEPOSITIONS AND DOCUMENT PRODUCTION

There is a deep historical divide between civil law practice and common law practice relating to discovery. Under civil law, each party is expected to provide evidence to support its own case, with no obligation to provide evidence (damaging or not) to the other side. While common law practice is not uniform—English practice, for example, does not foresee the deposition practice that is common in the United States—it does generally contemplate various forms of discovery that are intended to avoid surprise and to identify all the evidence. Notably, in the field of international arbitration, there is a trend toward harmonization of these conflicting approaches, with widespread, but not universal, acceptance of the IBA Rules on the Taking of Evidence in International Commercial Arbitration. Some experienced arbitrators thus refer to the IBA Rules explicitly, but only as "guidelines," in the Terms of Reference or other procedural orders, whereas others prefer not to refer to them formally, so as to retain flexibility, and certain others do not accept the IBA Rules at all.

A. Depositions

International arbitrators should permit depositions only in rare instances, usually relating to the inability of a witness to appear and testify at the hearing.

Pre-trial depositions (à l'américaine!) are generally not used or authorized in international arbitration, unless all parties request them. Arbitrators occasionally grant an exception, however, when unusual circumstances, such as illness or inability to travel, are presented. More often than not, neither the arbitrator nor a court will have the power to issue local subpoenas for the purpose of taking depositions.

In the absence of depositions and other elaborate discovery procedures, there are other available procedural mechanisms that can assist in avoiding undue surprise and which provide the parties with some of the benefits of deposition discovery. For example, it has become common in international arbitration for each party to prepare and submit in advance written witness statements that accompany the party's principal written submissions.   An early procedural order should provide for such written witness statements, and should set out the applicable conditions, for example, a proviso that no witness statements will be considered unless the witness is present to be examined at hearing. With regard to witnesses, it should be noted that in some civil law countries a distinction is made between party representatives, such as employees and directors, and third-party witnesses. Arbitrators may wish to determine in advance whether to consider all individuals who will testify to be witnesses for these purposes. While it is common, but not universal, for lawyers to assist in preparation of witness statements, arbitrators must be aware that in some jurisdictions such lawyer-witness contact is deemed unethical. As a consequence, the arbitrators might desire to clarify, at an early time, whether such communications will be permitted.

B.   Document Production

International arbitrators should exercise restraint in authorizing document requests, limiting them to narrow, specific categories of relevant evidence that is in the control of the opposing party and not otherwise available to the requesting party.

In contrast to the rare utilization of pre-trial depositions in international arbitrations, it has become increasingly common for arbitrators, including those from civil law backgrounds, to authorize procedures for limited document production. In that regard, the guidelines set out in Article 3 of the IBA Rules are frequently applied. Those guidelines require (1) the description of a narrow and specific category of documents reasonably believed to exist; (2) a statement of why the documents are relevant; and (3) a statement that the documents are not in the control of the requesting party and are assumed to be within the control of the other party. Experienced arbitrators set a specific time schedule, usually in the initial timetable, for document production, including the service of the request for production, the response (including objections), the reply/justification, and any decision by the arbitrators relating to objections to the document requests.

As in domestic arbitrations, arbitrators should encourage the parties to discuss, and attempt to agree on, document production; such a process, however, might require more patience and persuasion on the part of the arbitrators when the parties are unaccustomed to such a process. In some cases an actual hearing—whether in person or by telephone—might be useful or even necessary in order to resolve document production issues. Legal sanctions or court enforcement often will not be available to enforce arbitrator orders relating to document production, but the threat of "adverse inferences" remains a powerful tool.

Issues relating to confidentiality and privilege frequently pose difficult problems in connection with document productions. The best solutions to concerns about "confidentiality" are largely the same as in domestic arbitration: arbitrators should consider issuing a protective order that, depending on the circumstances, might provide that only the parties' lawyers and/or expert(s) are permitted to review the documents, or that, in the first instance, only the arbitrators or an independent expert will be permitted to review the documents to determine confidentiality.

The issues and solutions relating to privilege tend to be more complex. The rules pertaining to privilege differ between many countries in a variety of respects, including the material and persons (for example, in-house counsel) covered by the privilege, the ethical obligations of lawyers, and the general scope of the privilege. These matters are difficult to anticipate and address in general procedural orders. A frequent solution, which is not entirely satisfactory and yet is equitable, is to apply, in an equal fashion, the most restrictive rule under any applicable system.

VIII. EXPERT WITNESSES

The use of experts differs considerably between different legal systems, and arbitrators thus should consult with the parties to agree on an appropriate procedure.

Common law practitioners are used to presenting their own expert testimony, on technical aspects, quantum of damages, economics, and many other specialized areas. Such experts are treated like witnesses, subject to examination and cross-examination, and are usually expected to provide written expert reports in advance. Civil law practitioners and arbitrators, on the other hand, are very skeptical about the use of "party-presented experts"—whom they consider "hired guns"—and prefer that arbitrators appoint their own totally independent "expert." Arbitrators should address this issue at the preliminary meeting or in an early procedural order. It may be possible to use a combination of both types of procedure, or to add others, such as expert "conferencing." In some instances, it also might be appropriate for the parties to present experts on foreign law. In most cases, if one member of the arbitral tribunal is expert in such foreign law, the arbitrators will prefer to dispense with expert testimony and, instead, rely on legal argument.

IX.   WRITTEN SUBMISSIONS

Formal written submissions by the parties play a critical role in international arbitration, and arbitrators therefore should establish procedures that will guide the parties on the content and the format of such submissions.

Pre-hearing written submissions, setting out each party's full case, both as to facts and as to law, are expected under almost all systems of law. Indeed, in civil law they are given far more importance than hearings. However, the expected contents, the timing, and the sequence of such submissions may differ considerably from one arbitration to the next, and arbitrators therefore should address such issues at an early stage in one or more procedural orders.

Questions regarding the deadlines for the filing of submissions often reveal tension between the parties' wishes and the need to conduct expeditious and efficient proceedings. For example, some parties might desire sequential submissions, whereas an opposing party might prefer that submissions be simultaneous. The best solution might depend on how fully the respective cases have already been set out in the claim and answer/counterclaim; if the parties' cases are already fully stated, simultaneous submissions might avoid unnecessary delay. In this regard it is noteworthy that some English practitioners expect written "Statements of Case" from each party before the full written submissions are provided.

Another typical issue relates to how many rounds of written submissions will be required--one round only, or rebuttal rounds? When multiple rounds are permitted, the first round should normally cover each party's entire case, including all claims and counterclaims, and all factual and legal aspects relating to such claims. Arbitrators should insist that rebuttals, if any, be limited to responding materials, so that the parties do not withhold information with the intention of "ambushing" their adversary in the second round.

When submissions are to be filed sequentially, arbitrators will also need to determine which party files the first submission, and which party will be entitled to file the last submission. In most systems, the claimant files its submission first, and the counterclaimant files first with respect to matters relating to any counterclaim. In common law procedure, the claimant (and counterclaimant) may also have last word in reply; in civil law procedure, however, and increasingly in international arbitration, the respondent (or counter-respondent) has the final word in sur-reply. Thus, if submissions are filed sequentially, there may be as many as five rounds--claim, answer and counterclaim, reply and answer to counterclaim, sur-reply and reply to counterclaim, and sur-reply to counterclaim. In such circumstances, arbitrators might want to seek a means of compressing the filing sequence. Moreover, some local practices or nuances may be expected, or even expressly agreed, by the parties. For example, some English practitioners expect an exchange of witness statements and expert reports prior to the filing of any written submissions.

Because counsel may come from very different cultures, experienced arbitrators give explicit directions relating to the form and content of written submissions. Normally, submissions should include a table of contents and list of exhibits. A chronology might also be helpful. Submissions should include all exhibits and legal materials on which the party intends to rely. Exhibits should be sequentially numbered, one series for the claimant, and one for the respondent. Typically, arbitrators will require the parties to avoid the duplication of exhibits contained in the claim or answer/counterclaim and, in most instances, will ask the parties to continue any prior numbering of exhibits. Consideration must also be given to what requirements, if any, are necessary relating to the translation of documents, and whether such translations may be unofficial or must be certified.

Submissions should normally also include all written witness statements and expert reports, and should provide for limited rebuttal witness statements and rebuttal expert reports, if any. The arbitrators will need to determine whether witness statements should include separate exhibits or whether such statements should refer to the general exhibit list. Expert reports usually include separate supporting materials that are separately numbered. Submissions should further include all legal materials on which the party intends to rely. In that regard, arbitrators should be aware that, in many cultures, academic writings, articles, and commentaries ("doctrine") are as important as jurisprudence/case law. Given the length of some articles and judicial decisions, arbitrators should consider whether to eliminate unnecessary material by providing that the submissions should only include relevant excerpts, and/or that relevant sections be highlighted. As is the case with regard to general documents, arbitrators will also need to take into account any need to have legal material translated.

Finally, guidance should also be given as to the format in which the submissions and exhibits are to be presented. For example, many arbitrators prefer particular types of binders, document separators, and outside tabs for easy use. Arbitrators should also consider whether, and under what circumstances, the submissions may be exchanged by electronic transmission and/or data storage devices.

X. THE MERITS HEARING

Certain hearing matters are covered in the various international arbitration rules, as well as in the arbitration law of the place of arbitration. It is imperative that arbitrators be familiar with both. Overall, arbitrators must ensure that the hearing is a fair but also efficient process. The chairperson has the overriding responsibility for balancing the tension between due process and expediency. The party-appointed arbitrators have the delicate obligation to ensure that the parties' positions are fully understood by the tribunal, taking into account language, legal tradition and culture.

International arbitration hearings generally are substantially shorter than domestic U.S. arbitration hearings. As previously noted, this is because the parties will have submitted one or more rounds of detailed submissions, written witness statements, and supporting documents prior to the hearing. A hearing of three days to a week is normal. A hearing exceeding two weeks is long for even the most complex cases.

A. Advance Preparations

Because pre-hearing procedures and preparations play a particularly important role in international arbitrations, arbitrators should ensure in advance of the commencement of the hearing that those procedures have been followed.

Well before the opening of the hearing, arbitrators should review the procedural orders and confirm that the parties have performed all necessary steps. In a short hearing, there is little time to invest in "old business." Arbitrators may wish to take an active role in the pre-hearing stage in scheduling the order of witness appearances, as this can expedite proceedings.

Administrative preparation for the hearing must take account of the different language skills needed. There may be a need for sequential or simultaneous translation and bi- or even tri-lingual court reporters.

International arbitration hearings, in general, have become a mix of common and civil law procedures. The exception tends to be when both parties are U.S. parties or are represented by U.S. law firms, who normally follow a U.S. style hearing practice. To avoid any misunderstandings, arbitrators must establish the rules for the hearing, including especially the rules for the examination of witnesses, well in advance. The absolutely critical procedural consideration during the hearing is equality, because the validity of the ultimate award is dependent on a fundamentally fair hearing.

B.   Structuring the Hearing

Arbitrators should structure the hearing in a manner that fully exploits the nature and extent of the pre-hearing process.

If the pre-hearing orders are clear, the hearing should go smoothly. When counsel have submitted detailed pre-hearing submissions, opening argument should be short, perhaps one hour to each side. Similarly, unless there are to be no post-hearing submissions, closing argument may be brief or skipped altogether. Given that each fact witness has submitted a written witness statement, direct examination is non-existent or truncated, although experienced arbitrators recognize the advantages of allowing at least a short direct to relax the witness. There typically is cross-examination, but with the chair responsible for ensuring that it does not become overly aggressive or abusive. International arbitrators are free to ask questions of witnesses, although—depending on their own legal traditions—not all do. Generally, arbitrators withhold their questions for a witness until after direct, cross and re-direct examination, in order to allow counsel to develop the evidence. Arbitrators may be particularly active in questioning expert witnesses. Expert witness conferencing is becoming increasingly common in international hearings. Arbitrators obviously should give no indication through the questions as to their assessment of the merits of witness testimony.

International arbitrators are also free to ask questions of counsel. Experienced counsel will urge arbitrators to pose questions both in advance of the hearing and at the end of the hearing. Such counsel recognize that the hearing is not their chance to perform but, instead, presents the best opportunity to address and put to rest any doubts in the arbitrators' minds.

Arbitrators should determine in advance of the commencement of the hearing how they will address evidentiary objections. The IBA Rules prove useful in this regard; arbitrators might seek to adopt them explicitly or, alternatively, to generally refer to them when resolving evidentiary issues. As with U.S. domestic arbitration, arbitrators can admit otherwise questionable evidence "for what it is worth." Usually, the chairperson will decide evidentiary matters, with more or less input from the co-arbitrators.

The most problematic procedural issue often relates to the administration of time. Typically, the available time will be allocated equally to the opposing sides and the arbitrators will then conduct the hearing on a "chess clock" basis. Each side's allocated time includes not only its opening and closing statements and direct examination of its own witnesses, but also the cross-examination of the opponent's witnesses. This process is often misunderstood by U.S. litigation counsel who assume they have unlimited cross-examination time and thus are surprised to find their time quickly exhausted. The chairperson should monitor time closely, and announce at least at the end of each hearing day—on the record, if necessary—how much time each side has used and how much remains. When it proves absolutely necessary to allocate additional time to the parties, international arbitrators frequently sit into the evening and on weekends. In light of the importance of time, it is a given that the chairperson should tactfully speak up when witness testimony is irrelevant or repetitive.

If a witness fails to appear, arbitrators should invite counsel to give their views on the appropriate action to be taken. In general, and in the absence of a waiver of the right to cross-examine, a witness statement that has not been subject to cross-examination bears no weight.

At the end of the hearing, arbitrators should discuss with counsel what post-hearing steps are to follow. Subject to the agreed schedule, the chair must close the proceedings. After the closure of the proceedings, a party may not submit further evidence or argument without authorization from the arbitrators.

XI. THE AWARD

Arbitrators must ensure that the contents of the award satisfy the requirements of the applicable law and rules and the parties' arbitration agreement, and should only label an award as "final" when all of the issues relating to the award have been finally determined.

International arbitrators must be familiar with mandatory provisions of the applicable procedural law and the relevant international arbitration rules governing awards. The award in an international arbitration is a written and reasoned award unless the parties agree otherwise. In other words, the "default" is the opposite of the summary award that, at least in the past, has been the general practice in traditional U.S. domestic arbitration. The key distinction between an award and a procedural decision is that the former finally disposes of one or more issues. An award can be an interim award, a partial award or a final award. Interim and partial awards may deal with questions such as jurisdiction, applicable law, interim measures, and even substantive claims. In deciding whether to render an interim or partial award, arbitrators must consider whether it will be more efficient to render partial awards or a single final award. Additionally, arbitrators should consider the treatment of partial and interim awards under the applicable law. If the award is partial, provisions must be made for necessary further proceedings.

Just as the chairperson leads deliberations, the chair is responsible for the drafting of the award. Some chairpersons do all the drafting, while others delegate sections to the co-arbitrators. Although no set formula exists, a final award normally encompasses (1) an introductory section, which includes the basis for the tribunal's jurisdiction; (2) a section setting out the background facts of the case (sometimes comparable to "findings of fact" in a U.S. court decision); (3) a section on the applicable law; (4) the heart of the award, meaning the tribunal's application of the law to the facts as found by the tribunal; and (5) the formal concluding section—labeled either "award" or "dispositif"—setting out the relief granted. It is in this final section that the arbitrators must set out their definitive jurisdictional rulings, the award of monetary damages and/or declaratory relief, and the assessment of costs and fees. All arbitrators must physically sign the award, which should be dated and should indicate the place of arbitration. If one or more of the arbitrators must sign the award at a locale other than that of the agreed place of arbitration, it is a good precaution to have prior written permission from the parties. Unanimity is considered desirable but not essential. It is uncommon, but not unheard of, for there to be dissenting and concurring decisions in international arbitration.

XII. POST-AWARD PROCEEDINGS

Subsequent to the issuance of the final award, arbitrators are *"functus officio,"* with the result that arbitrators normally are only allowed to grant those forms of post-award relief that fall within the traditional exceptions to the *functus officio* doctrine.

Most international arbitration rules provide for very limited post-award proceedings by the arbitral tribunal itself. Typically, the institutional rules provide that the parties are entitled to ask arbitrators to (1) correct clerical, typographical, or computational errors in the award, (2) issue an interpretation (*i.e.*, a clarification) of the award, or (3) make an additional award as to claims presented but not addressed in the award. The time limits under most arbitration rules for all three forms of post-award relief are short. The second two categories of post-award relief are rarely granted, in part for the reason that such requests sometimes actually seek relief that would require a reconsideration of the merits of the parties' claims and defenses. The main avenues of post-award relief for the losing party are to either commence a court proceeding at the place of arbitration seeking to set aside (*i.e.,* vacate) the award or, alternatively, to resist the recognition and enforcement of the award in recognition and enforcement proceedings instituted by the prevailing party in the foreign courts of one or more jurisdictions located in countries other than the country in which the award was made.

As previously discussed, proceedings to confirm or vacate an international arbitration award are governed by the pertinent arbitration statutes of the nation in which the award was made, whereas recognition and enforcement proceedings, conducted in the national courts of nations other than the nation in which the award was made, are governed by international treaties as adopted by nation states. In the United States such treaties include both the New York Convention and the Inter-American Convention on International Commercial Arbitration (the "Panama Convention"), the latter of which has been implemented as Chapter Three of the FAA. Importantly, and insofar as foreign awards (as opposed to nondomestic awards) are concerned, neither convention allows courts to undertake a substantive review of the foreign award on the merits in connection with a recognition and enforcement proceeding. Instead, the conventions allow for a refusal of recognition and enforcement only on the basis of circumscribed grounds, which focus on due process. Although arbitrators have no role in confirmation, vacatur, and recognition and enforcement proceedings, it is critical for them to be familiar with, and ever alert to, the permissible grounds for such relief in order to protect the validity of the award.

Article V of the New York Convention, which provides as follows, establishes five narrow grounds upon which a court may refuse to recognize and enforce a foreign award:

1. The parties to the agreement . . . were, under the law applicable to them, under some incapacity, or the said agreement is not valid under the law to which the parties

have subjected it or, failing any indication thereon, under the law of the country where the award was made; or

2. The party against whom the award is invoked was not given proper notice of the appointment of the arbitrator or of the arbitration proceedings or was otherwise unable to present his case; or

3. The award deals with a difference not contemplated by or not falling within the terms of the submission to arbitration, or it contains decisions on matters beyond the scope of the submission to arbitration, provided that, if the decisions on matters submitted to arbitration can be separated from those not so submitted, that part of the award which contains decisions on matters submitted to arbitration may be recognized and enforced;

4. The composition of the arbitral authority or the arbitral procedure was not in accordance with the agreement of the parties, or, failing such agreement, was not in accordance with the law of the country where the arbitration took place; or

5. The award has not yet become binding on the parties, or has been set aside or suspended by a competent authority of the country in which, or under the law of which, the award was made.

Recognition and enforcement of an arbitral award may also be refused if a competent court finds that the subject matter of the parties' dispute is not capable of settlement by arbitration under the law of the country in which enforcement is sought, or that the recognition or enforcement of the award would be contrary to the public policy of that country.

Following issuance of the award, and, indeed, at all times, arbitrators must be careful not to disclose confidential matters. International arbitration rules and codes of ethics generally require arbitrators to keep all matters relating to the arbitration or the award confidential except as required by law or agreed by the parties. Deliberations are particularly sacrosanct. Experienced international arbitrators destroy their notes and other deliberative material shortly after issuance of the final award. They also scrupulously avoid discussing the case with the parties or counsel, no matter how much time has passed.

XIII. CONCLUSION

For a broad variety of reasons, international arbitration procedures and practices vary substantially from those utilized in domestic arbitrations in the United States. Those variations pertain not only to the formal aspects of international arbitrations, but also to legal issues concerning the confirmation, vacatur, and enforcement of international awards. Indeed, the very nature of international arbitration dictates that arbitrators and counsel must constantly be alert to considerations that might require innovative processes in order to transcend language and cultural barriers. As a result, the most effective international arbitrations are those that avoid the parochial practices of a particular nation and, instead, adopt a truly international approach.

INDEX

C

California Law,
  Arbitrator disclosure requirements, 19, 35
    Continuance during pendency of case, 25
  Disqualification of arbitrators, 23
Certification of class arbitration, 62
Chairperson's role in determining status of party-appointed arbitrators, 32
Change in arbitrator status, 36
Class arbitration, 53
  Applicability of general arbitration procedures and principles, 55
  Arbitrator appointment, applicable rules and procedures, 53
  Arbitrator determination on availability, 56
  Attorneys' fees awards, 67
  Class action preclusion clauses, 58
  Class certification, 62
  Compromise of claim, arbitrator approval, 69
  Confidentiality, 70
  Disclosures, 54
  Final award, 68
  Lack of mention in arbitration clauses, 59
  Management of the pre-hearing and hearing process, 66
  Notice of class determination, 66
  Partial final awards on the class certification issue, 64
  Settlement of claim, arbitrator approval, 69
  Voluntary dismissal of claim, arbitrator approval, 69
Clear and unmistakable evidence doctrine, parties' intent, 45
Communication of arbitrators with parties, limitations,
  Ex parte communications, 17, 38
  Initial communications, 8
Compensation of arbitrators, 11
Competence of arbitrators to serve, determination, 10
Conditions precedent to arbitration, power of arbitrator to resolve, 47
Confidentiality,
  Class arbitration, 70
  Discovery, 130
Court as decision maker,
  Validity of the arbitration agreement, question of illegality or similar defense, 50
  Procedural vs. substantive arbitrability issues, 47
CPR International Institute for Conflict Prevention and Resolution Rules. See
    CPR Rules
CPR Rules,
  Ad hoc arbitrations, arbitrator appointments, 15

H